Surviving Illumination
Breaking through Crisis

Kathrina Kasha Peterson

A Memoir & Teachings from a Kundalini Rising

DEDICATION

This book is dedicated to my family. Only love heals the brokenness.
May everyone experience being witnessed with love.
To Bonga, thank you for gracing my life.

Kathrina Kasha Peterson

When the leaves fall from the tree,
does one ask the suffering of the leaf
or the suffering of the tree?

CONTENTS

ACKNOWLEDGMENTS

I call forth the Grandmothers and Grandfathers of the north and south. I call forth the Grandmothers and Grandfathers of the east and west. I offer gratitude to the mountains, the oceans, the air and the fire. I thank beings, seen and unseen. I thank the two legged, the four legged and the many legged. I thank the beings that swim and the beings that fly. I thank the beings rooted to the earth, the trees and plants that give us life. I thank my teachers, elders and guides from the past, the present and the future. I thank the luminous. I thank the Kundalini.

I thank my family members who believe in me even when they didn't understand me. I thank my teachers who graciously shared their wisdom and compassion with me. I thank my friends who accepted and loved me. Thank you Claire, Carol, Eve, Marty and Jennifer. This book is a recollection of events and I've related them as best I could based on my knowledge. I recognize that the memories of others of the events described in this book may be different than my own. They are each fine, decent and hard-working people. I have changed some of the identities and names in this book.

I offer gratitude to all my relations.

Kathrina Kasha Peterson.

INTRODUCTION

"God has opened my eyes; for I saw the nobility of the vulgar, the attractiveness of the repellent, the perfection of the maimed and the beauty of the hideous." -Aurobindo

At first I was hesitant to write my story. As the decades passed and my life's journey spiraled through dark nights of the soul, I began to see that I may actually have something to offer others based on the ways I have found light through places of hopelessness and despair. My journey to the underworld many times over required a maturation over time. It necessitated a cultivation of qualities that could withstand the seasons of life with its ever changing circumstances. It is from these places that these writings come to you with an intention that it will shed light on a fuller and more meaningful life for you.

This book is a multimodal approach to individuation. I took an honest assessment of how my belief structures have come to be. I saw through the challenges of a spiritual emergency, chronic illness and grief how I am not any of my belief structures either. The spiritual cultivation and development needed time and space, and a lot of tending, and of course, grace. The book is a weaving of story and within this weaving, not only is the finished carpet presented, but also the way of gathering the wool, gathering the dyes from the rocks, feeling the weather and touching the clay by the riverbank on the soles of my feet. It brings forth the aroma of the peppermint tea on the kitchen table, and the prayers uttered between the sighs of stories shared between men and women. So in the kitchen table of love, all is welcomed: joy, dread, sorrow, shame, elation, bliss, sexual liberation, self-doubt, success, etc.

Very early in my life, I began to ask the big questions from deep inside myself. Who lives? Who dies? What is the meaning of life? What is the purpose of pain and suffering? I never really thought "Why me?" Instead, "Why not me?" Perhaps, this was part of the solution, the bigger space that held meaning for me to go through so much in my life. I didn't feel that I was special in a way that I should be spared pain. I was born an intuitive and an empath. I saw so much dysfunction early in my life, in my family and the community I grew up in. I saw people's pain in their faces and felt the pangs of anxiety in their bellies. There was a lot of violence, both inflicted to self as well as unto others. I wondered why do people who love each other hurt each other. I wondered why existence was dry for many, and the lubrication of love did not reach the thick leather of wounding.

I was a millionaire in emotions. "This is the purpose of emotion - to let a streaming beauty flow through you. Call it spirit, elixir, or the original agreement between yourself and God. Opening into that gives peace, a song of being empty, pure silence." A friend copied it from an inspirational book and used it to connect with me in a time when I felt overwhelmed. My journey is not an easy one. Neither is it one I'd recommend anyone take. But for all purposes, I would choose no other. It is my path unfolding.

There are different possibilities in reading this memoir. I invite you to read it in parts and not as a whole. Please do not read this in one go. Because parts of it carry an intensity, it is best for the reader to take pauses. Like you take a pause after a poem, or at a red light, or the pauses between an in breath and an out breath or the pause between the thunderstorm and the rainbow or the pause after an orgasm. Often times material with gravity is habitually met with a disassociated stance. I invite you to be present. Allow space to feel what you feel, your internal images to paint your inner scape, for sensations to bubble and let them all go. It is within presence where the creative moment lies. Drink it in and savor it.

It is my story, and also the story of every man and woman in the journey of life. The book is meant as a guide to be received and your responses allowed to ferment, come alive in your own experiences and internal landscape. I have liberally peppered the book with questions for the reader to reflect upon in their life, and hopefully bring forth a level of clarity that may be helpful in your life. Allow yourself to take in what is presented, let it dance within and then release it. In this way, it has the best potential to shift and transform the consciousness of the reader. It is a transmission.

Kathrina Kasha Peterson
Marin, CA
Apricot blossoms, March 2015

Part I: First stirrings of emergence

CHAPTER 1: CALLING ALL MY RELATIONS

"To the growing soul, to the spirit within us, may not difficulties, obstacles, attacks be a means of growth, added strength, enlarged experience, training for spiritual victory."
-Aurobindo

If your deepest yearning is to be alive and awake, then this book is for you. If you are navigating the perils of a spiritual emergency or an intense spiritual awakening, then the very human, nuanced and sober stories here will touch your heart. This intimate handbook invites you to the potency of the kundalini (life force) that is in all of us. Kundalini is a Sanskrit word for "coiled up" or "coiling like a snake". It is the spiritual power in a person, whether it is in its static or dynamic state. The snake is not only a symbol, but also illustrates the movement of this transformative essence and subtle bio-energy leading one into a higher form of consciousness. It is inherent in being a human being.

The book also demystifies the spiritual path as I speak of the most ordinary in our lives as the path. Often, it is in times of crisis that we find our biggest openings. Somehow, when things fall apart, we are more ready to change. In my own journey, the continual integration of personality and being was the key. The kundalini rising kept insisting me to be true in the ways I didn't even know how. Because it kept bringing up my blocks to what is authentic, I was forced to look into what I didn't want to see of myself. When the reservoir of my unconscious exploded, I was lost. I wanted to be found. I accepted the journey of finding myself. This meant walking into my deepest darkness - into those places in myself I had turned my back on. I grew up in a family with a lot of dysfunction, so early on my life I chose to just be in the light. Well, it worked for a while, but the truth of existence is that light and dark are really not separate. By choosing only light over dark, I chose separation of self. The journey the kundalini invited me into was about the union, the non-separation, the totality.

So if you are driving a car with a flat tire, at what point do you stop and do something different? You can keep putting differ-

3

ent kinds of fuel in the car, but it still has a flat tire. The shadows of our lives rule us as a general rules his soldiers. Shadows are those parts of ourselves we don't own. We usually are afraid of them, disown them, yet they keep showing up in our lives. The unconscious will loom bigger until we listen to its wisdom with love. The humorous play of light and shadow that a kundalini purification insists will touch your compassion for your humanity, which is no different than your divinity. The kundalini process is about waking up what is asleep in you. So put on your seatbelt as this journey traverses terrain that is mercurial. Remember that it is in the alchemical forging ground the phoenix rises. Welcome aboard!

This book talks of crisis, but it is not about staying in crisis. There is a redeeming value, a wisdom that is inherent in crisis that presents opportunities not just for us to break down, but to break through. This is what maturation does. The lessons of the seasons make us stronger, wiser, kinder and more loving. One, however, doesn't have to be in a crisis to be touched by grace and love either. Every moment everyday everywhere is filled with spirit. We are it. We just have to be conscious.

May this teaching memoir also inspire and allow your deepest yearnings to birth. May it quiet your mind, and wake up your heart. Because I wasn't in a sensory deprivation tank, the kundalini rising for me happened in the ordinaries of life. The blocks I encountered as part of the purification process as well as the cultivation and integration can't be separated from my history which is interpersonally based. I had disassociated very much as a younger person because of trauma. The kundalini process included owning again what I didn't fully feel earlier in my life. This book speaks to the process of my taking back what I rejected of myself. My struggles with both light and dark are inherently part of the development. My whole humanity was and is part of the whole kundalini rising.

Different people experience kundalini differently depending on different stages of rising as well as what blocks are in the physio-psycho-spiritual system. By sharing my experiences of initially plowing through the purification process of a kundalini rising (only to come to surrender each time), my wish is that this may serve as a guide for the reader on how to be with your vital essence in a most graceful way. If it is not graceful, then may my experiences shed light for you to discover what you can do to make it more graceful. May it be an inspiration for you to trust your own path of awakening. Kundalini can be explosive and rapid as a fire razes through a dry forest of beliefs and world views. It can also be smooth like mist. Over the decades, I have learnt and familiarized myself with the various ways of operating as a system. This meant learning how I used my human electromagnetic field as well as my entire human energetic system. I also used the knowledge and experience of the elements as medicine. Elements are air, fire, earth and water. Every food we eat, color we wear, scent, people's moods, seasons, and everything in the world has a predominance of element. I experientially practiced following my fluid body as well to work through the unwinding of trauma from the cellular level. This was in addition to years of Jungian psychology. Because kundalini rising is an alchemical process, I needed to be an alchemist to find balance that brought the greatest ease. There was a whole lot of trial and error. Life is like that.

Surrender honed over decades has allowed me to listen to the teachings of the Shakti (Divine Power Consciousness). There were times that my ego personality desperately wanted to control and manage the phenomena that was very disturbing. This grasping created more problems with the kundalini process. Think of BIG energy moving up your spine, and then LITTLE energy (ego) trying to micromanage the direction of big energy. It doesn't work. Part of my development was seeing directly these distinctions as energy patterns, and then translating them into the integration of being and non-being. There is a necessary place for the ego, but I found it wasn't the way we usually think about it.

This is not a didactic manual, but rather a compilation of teachings offered as stories. I share a life that spans decades and so the ways of supporting a kundalini process vary depending on the emergence phase I was in. Sometimes I was a vegetarian; other times, I ate double burgers and drank cream to help ground me. The kundalini process can be mild, moderate or intense depending on the toxicity in the subtle body. The level of discomfort in the process can also be due to this as well as to reactionary beliefs to the process itself. If you fight it in any way, then it becomes a battlefield. There were many times I experienced my body as not mine especially when the energy threw me from one side of the room to the other. The force was way greater than my personality. My personality included the fact that I am also a cultural product of my time in a female body. I had began a negotiating process with it which included giving ample time for it to do its work of purification. The exchange on the side of the personality was being able to go to work or school without the heat and the energy shooting up and going into convulsions in front of other people in public. Early on, I became very intimate with the public bathroom stalls to pass these spontaneous kriyas in semi privacy. I had to look at my beliefs and values around being liked by others. I didn't want to look weird or crazy. I had beliefs around normalcy and I knew I wasn't exhibiting normal behavior.

Although there were many extremely trying experiences, every time I would look at the mirror, I also saw illumination. I trusted. There was a part of me that kept surrendering into the luminous, even when my ego screamed of its annihilation. That is what kept me going through all the years. There was a push and pull internally between "this is terrible" to "this is great" to "is this okay?" There was a forging, a tempering that was burning away what wasn't me. The fire was hot, but it also illuminated. Of course, I went through phases when I wanted to understand, but it was so clear that this wasn't about the mind. The mind was too small, too narrow to comprehend. It was trying to catch something it simply couldn't catch. My spirit was being itself. There was surrender. Both potency and gentleness are key factors in my path. Kundalini rising will be different for each seeker as each individual path is unique.

This is my story but it is also the story of what it means to be a human being. Although I share my personal history, it is patterns of energetic holdings and movements that I look at to examine and transform. With our predisposition in the west to look at psychology, we point to them in terms of personality factors. It has its value, but it is limiting. However, if we see them as simply energetic bundles that move and flow as fields, then this dance of energy reveals more. For the most of these last decades, I've looked at these as just phenomena that come and go. The least invested personally I was, the more I could witness just the comings and going. As long as I saw me in it, both in gain and loss, I was in trouble. Over the years, I've learnt to experience them directly as simply space and variations of densities. It's literally a dynamic dance. Some places in ourselves are more stuck than others, and thus movement is less differentiated. This, however, is not a problem. It becomes an invitation like a puzzle as to how to help bring more life to these places that have forgotten their own way to optimal aliveness. Now, do we recognize that invitation and then take it? Do you still drive the car with a flat tire?

I've worked as a teacher, and my experience of teaching others, no matter what age group, is simply reminding students with many different variations and differentiations on how to remember. Remembering is both recalling from the past, but also putting together pieces of a puzzle to arrive at something new. This is what learning is on whatever level. This is true when I've taught dyslexic children how to recognize lines and curves and translate them into recognizable patterns we call letters in the alphabet, and then attaching these symbols to sounds that we've all agreed to mean something. This is no different when I touch clients, and together come up with a new movement of their heads in relationship to their pelvis in order to relieve back pain or for a client recovering from a stroke to recall a differentiated spine. It is the same pattern of learning when we let go of a habitual pattern of addiction because we discover another piece of the puzzle that can give us the core reward that previous behavior was seeking. My work as a healer now is founded on my kundalini process of how I've come to directly experience reality. I'm not different than anybody else, and so the body-mind system pretty much works under the same principles as I've described above. Learning is simply a process of breaking down and putting together. In other words, it is a movement from destabilization to stabilization and so forth. It is a dynamic dance of movement. It is like a river. The river is not one piece. The river constantly moves. If you were to catch a river, which part would you catch? This is who we are. You are movement. The whole creation is movement. We forget. We don't see. We think we are separate. We think we are one piece separate from the other, separate from the world. We are dynamic flux.

This is not a technical manual on nadis (subtle energy channels), vayus (winds) and chakras (matrix of nadis/energetic centers) though I speak about them in connection to the totality of spiritual emergence in the living of one's life. Throughout the book, I will refer to the elements in the pathways shifting and moving. The kundalini process for me has been about mastering the subtle body in order that my daily life is more joyful, harmonious, easier and at peace. It is not about psychic phenomena, but the ordinary in life. Spiritual here includes the most ordinary facets of life: loving, working, playing, getting sick, dying. In between all these daily cycles is my personal experience with the bliss and challenges of a kundalini rising.

The call of the kundalini is potent, highly flammable and must be handled with care. I don't want to glorify or romanticize kundalini either positively or negatively. It was the context in and of my life. I am simply giving a description of a life living with kundalini. I spent decades of spontaneous detoxification and purification including kriyas (spontaneous movements of my body), intense heat, glossalalia (singing spontaneous songs, foreign languages, poems), increased electrical voltage resulting in full body spasms, a plethora of multi-dimensional images/stories that questioned my beliefs of reality, psychic phenomena as well as expulsion of body fluids and elements as this accelerated spiritual emergence did and continues to do its spring cleaning of the perceptual, psychological, vibrational, physical, and bio-chemical pathways of this self called "me". There were many times that I couldn't control what the pathways did, but I could develop my awareness of the experiences. I have learnt to live a lifestyle that supports this process in a gentler and smoother way. I have accepted that this is a blessing leading to deep spiritual transformation and maturity. Over the decades since the initial rising, I have seen the shifts and the fruition of how I relate with others in my life.

Let me backtrack a little for now. When I was younger, what others saw of me was this adventuress who traveled to continents far away and brought home many exotic stories. I was involved with service work with the poor and destitute in India and

Africa. I also worked with different populations of people with special needs in the United States. I found myself in the most beautiful places in this earth as well as in the horrid realities of war zones.

Soon the outward journeys held not much meaning to me though. My travels turned inward, to the road less traveled. I led a monastic life and then to a life as a healer and teacher. In between life cycles, I struggled with the bliss and shadows of a kundalini rising. My experience of kundalini is that it is life force (felt somatically, chemically and energetically) whose purpose is complete wholeness (annihilation of what is not true is another side of it). I have felt the energetic pathways like a garden hose and when something is stuck in a garden hose, there is a kink. Where there is a kink, the force of the water pushes through many directions until there is no more block or kink. Similarly as kundalini awakens and rises, whatever blocks it meets in the subtle body pathways are energetically pushed in order to clear its pathway. It is part of an evolutionary development just as puberty is part of transitioning from a child to an adult. Non-ordinary states of being were the norm in my life as I navigated the arc from destabilization to stabilization over and over again during its crucial stages of development and restoration. Shakti or energy is not only tumultuous though. It is also soft and nurturing. The years that followed became the training ground for me to create a life that supported the transformation I was in. If it was a rocky roller coaster ride, I investigated deeply what could I do to shift. I was willing to change. I entered a renovation and restoration phase that purified, fortified and repaired my subtle body system. It was to last for years. It continues its dance. There were many levels of initiations and the corresponding unloading and shifting of my physio-psycho-spiritual body.

Throughout the years since the initial rising, my physical health met with a sudden back injury where I had to learn how to walk again, daily severe migraines (thankfully it was not a brain tumor) extreme light sensitivity, chronic pain (my body feeling like it was two sizes smaller), environmental illness and a spiritual emergency questioned further "what is real?" and "what really mattered?" As loved ones were born and died within a short span,

9

life's lessons were delivered to me in a compressed intensive way. In this journey I saw the full spectrum of beauty to ugliness, within myself and others. The higher I went into the light, the lower I sank into shadows. I found that light and dark were really not so different. I underwent several dark nights of the soul as I went through an awakening process into occupying my authentic nature.

This book is about emancipation, liberation, freedom to live a life with choices that bring more joy and peace. This book is a spiritual love story. It is the love story with the divine. It is the love story with the self. It is a guide into using whatever comes into your life as a path of transformation. I speak directly to many issues and situations that are taboo in our cultures. I speak directly and honestly about suicide, mental illness, chronic pain and dysfunction. I am writing this book to inspire people into a more elevated life, no matter what situation you find yourself living. I give practical wisdoms handed through the ages and transmitted to me from my spiritual teachers. I am now a happy person and others have commented on the peace and lightness they feel when they are around me. These qualities, however, did not come easy. They have been cultivated over a lifetime(s).

My journey is a heroine's journey, not a hero's journey. Though if you are a hero, you may also relate to it. A heroine's journey is based on relationships. Relationship is love. The heroine's journey is about love. It is about connections. There were times I went away to many parts of the world, yet it was always to find my way into relationship, whether internal or external. The heroine's journey is a woman's upbringing of being a pleaser and a gatherer, not a hunter. It is from these qualities that women through ages were honored. Some may even say it is biologically induced social behavior over time. It is a journey from invisibility to presence, from silence to finding my true voice. It is a coming back to courage repeatedly to fully embody feelings and senses and recognize that I am a gatherer. It is how I cultivate information as a woman.

This process of speaking my voice entails an ability and capacity to tolerate all manners of affect, mine and others. It requires a toleration for disharmony in relationships which goes against the basic tenet of my Filipino beliefs of "pakikisama"(to get along well together) and "tiis" (forbearance/endurance). It requires one to be in the "unknown" - a place of ambivalence and ambiguity without running into the familiar feeling of being "small." It is about setting down the war between my aliveness in the moment and the belief that my survival rests on being dishonest to self and other. It is truly taking responsibility for self. It is fully accepting and living from a place whereby I am responsible for all my interactions and choices. The heroine's journey is a "knowing" that we are interconnected, not just solitary islands or arrows that shoot in the air to meet a particular target. It recognizes that when you move one part, the whole moves. What we do affects the other. We are one living system. It calls forth those places within ourselves of "not being enough" in order that we may fall into the "knowing" we are always whole. It welcomes everyone on the table to have a voice to be heard, and then come to a negotiation of something new that benefits all. It is based on the truth of collaboration and that we are a network. We share the same net. It is dynamic, ever changing. Bridges are always being created for life is a creative process. Relationships are creative living systems. This is the heroine's journey. It is my journey.

CHAPTER 2: FIRST STIRRINGS

Men go abroad to admire the heights of mountains, the mighty billows of the sea, the long course of rivers, the vast compass of the ocean and the circular motion of the stars, and yet pass themselves by. – St. Augustine

The miracle of life waiting in the heart of a seed cannot be proved at once. By Kabir

I was twenty-two years old when I met my first Buddhist teacher. He was the elder Kirti Tsenshab Rinpoche. He was so patient, kind, gracious and joyful in teaching us. He was so generous in sharing the dharma with us. He was the Kalachakra teacher of the Dalai Lama. I feel very fortunate to be introduced to the teachings from a veteran monk who spent 25 years in a cave meditating. Although he was a scholar too, it really was his presence, warmth and kindness that drew me to him. He introduced me to the nature of mind. Commitment and dedication to the practice of awakening were born here. And so I studied and meditated in the lineage of Tibetan Buddhism and did ChiGong every morning for one month in my first formal retreat.

There were many insights and experiences back then that began a purification process for me. I would come in for interviews with the Rinpoche in the tiny room above the hill in Nepal, and in his warmth, would guide me, "The seed has been planted. Now water it." I would leave and walk down the stairs in a daze as to what he meant. Yet, somehow, something inside me knew exactly what he encouraged. There were divinations and conversations. There were many openings for me: non-ordinary experiences, shakings (the energy wanted me to move and there was so much electricity in my body), lots of light shows, past life remembrances, profound emotional access, heightened sensitivity to all perceptions, crying (Why do I cry? I never cry.) Experiences of ecstasy and energy surges were my daily bread. This was the first time I tracked the kundalini rising in this form.

In my journal back then I wrote, "The Ferrari is here and I don't know how to drive it. My chakras are all open. I have so much energy. Today I feel so different as though a force has taken over me. It is so strong and I've just begun to tap into it. There was a shield of force around me. The water and the sun will be used for healing. It was good, but also scary. There is a realization.

"I looked at my feet but they didn't look like my feet and my hands also looked as though they belong to someone else. There is an intense awareness. My hands grew bigger. I can see exactly and precisely every finger print, every pore. I feel wonderful. It's like a toy." A whole new world opened up. My habitual way of perceiving myself and the world dropped. I remained with the mantras and meditation I was given.

It was also overwhelming on another level. There was a floodgate of information access available and I didn't know what to make with it. "My pores have all opened up to hear. Acute awareness. What for? It's not all linear. There is no time, no space…You are empty. The 'I' in you doesn't exist. Empty or full. Depends on how perception is taken. The record stopped, and is playing the same line. I hear the bees, the flies, the minds of men."

It was clear in my self that watering the seed meant going the way of wisdom. I wasn't interested in the psychic experiences. As a child, I grew up with my mother being a psychic and a healer. The realization that really came through was that there was not a solid "I". My task now was how to live life from that place. The years that came afterwards focused on building confidence in the view. All the dharma teachers I was to meet agreed to this. They simply reminded me that many kinds of phenomena come and go. I just need to be steadfast in the practice. And so I did. I took everything in life as phenomena. Many pleasant experiences came, many unpleasant experiences came and of course many neutral ones as well.

It's funny, I only remembered one word after one month of the teachings. This was highly unusual for my bright mind, yet it is so true. What I did remember thoroughly was to water the seed, and I haven't stopped meditating since then. I began a contemplative life from that day forward.

The solitary word I remembered was "skandhas", and it was to guide my practice for the next decades of my life. I vividly remembered the Rinpoche holding an orange fruit in his hand while he asked us, "What is the orange? Is it the rind, the juice, the pulp, the seed and so forth?" He then elucidated how the "self" is to be seen and examined similarly. What is the self? Skandhas means heaps in Sanskrit. In Pali, the ancient language of the Buddha, it is khanda. The five heaps or aggregates, the Buddha taught, are what make up the experience of self.

They are:
1. Form
2. Feeling
3. Perception/Discrimination
4. Mental formations/Volition
5. Consciousness

Form refers to the body which includes the six senses: eyes, nose, ears, tongue, skin plus the mind sense. It is composed of four elements: air, water, fire, and earth. Feeling is pleasant, unpleasant and neutral. Feeling refers to the sensation, whether emotional or physical, that results with the form contacting an object. This is not emotion, but rather the sensation, and the resultant pleasant, unpleasant or neither pleasant/unpleasant. Are you feeling pain or pleasure? When the ear hears a sound, what is the next train in the line up. Does it sound pleasant, unpleasant, neutral? Perception refers to the first contact of form to sense object and what is the immediate thought that arises. Do we name a sound as a bird song, a noise from a jackhammer, etc? Perception discriminates whether the incoming sensory object is white or black. Mental formations is roughly what we refer to as thinking or mental states: conceptualization, psychological understandings, stories, virtues and volition. Volition is also a potential for a seed to flower, for example. Have we made a whole story of why we like it, and what does it mean, or it shouldn't be there, etc. Then lastly, the fifth part that compromises what we call as self is consciousness . It is awareness itself. It is what ties it all together. These aggregates coming together happen pretty much every moment of the day, and it is what we call self. Because it goes by so fast, we don't even recognize it as conditions that cycle one into another. We just think here we are. Buddhist meditation is seeing the truth of self. It is like watching a movie on a screen. We think it as one story, yet if we go to the projector, we examine it as many frames of photos spliced together. Or in our digital age, many pixels comprise an image we see on the computer screen.

We studied about the mind and liberation. "It is the mind that makes problems out of outside phenomena. What/how you see what is outside depends on the quality of your mind. You see a person/place according to how you judge. Our view is only one view, therefore, we can't say this exist because this is how I see it. It is not a valid base." If an event is a point in space, there are multiple ways (in fact infinite ways from 360 degrees) of how to approach it. The mind puts labels according to mental state of mind (projection).

Practical Application for you:

1. Look around you, to the sides, above and below, also behind and back to front. What do you see? What in your life right now can you invite a 360 degree view?
2. Can you feel the chair you are sitting on right now? What are the sensations arising from you? Is it pleasant, unpleasant or neither pleasant or unpleasant? Did a story immediately arise with that?
3. Think back to when you were twenty-two years old. What were your concerns and values then? What are your concerns and values now? Do you see a connection between the you then and the you now?
4. Was there a time in your life that you experienced a dramatic perceptual change? Did you share it with others? How was that? What did you feel? How did it change your life?
5. Feel your sitting bones on the chair. Are both the right and left side sitting bones supporting you equally?

CHAPTER 3: HUNGRY FOR LIFE

With this view in mind, I introduce you to my personal history as to how I have come to be writing and sharing my insights now. It wasn't out of the blue that I began a monastic life at such a young age. There were many significant experiences all my life that created the steps of a ladder that made me become disillusioned with the world. I had traveled extensively and had experienced a full life by that time. I was like a fruit – ripe for a picking! Let us go on a journey that traverses the world across socio-economic and religious terrains.

<u>Grandma Elsie and this little toe went to market</u>

The message on the yellow sticky note said to call your mom. I was a first year student in the University of California, San Diego, having barely settled in. I deliberated, noticing how my breath had both stopped and then quickened, the afternoon light somehow having shifted.

I knew before I picked up the phone that something terrible had happened. "Your grandma just died," my mother said. My mind registered these words while my heart stopped its beat for a second. "She's dead. She's 90. I too can die. I'm 18 and I haven't done what I've come here for." I stood in front of an abyss and everything I had prepared my young life for didn't seem to matter. "I too can die right now as she had died just right now," these words dawned on me like sunrise. It took me a while to realize that her death was my birth.

I relayed the funeral arrangements over the phone to my mother just as Grandma had prepared me throughout the six years I took care of her. She wanted to be dressed in her torquoise blue dress with the sequins around her collar and to be buried back in New Jersey, across the country, to be laid alongside her husband who died 12 years previous. The last picture they had together was her wearing this blue dress. She had twenty more pounds on her frame then, and her face rounder than the bony ridges of her cheekbones that now prominently hung the thin white skin along itself.

My Grandma was born near one of the many lakes in Finland in 1896. Another century. Another time. Life was extremely hard as the photos of her parents' faces illustrated. Their leather faces carved with determined wrinkles - determined to grab unto life. Staring at the picture, I imagined their hands penetrating iced lakes grabbing the fishes that would feed the family throughout the long winters and mosquito filled summers. These were people who knew how to survive and peered unapologetically to the world. When I first saw these pictures as a twelve-year-old girl, I wondered whether we were really related. My grandmother's mother sat like a mountain while her husband's bushy mustache did not conceal the darkness and bitterness of the harshness of his life.

My grandmother married a Dane, a handsome young man whose picture showed him holding a sword he had used while he fought in WWI. They had separately immigrated to the US early in the century, via Ellis Island. They had worked in a mansion. He was the gardener and she was the cook. My grandmother mischievously narrated to me that they married secretly on a long weekend. Their employer did not allow their employees to have relations with each other and they kept their marriage a secret for a while.

My grandmother was a gentle soul, and only had kind words to say about her husband. She was so generous that when a visitor would comment on how beautiful an object in the home was, she was known to give that object as a gift to the visitor on the spot.

Elsie was her name and it is also my middle name. It means "My God is a vow". I remember her with her red vinyl covered Finnish bible on her lap. She read it every day. She'd sit on the lounge chair on the driveway, the gray cat curled on her lap, her thick glasses with the curl on the top edges, contemplating what she's just read. She was quiet and delicate. She was fiercely independent as well. By the time she was 84, I assisted her in getting in and out of the bathtub. We had this ritual that was to last six years.

I washed her short white hair gently and scrubbed her thin back, along the curvature of her spine. She'd then washed herself alone. I'd wait outside by the couch until she called me to help her get up. I remember her sagging breasts that swam in her bra just as my own breasts were starting to grow and not yet accustomed to being bounded. I still feel the lack of elasticity of her skin as I oiled her legs and trimmed her toenails. Once she saw me giving a haircut to my Barbie doll and she asked that I give her one too. I did, and my grandmother had a punk rocker hairstyle for the first time in her life.

I learned to cook American food from my grandmother: beef stew, roast beef, Yorkshire pudding, etc. In my home, we ate American and Filipino food together. Although she enjoyed all kinds of good food, I remember her eating a lot of applesauce and graham crackers, and how much delight she took in eating anchovies. She'd wait for me to come home from school and would prepare bowls of ice cream while we sat on the old couch. I'd curl next to her and she'd sing, "This little piggy went to market. This little piggy went home..." as she touched my toes one by one.

I had a deep affection and love for my grandmother. I generously kissed her cheeks and embraced her. Every evening, I'd walk her to her bedroom, and we'd lie side by side on the single bed while the dancing girl in the jewelry box danced to the tune of the entrancing song. She'd then tell me stories of her youth in Finland, in the East Coast, her marriage. I shared in her joy, and she cried tears of sadness when my own parents fought. "I never had fights like that with my husband," she would tell me. I am glad she planted another alternative in my mind and heart.

As the white flowers had fallen from the apricot tree that grazed her bedroom window, my grandmother's health took a turn for the worse. She had to used a walker and did not walk past the mailbox. She loved collecting the mail, though as her friends died one by one, there were fewer and fewer handwritten letters. Then she couldn't write anymore, and I wrote her letters for her. I wrote to relatives and friends I had never met and only knew through her stories. How different her life had changed. Here, she lived in the desert of sand while her letters arrived in the desert of snow up in Scandinavia.

The summer bore fruits and one morning, she fell and broke her thigh bone. Her aged mahogany headboard was replaced by a hospital bed with rails that imprisoned her. She scratched her stapled surgical wound and was in an altered state from her medications. The doctor insisted that I tie her hands to the bed rail for a period of time. "Kathrina, how can you do this to me?" she pleaded. We both were crying.

One early morning at three o'clock, my grandmother was vocally excited. I ran to her room, her wound bleeding. As I dressed her wound, she began singing in the loudest voice, "Happy Birthday to you, Happy Birthday to you, Happy Birthday dear Kathrina, Happy Birthday to you." It was my 18th birthday. She remembered even then.

As I packed my suitcases to go to college, my grandmother looked at me with confusion. "Where are you going?" she half begged, her eyes pleading, "Please stay." "To school, Grandma", I held back my tears. My grandmother died three months later.

Her death was a shock that rippled through my life. As I packed her personal belongings and opened her bible, I saw my picture there, smiling at her. It was a winter of quiet despair for me: an inward turning, a query into what really matters when death comes, and when the one I love the most had disappeared.

Finding myself through Solitary Travel – 18 years onward

Even though intellectually I understood that old people die, I was dismayed with the news of her passing. We were extremely close, and her sudden death reminded me that I must live my life. I took my savings and bought an airline ticket to Europe. My mother frantically screamed at me as I packed, "You're going to get raped!" I had never traveled alone nor was even allowed to spend the night at a slumber party a mile from my home. " What about money?" my friends chimed. My then boyfriend sadly handed me travel medications in little pouches just in case I have diarrhea or constipation in the travel. "I miss you already," his doe liked eyes watered. At that moment, I connected to my determination that was a hallmark of my history.

Here's a good place for a side note meander. When I was seventeen years old, I and four other boys who graduated at the top of our class were interviewed for the newspaper. Each of us was asked about our future aspirations. Each of the boys said, "engineer, doctor, pilot," but I said from my heart, "I want to travel around the world as a hobo." Everyone who read the article laughed. I began traveling alone at eighteen, backpacking in Europe for 10 weeks as a vagabond! So when my grandmother died, I did it!

I spent the next 10 weeks alone as a vagabond traveling through Communist Poland, Sicily, France, Greece, Holland and England. It wasn't important where I was going. It only mattered that I was going. I had to do it then, not later, because I had a thought that tomorrow I may not want to do it anymore.

In retrospect, it was a spiritual quest and pilgrimage that I had undertaken. At that time, all I knew was that I didn't want to play dead before I had to. I slept in beaches, train stations, nudist islands. I gallivanted in museums, took trains, met hundreds of people. I came from a family that was very protective in many ways and I had not even been in a slumber party, yet here I was, alone, experiencing the many ways people live. It was an awakening.

I didn't know why I was going. I just knew I had to go. I intuited that the journey will reveal the chambers of my heart. I was so young, naïve and innocent. These qualities somehow drew the people I met close to me. I saw in their eyes protectiveness and an admiration for they recognized the quest, even if I didn't recognize it at times. I didn't have a map to the journey, no itinerary, no shoulds, coulds or woulds. I didn't have to be anybody or somebody. I had just to be me... and the beautiful wonder of it all was I had no idea who me was. So I kept opened and met me again and again and again.

I marveled at everything. The people I met with their kaledioscopic visions. The different countries whose inhabitants matched the temperatures of their land delighted me. The cathedrals beckoned and dwarfed my identity and forced me to expand into my birthright up and into the heavens. The train stations became my home and carried the hopes and fears of mankind. The old with their luggage, and the young hungry, greedy for experience were my teachers.

I stumbled on a nudist beach in a Greek island in my journey. I had a bright neon blue one piece swimsuit and I stuck out like a sore thumb. Day by day, I peeled my suit lower and lower until I was bare naked as the day I was born. I was perched on a rock in Greece watching the moonrise when this silence dawned upon me and I realized that I was experiencing at that moment what I had been searching for all my life. I didn't even realized how lost I was, and now I have been found!!!

And funnily, I didn't even know I was looking. All the questions of my adolescent years that only my eyes revealed opened like an accordion: Moses' exodus, the Lama's Shangri-la, Thoreau's wilderness, Emerson's yearnings, Ayn Rand's objectivism. Here I was, butt naked, half hungry from eating only plums and sleeping under an upturn boat. And I felt like a queen!

It was subtle, yet monumental. It was as though I opened a book of life, from a long, long time ago. I began to take certain postures, and hum, and do gestures with my hands and fingers (mudras) spontaneously. I entered deep states of meditation. I became a vegetarian. My life dramatically shifted internally. At that point in my life, I had not been exposed scholarly to Eastern mysticism.

Communist Poland

I was part of an educational work exchange in Poland when I was eighteen years old. It was still Communist before when I had landed in Warsaw. It was distinctive the landing. Everyone clapped in the airplane as the wheels hit the ground. The passengers were so happy to be arriving in Poland. I felt their love of their mother land.

I traveled from Warsaw all the way to south of Poland. I didn't speak Polish, yet the people helped me arrive where I needed to go. I was handed hand to hand from one Polish person to the next until I arrived at my destination. I remember boarding the old steam train, the dark smoke bellowing in the air, the hard benches, the Polish countryside with parceled farm lands in different rectangular shapes, each a different hue of a color. It was summer, and it was warm. I was glad to leave the city of Warsaw and its grayness. The countryside had more life, less repression.

Life was hard there. Everything was rationed. There were coupons for milk, for chocolate for children. We ate mostly potatoes. Once I saw many people running towards an old cart. It was horse sausage being sold in the black market. No western product was allowed into Poland then. Those that spoke English were very eager to know about the life outside of Poland.

I stayed for three weeks in the Beskidy mountains bordering Czechoslovakia. We were doing forest restoration work, except there were no supplies. One of the projects was building foot bridges across the creeks. There were only rusty, bent used nails that had to be hammered straight to be used again to make the bridge. There was a cellar underneath the house with a fireplace and a long table in the narrow room. One night, all the students were there and vodka was passed one after the other until the fire no longer was burning and everyone was dead drunk.

There was a special treat of spaghetti cooked in blueberries as a meal. There were lots of laughter and shared facial expressions. It was really not about the work, but more the exchange of young people with each other.

Towards the end, we went to the Auschwitz and Dachau Concentration camps. It was eerie and disturbing. I have only read about the camps as a general historical fact of WWII in my high school history class. Holocaust meant something else to me after going there. Nothing could have prepared me for what I saw. According to history, "Auschwitz, also known as Auschwitz-Birkenau, opened in 1940 and was the largest of the Nazi concentration and death camps. Located in southern Poland, Auschwitz initially served as a detention center for political prisoners. However, it evolved into a network of camps where Jewish people and other perceived enemies of the Nazi state were exterminated, often in gas chambers, or used as slave labor. Some prisoners were also subjected to barbaric medical experiments led by Josef Mengele (1911-79). During World War II (1939-45), more than 1 million people, by some accounts, lost their lives at Auschwitz. In January 1945, with the Soviet army approaching, Nazi officials ordered the camp abandoned and sent an estimated 60,000 prisoners on a forced march to other locations. When the Soviets entered

Auschwitz, they found thousands of emaciated detainees and piles of corpses left behind."

"For those prisoners who initially escaped the gas chambers, an undetermined number died from overwork, disease, insufficient nutrition or the daily struggle for survival in brutal living conditions. Arbitrary executions, torture and retribution happened daily, in front of the other prisoners. Some Auschwitz prisoners were subjected to inhumane medical experimentation. The chief perpetrator of this barbaric research was Josef Mengele (1911-79), a German physician who began working at Auschwitz in 1943. Mengele, who came to be known as the "Angel of Death," performed a range of experiments on detainees. For example, in an effort to study eye color, he injected serum into the eyeballs of dozens of children, causing them excruciating pain. He also injected chloroform into the hearts of twins, to determine if both siblings would die at the same time and in the same manner. When the Soviet army entered Auschwitz on January 27, they found approximately 7,600 sick or emaciated detainees who had been left behind. The liberators also discovered mounds of corpses, hundreds of thousands of pieces of clothing and pairs of shoes and seven tons of human hair that had been shaved from detainees before their liquidation. According to some estimates, between 1.1 million to 1.5 million people, the vast majority of them Jews, died at Auschwitz during its years of operation. An estimated 70,000 to 80,000 Poles perished at the camp, along with 19,000 to 20,000 Gypsies and smaller numbers of Soviet prisoners of war and other individuals."

I wrote this in my journal at the time: "There were barracks - gray, long buildings in a row. It was silent. Dead. I went inside one room and it was filled with shoes, from floor to ceiling. I went inside another room, and it was filled with suitcases with people's names on it, coming from different places. Another room filled with human hair, from floor to ceiling. I went to the gas chambers, and swallowed hard, and prayed for peace for all the souls. I saw the films of 'liberation' when the Russians came to end the concentration camps, and released the Jews that were still alive. There were slides and pictures of skeletons with smiles, and numbered tattoos and white and black striped clothes. It was hard to believe that I belong to this humanity that is capable of such atrocity to each other."

Practical Application for you:

1. What are you feeling right now just after reading about the concentration camp Auschwitz?
2. What comes to mind when you think of your grandparents? How were you influenced by them? What smells come to you?
3. Do you remember your first yearnings for travel to another land? What was that like? What does it bring up for you now?
4. When images of war arise in the media, what happens to you? How do you receive it?
5. Feel your feet on the floor. Is there more weight on the heel or the toes? Is the floor hard or soft? I invite you do a movement like a windshield wiper with your feet. Breathe.

CHAPTER 4: DEATH AS MY TEACHERS

My brother committed suicide when he was 22-year-old. He was really a sensitive artist that none of us could really see through. He self-medicated and did everything to call attention to the big wound of life. He was the saddest person I knew back then. We had our last supper before he took his own life. I remember because I even wrote a paper in Spanish about his loneliness. Yet, there was not an ounce of knowing in me that his pain was so grave that he would soon shoot himself to still the pain in his heart. He blew his brains out with a shotgun and I cleaned the fresh blood and gray matter that once was in his skull. How could a 19 year old me comprehend such despairing action whose purpose was to quiet that which hurts the most? His death shook the foundations of my family, and my understanding of life. At that time, I was angry with God yet I couldn't be too angry because my brother was with God now. It was sort of a deal that he would take care of him. I was just thankful that he was free of pain. At least, I hoped that it was true.

Later in life as a 44-year-old aunt, my young niece and nephew who never met my oldest brother asked me why he killed himself. I said that he was in so much pain, and sometimes people want to stop the pain by killing themselves. I said to them that it is important to speak to friends and family and get help if you have pain. That killing one's self is not the only solution. I feel sad right now that they never met him and that they only know that he was dead. I don't know if their father (my other brother) ever speaks to them about him. He still feels the pain in his heart. So do I. I wondered too how an older brother would look after a younger sister as we aged in life.

It took me many years to heal and accept his choices. I wanted to show him how to live a life to the fullest. I wanted to show him how it could be done. I didn't want to be defeated. I didn't want to succumb to despair, loss, disappointment and failure. I flew into my magical world of flowers as solace. After all, they were open and blooming and had no problem showing their hearts. I knew I was one of them. They reminded me of my birthright. This too is our birthright. To be open, held, vulnerable and awake. My duality widened as I disassociated further from the deep feelings of grief. I wanted to feel the opposite. I ran away from my sense of shame.

I ran to Africa to escape my pain.

It was befitting that I arrived in Nairobi airport in the darkness just before dawn breaks. It was silent except the chorus of cicadas that joined the squeaky soprano sounds of the wheels of my two suitcases. I, along with other Californian students, began what was to be a year as exchanged students. Directly from the airport, a bus drove us to the National Park to witness dawn breaking and the animals coming out into the day. My breath stopped with marvel at the vast horizon and the huge African sky. I felt it was my first sunrise, ever. Nothing prepared me for what was to come.

I was twenty years old when I walked up the hill towards the museum in Nairobi where the director's office was. I had barely arrived in Kenya from San Diego and was still disoriented by the change of the sea of skin color enveloping me. I was impressed by the different variations of blackness, and fascinated with the mystery it had awakened in me. Chocolate, charcoal, indigo, ink, nutmeg, molasses, evening, ebony, raven, sable – my nuance of black widened. Images of oil and petroleum mixed in with dark jewels. My eyes drank the velvety texture of others and my belly churned with a yearning new to me. Excitement and fear danced as I entered the African continent.

Unbeknownst to me at the time, I was to enter different layers of darkness within myself. One of them would be the great divide of the gender inequality in Kenya. "I was struck at how this man ignored us for the first part of the conversation because we were women. I don't need a guy to escort me to the alley, to anywhere! I feel so caged. The only thing I value the most is my independence and it is being threatened." I bumped against this repeatedly. Ignored for my intelligence, yet leered at for my beauty.

My travels were to teach me by experience the dos and don'ts of men and women. Women were objectified so blatantly here, everywhere in the world really. Here in instinctual Africa, I became very conscious of this. My simple, warm friendliness was interpreted the wrong way. It was mistaken for something more. For the first time, I had to temper my sweetness. "I want the one in the red kikoy (skirt)." "I like your smell." "You can sleep in my boat." "I like the way you move." Men just looked women up and down as though as women were cargo or something. It brought up deep feelings of disgust and mistrust for me.

There were many double standards, and that I would be frustrated by them. Men of all kinds and ages would try to seduce me with their words and eyes, and when I didn't play along, got nasty and mean. I learnt really young the unruliness of these pre-sexual mating games, no matter what country I was in. Both men and women's sexuality were so tied up with their sense of insecurities. It was excruciating!

There were some women along the road to Lamu that were barefoot, and one of the Kenyans said that it was because the husbands required it of the women so that they knew everywhere they went. The men knew their wives' footprints and just followed them wherever they went. Women in Kenya worked very hard, while the men led more leisurely lives.

The blackness I encountered was not the villain against the white superhero that my western education groomed me in. Rather it was the mystery that a dark night invites and as one settles into its cloak, one begins to encounter the magic of the senses. There are creatures that emerge and thrive only in the night. Stars only twinkle when it is dark and the fireflies circle in their light. It is in the dark night that the moon in its fullness beckons me in all my nakedness. And it is also in the darkest night when the moon is black that my deepest fears and longings cry the loudest.

Little did I know that the girl who came to Africa was not going to be woman that left a year later. My eagerness for excitement and experience coupled with my innocence laid the foundation for a journey rich in its complexity and profundity. Wherever I went, the people welcomed me because of my easy and warm way to blend in the lifestyle.

"There is a feeling of Eternity in youth which makes us amends for everything. To be young is to be one of the Immortal Gods." - Hazlitt

I studied at the University of Nairobi in 1988. The Kenyan students were fabulous, welcoming and generous to us foreigners. I made deep friendships there and it was truly magical. I studied African literature and Anthropology. I tried many new things in my life. I was carefree. I was happy.

Once we hitched a ride on a truck carrying 40 tons of coffee from Rwanda. I even got featured in the Kenyan newspaper a couple of times and also in a trailer at the movie theatre. I acted in a play about social injustice in South Africa at the University of Nairobi. I traveled a lot during the weekends and the breaks. I was so thirsty to know of the world.

Another time, I went to Zanzibar and it took three days by dhow. "I was dropped off at the old Mombasa port and waited to be smuggled into the boat that was to take me to Zanzibar. I went inside this really old immigration building. It was like being transported in time. There was a long wooden table smoked with time. I wondered how my fingerprints had been on it. There was an elderly Moslem man in his white robe and cap. He had a big silver ring with a black stone on his pinky. He looked at me and with a firm hand, stamped my passport with a departure stamp. As I looked out of the window, I saw this huge wooden ship being filled with hundreds of brown sacks. Destination: Somalia. Next to it was a ship that had just arrived from India.

I went downstairs to look for my dhow. Gulam, Amir's friend, had been sent to "take care of me". I met Amir on the train from Nairobi. I am the same age as his daughter and so he took me under his wing. Anyways, another ship just came from Dubai, Saudi Arabia. I was mesmerized.

I waited nearly six hours for my dhow before we left at half an hour past midnight. There were lots of bribery happening in the dark of the night. I slept on the floor of a dhow with 20 other Swahili passengers on their way home to the island of Pemba. It took 16 hours to arrive there. There were thick ropes of tobacco and dried fish. The stars glistened in the night.

The town of Maokani in Pemba was at the peek of the mango season. I never saw such gigantic mangoes and the forest of cloves fragrantly scented the roads everywhere. I slept on the boat that night, despite the custom officials threat that he would arrest me if I did. I remembered as he paddled his skiff to our dhow. I quickly doctored my yellow immunization card. I didn't want to be given any injections there. I've seen the one jar with all the used needles in Uganda. Anyways, he came on board with his starched collared shirt and demanded that I take a hotel in Pemba. I didn't of course. I took the local bus (trucks that have been re-modeled with hard wooden benches) around Pemba and was astonished of this island that stood still in time with the clove smell hanging in the air. There were forests of cloves in Pemba (3.5 million trees). There is a quite large Arab community from Oman. The population is a mix of Arab and original Swahili people. The Shirazi people also lived here.

The crew was extremely kind and caring towards me. They brought a bucket of fresh water for me to take a shower. The only thin mattress was laid down on one side of the boat and sarongs were tied together to make a curtained private bedroom for myself. We ate lunch at the boat's stern and the men taught real Swahili : bodo (Lamu/Zanzibar) or Sima (Mombasa) or Ugali (Nairobi). We all laughed so much. I was so impressed by the respect the Moslem men in the boat showed me in this journey! I felt protected."

In Zanzibar, I kept meeting the locals and having conversations about their lives. Abu's father makes only $25 a month and there were 15 members in the family. Colin's father made the same amount, and he was a doctor.

In Dar Es Salaam (means piece of heaven), I stayed with a Bohora family. Even though the young woman was progressive in her thinking, she told me that she still has to abide by the rules there. If she didn't wear the purdah, the priest would see her and not marry her with her fiancée. They told me that the family would suffer and the family would be ostracized! The father will be refused entrance into the mosque.

I had planned a trip to Zimbabwe, via Mozambique at the time. I even had an agreement to write an article for the Associated Press about the war in Mozambique. I cancelled my trip and returned to Kenya instead.

There were also riots that the students were known for. Kenya was not a democratic country, and one was not to talk politics and it was forbidden to meet with more than three people at a time. Once I had dinner with a group and the police came to break it up. The neighbor came out and told the police that it was rude to send visitors away when there was still food on the table. Funnily, the police said we could finish the dinner then leave.

We were warned of these political maneuvers. Whenever a riot was impending, I would get a note requesting me to leave campus and find a safe place.

"The first year students are going back to NYS (National Youth Service) next weekend. None of them want to go back but the green buses are loading them. NYS is a 3 month long military training university students must go through before their first year. I've been told that NYS is torture – hell! They sleep at midnight only to wake up at 3 or 4 am. They run for miles without end and then eat lousy food. They develop circles under their eyes. I was told that the reason for this NYS is that President Moi wanted to control the riots. In the past 17 years, there has been 17 riots. By bringing and letting the students know what torture is then maybe they won't want to suffer the consequences of a riot!"

"There was a riot at another school (Gilgil) and it was ugly. The fight lasted 12 hours between the students using rocks against the corporals with batons and masks. Many were hurt. Women were raped. I just talked to a girl that came from Gilgil. I was told that it's always the girls that get hurt the most. They get raped. I don't want to get raped."

The realities of life there were stark. I studied and got to know the Kenyan people. I volunteered in a school at the slums. I traveled and tried many walks of life. For a day, I picked coffee berries with others. It was really hard work and I only got paid $2.50 for my labor. Global economics left the books and I saw experienced first hand more inequalities.

Because my skin was lighter in color, I could enter any establishment I wanted to in Kenya even if I didn't have money. That was the politics of skin color, the privilege of race. Apartheid wasn't just in the plays of Athol Fugard I read in my literature classes. I saw the color divide in Kenya first hand.

Zealous to jumpstart my career as an anthropologist, I raced to the archaeological office. I found the door ajar but the director not in sight. It was an unpretentious office, with many old, dusty books in disarray. I sauntered along the unassuming hall, passing time with reading old paper notices on a dilapidated board. Along came an elderly African man whose curly beard was peppered with gray. He was simply dressed. I evaluated him to be a janitor. He had deep dark eyes that bored into me and I didn't like being read without my permission. Under my politeness seared defiance. He missed nothing. Since he was the only one around, I hesitantly but pointedly enquired about the director. He simply dismissed me that he'll be back and I should wait in the office. I insisted in meandering outside, preparing my script as to how to impress this director in accepting me as a research assistant in the back country. I waited for an hour or so, impatient, nervous, irritated, strategizing to get what I want.

After what seemed like an eternity, this old man that I wanted to shake off like an unwanted fly on my forearm went inside the office and sat behind the desk. He was Mr. Omondi (not real name), the director I wanted to impress. With disbelief and resentment, I gathered my wits and meekly asked if there were research positions for me in the field. He simply dismissed me with "Nothing. Come back in 3 months." No smile. No welcome carpet. No, I'll take your name. I was the fly that was flickered from his arm!

My head was burning as I stampeded down the hill. I was determined to show him. I came back every month for the next nine months and was given the same cool answer. The tenth and last time I trudged up the hill, he said, "Where have you been? Your man has arrived and is waiting for you in Mombasa. The survey has begun." Mombasa was the coastal town an overnight's train journey from Nairobi. I raced home and walked the three flights of stairs one last time.

While holding the arm rail, I was reminded of having been stopped here several months earlier. I had known Raj only a few weeks then months ago and he was eager to get to know me. His questions were many and with my polite smile, I was able to reply with enough veil for my privacy.

"How many brothers do you have?" Raj asked, wanting to know more about me. "Two..." I hesitated, then added, " I have/had three brothers." It was an unfamiliar and uncomfortable question for me. I didn't know how much to reveal, how to answer without inviting more questions. The memory it evoked was so fresh and I hadn't made sense of it. "My brother died last year," I stammered. He looked at me quizzically, and I knew the question before he spoke. "How?" Up until that point, I had revealed no more than "my brother died" to my friends, if at that.

My brother shot himself with a Winchester. He was twenty-one years old. When I arrived in the scene of his departure, his two suitcases were packed. He had planned his suicide that it would be quick and easy, for him, for us. Except, it didn't work that way. I touched the empty shotgun box, newly bought. Quietly, I cleaned up the blood and brain parts on the wall and table. My parents and I let the fresh blood drained unto the roses in the front yard. The house was colder than usual, more silent and this time, we didn't look at each other.

Just the week before, Pekka and I were having a 12 course dinner at a Chinese restaurant. There was deep loneliness. I didn't realize that he was saying good-bye, or maybe he was waiting for me to say hello.

I saw my brother next after his autopsy while on a stretcher covered in a white sheet just before he was cremated. We didn't have money and could not afford the elaborate funerals typical of my culture. I was the only one who did not shed tears. I didn't know how to feel and what to make of my feelings. Instead I comforted my younger brother with his beseeching eyes, "He's in heaven now." I was angry with God. And at the same time, I wanted God to take care of my older brother. Looking at it now, I was making an emotional deal with God as though I was bargaining and brokering for love and care for my brother in the afterlife.

Going away to Kenya was a little of forgetting. It was a little of remembering life. It was a flying into possibilities of a lost youth, a lost life. Maybe a part of me wanted to show him that one can be happy too and be free. I often wondered about how confusing my relationship to him was when he was alive and how more confused I was when he died.

I spent my adolescence trying to be everything he wasn't. Pekka was the oldest child in my family, and he shunted the brunt of its dysfunctionality. He was the reason my family left the Philippines when I was twelve years old. He was sent to be with my estranged father in Louisiana after a run in with the law in the Philippines. Before he had left hurriedly, I remember finding him in the dark attic, shaking with fear. Only the white of his eyes held me steady.

Pekka ran away because of the abuse he received from my father. My mother then took the rest of the children from the P.I. to search for Pekka in the States. We found him. The harmony of the unification was short lived. Pekka was in and out of juvenile hall and he became the scapegoat and focus of my parents' arguments. Just as he was so visible, I decided to be invisible. Just as he was dark, I wanted to be light.

I don't remember Pekka as a person very much. Somehow, in the boxes of survival strategies I created, I didn't really see him. Later, upon years of inner reflection and therapy, I accepted that we shared the same wound and the same curiosity for life. Actually, I was surprised how much alike we were. I accepted that we loved each other and I couldn't bear this love. It took me many years after he died before I could cry. It took me longer still to allow myself to long for my big brother's protection and warm gaze.

Once, he spoke with my younger brother next to his old red pick-up. Pekka said, "Hold these three sticks in your hands and try to break it." So he did and had a hard time doing so. "Now just hold one stick and break it." Quickly and without effort, the single stick broke. "Now you see, you (brothers and sister) need to stick together because you're stronger that way."

Today I miss my eldest brother. When I was six, I would wake up and he would have already bought freshly-baked bread and eggs from the market. He would help the vegetable sellers carry their baskets on his wooden cart when the night was not yet day, and with this money, he'd buy breakfast for us. He was only a few years older than I back then. I wonder how he would have been as a man today if he had lived. Today I missed my eldest brother.

Practical Application for you:

1. Do you know anyone close to you that have taken his/her own life? What was that like?
2. What feelings arise for you right now?
3. Did you talk about it with others? Did that help?
4. Do you remember a time of deep loss when you couldn't cry? What did you do?
5. How has this changed your life in your relationship with people around you now?

CHAPTER 5: ARCHEOLOGY OF MY PSYCHE - AFRICA

Now in Nairobi, packing everything again and saying goodbye to a lover. I took the journey to the coast, swapping the coolness of higher elevation for the humid, sweltering heat of Moslem Mombasa.

I had taken this overnight train journey the first time a year previous as I traveled to the island of Lamu to study Kiswahili. The train journey was beautiful and magical as I leant on the open window and felt the breeze and the African dusk. The horizons were wide, and the sky big. I remember the trees with the space around. The trees were stately. They were unapologetic. I felt that I was in a magical book when I was there.

Lamu is the oldest town in Kenya, its history over a thousand year old. There was only one car allowed in Lamu, the governor's. People walked in ancient narrowed streets that winded the island like a maze. There were 5000 donkeys and twice as many cats. To this day, Lamu is a feeling rather than a place for me.

Elaborately carved wooden doors differentiated the white-washed lime washed-cemented walls that lined the tiny stone corridor. Women with mysterious and curious eyes watched me hidden in their black buibuis (a black veil that hid them from head to toe). Gorgeous darkened bronze men in colorful fabrics called kikoys wrapped around their waists navigated these beautiful old wooden boats with white sails called dhows. Swahili people are a mix of African Kenyan, Portuguese and people from Oman and Yemen. They were exquisitely beautiful.

"Once we were all in the boat for an excursion and we got stranded with only less than a loaf of bread and two tomatoes for 20 of us. Two hours later, another boat began to approach us and we thought, we would be rescued. To our surprise and laugher, they came just to drop a bag of oranges for us, and not to rescue us! So we spent the whole night under the stars and it was all so romantic...until I had to go pee. There was no bathroom as this was just a simple and functional old boat. So I sat on the edge and with everything and everyone being silent, peed into the ocean. Others followed. As the night progressed and I laid down, one of the Kenyans asked me, "Why did you take so long while your girlfriend so short?"

I had a crush on "Luke". We went on his dhow to visit the neighboring islands. Once, we went fishing late in the night. The tides were low and we hiked our skirts to our hips and trudged the mud towards the boat waiting to sail. The sky was dark like chocolate and the stars lit brilliantly inviting the fish to the surface. I dipped my hand onto the Indian Ocean as the boat sailed into the open sea, and to my biggest surprise, there were so many phosphorescent fish. My hand sparkled and I was electrified! The magic continued into fear as we were stranded in one of the uninhabited islands because the tide had receded.

The adventure turned out well and we were unharmed. Luke caught one fish and grilled it. We walked the whole day across the other side. It was scorching hot and we barely had drinking water. A search party found us.

Another time, we were caught in the dhow with the waves tossing us hither and thither. I didn't know that we were in danger of being overturned. I was so caught in the excitement and energy of the ocean and the sky and the storm. It was the kind of fear that was mesmerizing. It is the fear when life and death, calmness and calamity merge into one. It was an adrenaline rush that also put life and creation into a bigger perspective. I found stillness in the midst of the engulfing waves.

Luke was kind of a hero. He invited me to sleep in his dhow and I declined. "Haraka haraka haina baraka" - hurry hurry has no blessing, I mischievously said to him. The men told me that hurried people are in a lot of heat and must be cooled down with the ocean water.

In actuality, I was in a relationship with the only son of an Indian family. Raj and I had a relationship against his parents' wishes. It was a love that was doomed to end. My romantic idealism was shattered when Omar, a Pakistani friend who'd lost both his legs, sat me one day over dinner and explained the triangle of life. He drew a triangle on a paper and marked each corner with family, career, friends/religion. Then smacked in the middle of the triangle, he drew me. He proceeded to explain that everything in Raj's life was all connected except me. I was in the center but dangling, not belonging to his universe. Omar begged me to think of years ahead and how this union would impact both our lives and the children's lives in unfavorable ways. It was clear - compassion can be hard too.

While in Nairobi, I volunteered as a teacher in the slums of Matare. Matare was built on garbage and the homes made of flattened boxes and tin. White people do not come here alone. I was escorted to the school to teach. The school was 6 feet by 12 feet and 60 students crammed inside. The two windows lined with wire were jammed with eager children wanting to learn. I remember the curious and delighted eyes of the children, in the classroom and also through the wired windows. There was a thirst for knowledge and I wished I had water for all.

It was here that I realized I couldn't teach exactly how I was taught. There was no point reading Snow White and the seven dwarves. It became critically apparent that children's books are socializing agents and hold within them the seed of ideals and rules for society. If whiteness and beauty are the twin pinnacle of Eurocentric teaching, then what is the equivalent for black Africa? What do I teach the children born of abject poverty? Out of the mountain of garbage, how do I speak of hope? How do I speak of the wide ocean when they've never seen it? When sniffing gasoline from cars is equivalent to moments of glory? And children are born out of 2 shilling sexual intercourse or rape? Once I asked what freedom means. One student replied, "food on the table." They were teaching me.

Once I was in the countryside where the soil was the color of ochre. One child held my hands and was so puzzled. She then touched the soles of my feet and asked me, "Do you work?" more out of disbelief. Somehow, the idea that someone didn't have calloused hands and feet was inconceivable to her. It took me a while to realize how bizarre I must have been to them, with my cushioned life - a life that was a life of leisure. How was it that I could have skin the color of the ripe mangoes they picked from the trees?

I was to return to Lamu at the end of the archaeological expedition, this time deathly sick with malaria and hemolythic jaundice. It was again Luke who cared for me, bringing food, carrying me when I couldn't walk and making me laugh with his seductive attempts. But this time, he knew that I was just a sister and not a lover.

Luke was part of the archeological expedition along the islands on the coast of northern Kenya. Tinga, Mohammed, Kusimba, Karissa and I made the team. I was secretly called "Ice cream" by the team. I don't really know why. At the time, I felt somehow offended by this term. It connoted sweetness, but ice cream easily melts as well. I wanted to forge and present an image of toughness that was necessary to work in the African bush. I never confronted them about this nickname though my face revealed my initial displeasure regarding this term of endearment. It soon became apparent to me that they wouldn't have accepted me into the archaeological survey team along the Kenyan coast if they didn't think I'd make it.

Before arriving in the islands, we traveled in an old land rover all along the coast. Our goal was two fold: one to check the status of archaeological sites in this area and what needs to be done and the other, to find traces of iron ore development in Kenya's early history. We interviewed scholars, religious clerics, the elderly, blacksmiths. We searched for clues that would lead to more interviews. We weaved our way across different cultural and religious fronts. When with the Swahili Moslems, I wore a bui-bui. When with the Bohoras, I wore their version of purdah. With the blacksmiths, I was given special privileges as a woman to join them in their firing pits. Women were not allowed as we were considered impure. I was given an exception. Blacksmiths are considered magicians and alchemists. They belong to a special caste. They transform earth into metal.

This alchemical transformation of the earth into metal foreshadowed what my life's passion was to be: the alchemy inherent within the human psyche and body. Already, it was apparent in my life Kenya.

June 28, 2009

Yesterday, we were into Samburu, Chengoni. The craft of blacksmithing is fast disappearing in this part of the world. It is not merely about producing a product. In fact, the craft is something sacred with a lot of rituals and symbolism attached to it.

The bellow is made of the skin of the goat's legs (mivuo). One end has a clay tube called a chewa. They look like bagpipes. Inside is the fur and the outside the hide. Together it is what is used to blow air into the fire. There is the fire pit and an open rectangular hut around it. The fire pit varies in size depending where we went.

Today we interviewed the Mkendo-Giriama people. One of the men would speak in Geriama to Tinga, while Karissa translated it into Kiswahili and then Kusimba wrote it in English. We were outside under a tree and the children were playing and laughing. Bare breasted women were around. The girls wore a mini skirt made of pieces of material. Women wore many black bangles made of rubber all over the arms. Men and women find it sexy to amplify the hips and so women wear kangas around it. Wide hips are related to fertility.

The containers they used were made of water pipes. They put a wood stopper on one end and a rubber with thread on other as an opener. This one is used for snuff. I am fascinated by the combination of very ingenuitive incorporations of modern things with traditional life. A milk carton is flattened and used as a wallet by an old man.

There were times I would see a man carrying a chair, while the woman would carry the bed. The inequality of the sexes was very apparent in this part of the world."

The Giriama (also called Giryama) are one of the nine ethnic groups that make up the (which literally translates to "nine towns"). The Mijikenda occupy the coastal strip extending from Lamu in the north to the Kenya/Tanzania border in the south, and approximately 30 km inland. The Giriama are among the largest of these ethnic groups. They inhabit the area bordered by the coastal cities of Mombasa and Malindi, and the inland towns or Mariakani and Kaloleni.

Fieldwork had its ups and down. We had at times to chase the informers around. We would be told it is only 5 kilometers away or just around the bend when in actuality, the distance was 2 hours away by land rover. And when we got there, the informer didn't know what we were asking for. This was life as a researcher.

My project was to observe and take pictures of the black-smithing process. I've also taken on the study of the socialization of children amongst the Swahili children, specifically in terms of play.

June 29,1989

"A group of Swahili girls were playing hand-made dolls made out of foam. Only the female dolls had clothes because the children said they didn't know how to make guy clothes. There are no fathers in their play; only mothers. This is indicative of the Swahili family where there is a separation of men and women.

The boys made cars/buses out of wood. They use a can with a nail as a horn. They use rubber band to tie sticks together. The cars/buses, they said, carry ungmboga, sugar, maharagwe, ndezi from the store to the house everyday. They said only boys can do this because girls are not capable. Girls play house and cook.

I also noticed that girls tend to make toys of what's around them. They don't make anything – just say an object is something else. It's good enough. They always play in the vicinity of the houses – comfort and security.

Boys make things. They make a dhow (a boat) from wood. They make them by the house and then wonder off to the sea. It shows adventurous spirit.

In fact, men and women don't eat together. When there is a male guest, he only associates with the males. He can't go beyond the dining area, in the front of the house. This is opposed to the women who had access to the entire house. The women eat from the same plate – a huge plate. We all sit on the floor on a straw mat with a big round plate of food and with our hands, share the meal. There is also a type of lettuce that helps with easing gas. The men eat separately with the choices of meat with their rice and vegetable."

July 4, 1989

"We're in Msabaha, between Gede and Malindi, interviewing blacksmiths. There are three of them, one blowing the bagpipes in the middle of the foraging area, while the other two pounded the metal that is to be turned into a functional object.

It was very beautiful in the open walled hut under the coconut grove and the wind whistling softly. The goat skin bag pipe beats like a heart. The rhythmic high pitch pounding of metal against metal and the crackling of fire were mesmerizing. As I close my eyes, I feel a deep sense of comfort, especially from the sounds of the bellows. Drinking water is in the baobab fruit and calabash whose function now is to carry water.

It is dark inside amidst the ashes and dark skin of the blacksmiths, yet the orange color and liveliness of the fire jumps at the observer. The hot orange metal and how flickers of orange fly here and there. As my own hart synchronizes itself with the pounding, a rhythm is made. I, and the blacksmiths, the blacksmiths and nature, I and nature. Together we are one."

Blacksmiths are known as magicians. They are also feared as they partake in alchemical work. Today I understood this.

July 7, 1989

I am now in the town of Garsen on the way to Lamu. It's quite a colorful town and the people look more like Somalians. I gather that this is more a pastoralist society. Men wear sarongs, mostly green or blue, and a shirt. The men carry long sticks. The women wear huge bright blue scarves trailing from their beautiful hair all the way to the ground. It is called a Kishali. I think these people are called the Orma.

July 12, 1989

Ungwana: Will my friends in America understand this? What I see, what I hear, what I feel? Can they relate when I tell how the River Tana washes into the Indian Ocean, where the ocean is no longer salty and it is the color of the soil?How will they react when I convey how the hippopotamus emerge from the same water at sunset only to return during sunrise. How untamed is the land of

Ungwana! Drinking Orma chai, I watch the baboons hunt for crabs on the seashore.

July 17, 1989

In Pate Island, the people looked more like Portuguese or Arabs. Their skin is lighter. The women wear many gold earrings along the ear bridge and one big black circle on the earlobe. The shortcut to Pate is the channel of Chungoni. The water must have been just 2 feet deep as we passed through. One does not want to be caught here overnight as the mosquitoes will feast on you. I also got very ill here with malaria, hemolytic jaundice and gastrointestinal infection at the same time. The team of researchers was simply amazing. I didn't know how sick I was. They carried me to the boat and took turns holding my hand. My urine was the color of coca cola. It took a while for me to recover.

I remember waking up in the simple room in the island and it felt like a huge skyscraper was heavy on my chest. For a minute, I thought, "Wow, the humidity really changed dramatically that I could barely breath." I thought I was having a heart attack at the age of 20. I slowly opened my eyes and saw I was covered with red spots everywhere. I couldn't move. As the days progressed, it became worse. Once someone knocked on the door and I was awakened. I rapidly stood up, only to fall on the ground. I tried to feed myself, except the spoon kept missing my mouth. I had lost eye-hand coordination. Others had to feed me, though I had no appetite. The only doctor in the island came to my bedside and said he had no medicine. I simply stated that I had Fansidar with me if it was malaria. I took the thick pills not knowing if I would have an allergic reaction to it. I don't even remember how long it took as I was unconscious most of the time. I would go in and out, and would remember being drenched in sweat, shaking, the mosquito net around me. I was barely cognizant of the filtered light and darkness. I would hear Swahili spoken around by people who took turns watching over me.

Once I was in Mombasa again, a Bohora family took care of me, preparing the special food I needed to recover. I am indebted to the generosity of the Moslem people I met during this time.

Uganda:

I went to Uganda to visit Janet, whom I met when I was part of the theatre program at the University of Nairobi. She was a cultural dancer from the University of Kampala. I went to visit her in Kampala and then to her village near the Zairean border. Although Idi Amin was no longer the ruler of Uganda at the time, there was still unrest in the country. His rule was laden with human rights abuse, political repression, ethnic persecution and corruption.

I saw many child soldiers with guns bigger than themselves. There were curfews in the evenings and I heard gunshots. Besides that, I loved the Ugandan people. They are so generous, giving so much even though they owned so little. They were very warm. Even though life was very poor, there was a certain joy. I have noticed that in poor countries, there is a coming together of community that I don't see in richer countries in the world.

"On our way to Rukunjiri, in Western Uganda, the car again had a flat tire – a normal occurrence on African roads. It was Christmas time and we had stopped for the evening as we got word that night robbers are on the prowl. We stayed in Mbarara. At first I didn't realized that they were rationing everything amongst themselves so they could give me the best food, the best bed, first in the bathroom, etc. Janet was very kind to me. When we sleep, she holds me like a child. She always makes me sleep next to the wall so I won't fall down the bed (it was small). She'd hold my hand to usher me to the bathroom in the dark or hold my hand as we crossed the street. She was so amazingly kind and generous with me. She was only twenty-three years old then and I was twenty years old. I thought then she'd make a wonderful mother for a child one day!

The staple food in Uganda is matoke, boiled bananas, with stewed peanuts and maybe vegetables. I saw so many miles of banana plantations!

The villagers had never seen a mzungu (white person) before. Everyone was very curious about me. Everyone loved me there, eating on the roadside with the Ugandans. They killed a goat as a celebration. I ate all kinds of new fruits. There was lot of learning for me. The cows there had horns 2 to 3 feet long. The bathroom was an outhouse, and one night with a lantern, I went to pee and as I entered, I was startled as two goats exited between my legs!

Janet was given a graduation party by her family. Everyone gave a speech in honor of her. It was so touching. As graduation gifts, she was offered 2 cows, 3 goats and 2 chickens.

I saw Lake Victoria and I thought I was seeing an ocean. Lake Edwards was only 20 miles from Rukungiri and I got a glimpse of it as well. The closest trading center to where her family lived was Bugangale. It is surrounded by rolling hills just like parts of Switzerland. There was no electricity. The houses are made of mud.

They had AIDS there too. It was called SLIM because people who had it got slimmer. There were many posters about it. Children were being taken of by grandparents because the middle generation was dying. They fear it so much in Uganda, unlike Kenya where the reality has not even sunk in yet.

On the way back to Kampala, the van was packed with 20 people, live chickens underneath the seat, and corrugated iron roofing on top of the van. The latter we were detained at a checkpoint because we didn't have a receipt for it and the army guys were saying that maybe we stole them!

Needless to say, I arrived safely to tell the stories of faraway lands. The people I met and their lives changed me. It made it clear that there were many different ways to be in this world. Possibilities abound, and nothing could stop me. So I thought, at that tender age!

As you can see, I traveled and worked in different countries before I was even in my twenties. I wanted to pack life in. I didn't know how long I was going to live and I didn't want to play dead before I had to.

I graduated cum laude from the University of California, San Diego with a double degree in Anthropology and Third World Studies. My doctoral appointment was waiting in the Fall of 1990 for UCLA in the filed of medical anthropology and psycho-cultural studies. I decided to travel the summer in between my undergraduate and graduate studies.

Practical Application for you:

1. Do you remember a time you were invited into someone's house and you felt so welcomed? How was that? Do you remember inviting someone as a guest in your house and they felt so welcomed? How was that for you?
2. Think of an adventurous time/event in your life where you felt so alive. What comes up for you?
3. What does freedom mean to you now? When you were twelve years old? When you were 20 years old? When you were 40 ?
4. How do you recognize your aliveness?
5. What brings up aliveness for you now?

CHAPTER 6: WORKING WITH MOTHER TERESA - PASSAGEWAY TO EXISTENTIALISM

Hoping to take a break from the intellectual climate, I went to Calcutta to work with dying people along with Mother Teresa. I worked at Prem Dan – a home for sick and mentally disabled women. The sisters took the better ones from Kalighat (home for dying) and place them in Prem Dan. There were many women who were dying too. Being in Bengal, walking in the monsoon flood, and spooning water on dying women's mouths shattered my world view and forced me into a corner where I could not reconcile all the contradictions emerging. I was taught that I could change the world, and here I was, I couldn't stop anyone from dying. I couldn't stop myself from dying. It was a big factory of destitute women with hair chopped off as to not spread lice. There were many beds one after the other, and everyone was at a different state of wellness. There was a woman whose uterus had to be pushed back in because it kept coming out. There were women who were mentally ill, and would scream. Some were very peaceful and happy. Some were waiting to die. This wasn't a hospital. It was a home for those that had no place.

July 10, 1990

"I went to mass at six o'clock this morning at the Mother House and saw Mother Theresa. She was a very small, white, wrinkled woman with a slight lean to one side. It was a chapel in a convent. Most of the worshippers were nuns dressed in white saris and long sleeves. They are not through their vows yet. Now they take a vow of silence. Once they're through, they will then wear white saris with blue stripes at the fringes. This symbolizes a nun that works for and with Mother Theresa. The saris were woven by the patients at Kalighat.

I worked at Prem Dan today. There was so much moaning. Some women were scared of the cold water being gently poured over them during their baths. We helped bathe them, dressed them. Some of them cried a lot. We had to carry them to their beds. This place housed only women. We then washed the beds – made of iron and metal. On top was a sort of a cushion covered with rice sac and then white and green checkered bedsheets. I've never seen so many mentally ill patients in one place. Hundreds. Not all were mentally ill though. Some were just old – abandoned by their families. Some spoke quite good English."

"I can't believe that I just walked through that flood up to my thighs with everything in it, including human feces floating. I was carrying a Chinese take out in a box for a friend who was ill in the hotel. I protected this box of food up above my head, while in disgust waded through the dirty water.

Someone died in Prem Dan and another one is dying. She can't drink water so I must place water teaspoon for teaspoon in her mouth, like a drip. Still there was another with cancer of the uterus. She's discharging a lot. She is only skin and bones. Only her eyes are alive. There were so many wounds all over. Another woman menstruated and we didn't know what to do. She had these sanitary napkins with a belt. I've never seen one before. We figured out how to use it."

"The two ladies died today. The cancer patient died too. I knew they were going to die. I cut fingernails the whole day. Some women were really picky about their nails. Some nails were already deteriorating, black, soft. One old woman kept singing."

July 16, 1990

"Prem Dan is exhausting…physical, but more emotional. Today another woman died. She doesn't have a name. We called her Maria. She has so many bed sores from lying on the bed too much. She must be moved often for she can't do it herself. Like the cancer patient, her cheeks are hollow. Her eyes have sunk and her mouth barely open to receive the drop of water. Today she will die. Her feet are cold. Her eyes are cold. Her face is cold. She will die. Her breathing becomes shorter. Her eyes no longer search me. Instead they are blurry with no aim. The sisters say she now looks to Jesus and Mary. The sisters surround her – holding her lifeless hand. They know, today she will die. She doesn't call out "pain", "bed pan" or "lunch". She doesn't say ouch when her wounds are cleaned. She lies still and instead clenches her teeth. Today she will die. A twitch that's all the life she will give. Her sores expose the inside of her body. More sores are developing. One sore shows her bone. Today she will die. I have never wished before that someone should die. But today I wish and I prayed she would die. It's not fair that she should suffer so much. Today she will die. She died at 2:30 in the afternoon."

July 17, 1990

"There was a lady that was burnt. There were lots of pus. The sisters had to squeeze the pus out. Her lip is swollen, her hands are swollen. She complained that her bed is hurting her – the mattress too thin. I looked at her back and she has a big tumour on her back and she doesn't know about it.

While giving baths to the women, I saw three with big pink tumors hanging out of their vaginas. My friend thinks it is their uterus. They just push them back in. Some women are so skinny that they have no breasts left. Their hair is cut off to prevent lice. The patients there need to get shots. Patients are crying about a lost love. Crying for a lost life. What should I do when one clutches unto my hand? I cry with them. Silently, I hold their hands. I say, "I'm by your side." Give them someone who loves, to share even at least death. It's lonely to die alone. While I'm there, they won't die alone.

The patients are recognizing me. The ones that used to yell don't anymore. The one next to Mary calls for me all the time because I understand her. I talk and sing to the women while I fiddle with them. It really soothes them. The women kept kissing my hands, as a sign of gratitude.

I see the women and it aches me how their dignities have been robbed, dragging themselves on the floor into the bathrooms. Some of the patients help other patients.

I keep getting these visions of wrinkled, crumpled, dark, emaciated Indian women with no hair in fetal positions."

July 19, 1990

"Today, I worked with Dr. Jack – the counter of Mother Theresa. The latter the Indian government approves of because they do things according to the law and Mother Theresa is a noble laureate. Dr. Jack, on the other hand, wanted to do things the "right" way even if it goes Indian bureaucracy. He has two clinic in Calcutta. One is by the Ganges and the other one in Middleton Street. It's literally on the sidewalk. It has plastic on tope to protect from rain. They cannot overflow into the street because it is illegal. He has been closed down a couple of times before by the police. The clinic has lots of medicine.

We bandaged patients today, mostly lepers (Hansen's disease). Indian women with their children were many – malnutrition is predominant. One baby was only 2 kilos 750 grams and she's seven months old! She had to be placed in a hospital. The patients came as far as two days away. Dr. Jack lures them into Calcutta. They don't necessarily come for the medicine. Instead, they come for the free milk and powdered biscuits the clinic gives away. He also reimburses the patients for the time they are there, bus faire, day's wage or beggar's wages. There are a lot of beggars.

Here, everyone has to queue. It's not the strongest man that goes in the front. They are given numbers and a file is kept for each recording their medical history.

Dr. Jack has 20,000 patients. They ask the patients to come back for check-ups and such. The children are given vaccinations against polio – very rampid here. There are translations as to how patients need to follow up to cure diseases. Not only are they given bandages, but they are actually told to exercise the leg for blood circulation. It's a clinic. Patients are processed one after the other.

I think Dr. Jack's clinic is a good idea. I think education should be the key – preventative medicine as well as health education in nutrition, sanitation and birth control."

July 23, 1990

"The women there will always have a place in my heart. Auntie Shanti Devi especially with her warmth. I recall the way she always sings and caresses my face and looks at me with her one good eye. She's been very sad the last 5 days as her best friend Badu is in a coma. Badu will soon and Auntie Shanti Devi will follow. For now she is singing for me, for her, for others at Prem Dan, for Badu. The others will watch, shed tears, try to comfort and take care of each other. They have no one else but themselves, and life in Prem Dan will continue."

It was a short time in Prem Dan yet extremely profound for me. It broke my heart open and my soul yearned for another kind of life. I saw so many people dying and die in such a short time. I was only twenty-one . It confounded many beliefs I had about life. It made me yearn to know myself deeply before I die. What is that we die into? When the women were about to die, they stared at something. What was that? What is that we are born into? There were no guarantees that family will be there at the moment we live this earth. Women were abandoned to dying. All the beauty and promise of youth paled into the distance as I washed women with no hair, screaming, afraid, lost in another world.

I was a mere two decades on this earth, and I had seen so much suffering already. Was that all there was to being born here? I've always wanted to help people and when I was in Calcutta, I realized that I didn't have to go far away to help others. Wherever we are, people are suffering. We can help right where we are. While in Calcutta, I faced the hardness of life. Once, a boy took a group of kittens in a bag and he was going to drown them. I thought about it so hard then. There was no food. Was it better for the kittens to survive and suffer that way? I looked around the streets in Calcutta. There were so many beggars. Many children had distented stomachs, big eyes. What life do they have look forward to? Everyone there seem to want a family, but if there is no food, no home, then what? Many of the life choices of people around me didn't make sense to me. I would go to work with dying women in the slums, arriving there in a taxi, coming home and having a nice meal in an expensive restaurant to get some respite from all the chaos. Nothing made sense. It was all like a whirlpool. The whole life was a paradox. I didn't know where I belong in the shifting paradigms.

I felt my self-absorption and my demons of self-judgment pulling me apart. I entered the passageway of existentialism. I questioned my faith and the justness of life. In two decades of life, I was already exhausted. What was there to look forward – truly? I was bright, kind, and beautiful, had a whole future ahead of me, yet these questions pierced my heart. This gnawing feeling was not easily dismissed.

Intuitively, I felt to enter solitude and silence in order that I may embrace my spirit, yet what about my dream as an anthropologist? It was in the midst of this ecstatic turmoil that I met a German man who gave me a clue. "Think of this not as a 21-year-old but as an 80 year old looking back at your life. How would you have liked to lived your life then?" I felt deeply, positively influenced by this meeting. It was clear that I had to stay behind in India.

I let go of my air ticket back to the United States and the doctorate appointment at UCLA as a medical anthropologist. I wanted to know what freedom meant and how it felt to lived it. At first, I struggled with this decision. After all, it was about my "security" and sense of "prestige" and "identity" for the rest of my life to be a professor and researcher. I had the all my research identity, place pegged. All I had to do was show up and eat off the silver platter. How easy could that be! It was a place none of my family members had been before. It was what I had worked very hard to get. It was also my passion and my gift. My identity as a scholar was very strong, and here I was at a crossroads and I wanted to leave it behind for what. The unknown beckoned me. It was my heart and soul calling me to answer. I chose to live my life without regret. At that moment, I turned my back on everything I knew: my career, my family, my roots, my religion, my sense of belonging. I made a funeral rite for myself and sent letters of gratitude to everyone I knew deeply saying my goodbyes. I didn't know at the time that is what a sannyasin (renunciate) does.

Practical Application for you:

1. Lean your hand and arm onto the floor or chair. How does that feel? Is it stable or not? Find a place of leaning that feels really stable. Now find another place that is not stable. Go back to stable.
2. When was a time in your life when you felt your basic beliefs in life were fundamentally challenged? What was that like? How did that change you?
3. Have you been with someone dying before? What was that like?

4. What do you think happens when someone dies? Are you afraid of dying? What does your heart feel now?
5. Make sure you find a leaning place with your hand and arm again and feels what stability feels like right now.

CHAPTER 7: MAHABHARAT AND HER GREAT LESSONS

During this time, I met many more people who influenced my thinking: both westerners and Indians. The social stratification of India was very evident in my travels. I met many kind, gentle and generous people who shared their homes, their food, their lifestyles with me, and in the process challenged my beliefs, and encouraged me to grow and expand. I was very well liked in my travels. I was charming, approachable, gentle, kind and very light hearted. I feel very blessed to have met so many beautiful people on the journey, for it is these meetings that I remember rather than the places of inanimate objects.

I stayed with one Tamil family whereby the women had been doing a fasting practice once a week for the last 37 years. I sat on the floor with them and ate my meals out of banana leaves. I met people who also were activists. "I will not drink milk from any woman but my mother," shared one who writes for an underground newspaper speaking against social injustices. He spoke of staying in a village in the middle of India where the poor people are uneducated. They didn't even know that India had gotten independence from Britain. That was in 1947 and it was now 1990! The people didn't know their rights so the rich people kept robbing them. He told them that they can run for elections. Because of this contact, each villager now owns a house, public road was built, a state run bus, electricity and water are now available in the village. They've become self-reliant.

I also met very arrogant Indians. Usually they were educated, wealthy and had a big case of attitude. In many ways, the Brahmins of the country just replaced the British in the pecking order according to one of its citizens. I met many young women my age already married and bearing children. I was 21 years old. It was rare to see a young woman traveling alone in India.

I made many friends, and they all wanted me to meet their families. I felt very honored to be included in their lives. At that time, India had a closed market and so the young Indians were especially curious about the life outside. I was approachable and a source of information. When I asked them about their thoughts of the United States, the reply was, "AIDS, power hungry and aggressive, 'butting their noses where they don't belong.'"

In my travels there, I was caught in several union strikes (trains, airplanes, buses) where all public transportation come to a halt, and buses couldn't move because the roads were blocked with logs. Strikes were enforced violently, some with students carrying sticks and burning buses. Self-immolations were happening. At times, it felt like a civil war was impending. Even stores and vendors were not allowed to sell food to the passengers of buses because they were breaking the strike! Bus drivers fears that we would get ambushed, stoned, set afire in the middle of the night. There was a strike and everything closed: hotels, buses, restaurants, shops, trains, etc. The Indians helped me by sharing their homemade food.

There were many stories of people looking after me and really wanting me to have a safe and happy journey in their country. One instance, I had a young business man gave up his business plans when he found out I was the only passenger on a boat. He felt it wouldn't be safe for me so he came along as a brother to protect me! He told me that rape was common in India and he wanted to make sure I was safe.

I met a medical student who spoke of belonging to a lower cast, and the shame around that. There was definitely a great divide in the socio-economic strata, but this is also seen in the gender stratification in India. I met people from all parts of the spectrum. I met a very independent woman who was a professor. She told me a story when she was studying in Germany many years before. A German child came to her and kept licking her hand and she wondered why. The aunt of the child asked, and with disgust, the child answered, "she looks like a chocolate, but she taste just like us!"

I traveled and saw some of the most beautiful valleys I had seen in the world. I marveled at the tradition, climbed isolated temples, and partook of religious parades of Gods and Goddesses that come out once in a blue moon. People made their living very creatively in India. While I waited in buses, many peddlers would sell different merchandise. It was fascinating the way they seduced you into buying their gadgets. There was one who sold silver necklaces at the front of the bus. He stood there telling us it wouldn't scratch as he exemplified it by scratching the chain next to the metal post of the bus chair. Then there was the one who sold watches. Then another one who sang songs. I met magicians who swallowed rocks, and with agility, regurgitate it back up, and snake charmers with cobras. I met astrologers who read my palm and my astrological chart. I met spiritual mendicants with piercing eyes, and nuns who lovingly shared their food and wisdom with me. I met sellers of chickpeas and lemon juicers, as well as deer musk sellers for sexual prowess. I also met travelers with a fascination for Eastern philosophy, alchemy, hashish, music, peace, orgasms. There were many who were searching. And still many who were lost, like zombies, completely wasted! I saw the whole of creation, and the big illusion of this kaleidoscope of colors in formations.

I stayed behind in India and let go of my doctorate program. My parents thought I was crazy for throwing everything away. I knew that I was following my heart!

I traveled up to Kashmir once again. This time, though, it was not the lush, yellow flowered mustard valleys of the honeymooners I had visited the year before. Srinigar is the picturesque summer capital of Jammu and Kashmir. It is located at 5,200 feet and had many lakes and waterways. It was surrounded by snow capped mountains and the shikara (boats) on Dal Lake were mesmerizing. That's why the Mughals settled here and built seven hundred gardens in the valley.

A year before, I had traveled there and learnt a lot about their ways of living. Women stayed home, and so it was mostly men I met on the streets. Once I joined a group of women washing clothes at the stream. Together we laughed and by hand wrung the dirty clothes. They called me "Zuni" for my round face. It reminded them of the moon. I was called many endearing names wherever I traveled. They covered their heads with colorful scarves and so did I. At the time, there was talk already of throwing acid at women who had faces exposed.

The men wore a shawl/blanket called a "ferin" and inside they carried "kahgri", a firepot with coal to warm them up. I was caught in a landslide back then and the buses couldn't pass. Once I got to Srinagar, the lake was adorned by these beautiful, ornately made houseboats the British had originally built for themselves when the Mughals forbade them to own land in Kashmir. There were shikaras, colorful canoes, the men pedaled with heart shaped oars. Remember that Srinigar is the honeymooners destination. So the language of love and the heart was everywhere! Most were for passengers, but a few are shopping centers unto themselves: chocolate, cigarette, soap, jewelry. Some shikaras were for washing clothes. I was told that a few years ago, the lake froze and no shikara could paddle. The townfolk played cricket on the frozen lake instead. I can imagine the mirth, the laughter, the carefreeness of those times.

There was the old town where with all its craftspeople. One shop had someone sharpening knives while another man worked like a horse making the sharpening wheel work. There was a silversmith on another while the next shop had four men hammering copper pans. They will be used for cooking pots. All cars back then were 1950's style of the black Ambassador model. There were also wagons pulled by horses.

A year previously, I had traveled freely throughout Kashmir. Then I heard the birds singing while the snow melting dripped melodiously. I stayed in guesthouses that had walls covered with Indian magazine sheets that didn't prevent the cold air from coming in. I was young and free spirited. A little cold didn't matter.

But now, the war was way colder. The heart grew thin.

September 4, 1990

"The curfew is from 6:30 p.m. to 6 a.m. There is gunfire at night. Machine guns. The war is between the freedom fighters of Kashmir vs the Indian army. Kashmir wants independence while India finds Kashmir an asset. Fighting has been going on for 8 months now. Srinigar is like a ghost town. Most of the shops are close, hardly anyone in the street except the Indian army in their khaki uniforms. 10 meters apart from each other are army men carrying guns and rifles. Their eyes were fearful and hungry for power. One mistake means a ticket to one's grave. The bridge where our houseboat is has been blown up. Srinigar was no longer a paradise."

There was war full blast happening. The red sky of Kashmir foreshadowed a bloody ground this year. It was dangerous. People were scared, unhappy. There was so much violence. There were Indian soldiers there, and there were many stops along the roadblocks. People were searched repeatedly. I was too. Even toothpaste was squeezed to check for any bombs. Bras were suspected to harbor bombs as well. There were curfews. People were struggling. It was hard.

The Himalayas are beautiful. The road from Srinagar to Leh is one of the most beautiful sights in the world. Leaving the lush Kashmir valley with the lakes and Moghul gardens into the dry, high mountain plateaus with colorful mineral landscapes everywhere. I hitched a ride on a lorry/truck and rode part time on the back so I can take it all in. The first day, a bomb exploded. The second day, the truck was stranded in Zogi la Pass, the most dangerous pass in the world. We hitched a ride with another truck, sitting on the back on the spare tire watching the full moon. The next day, we were part of a convoy. Thankfully, we befriended the lieutenant colonel and he wrote a note for us not to be bothered because we are running out of time. I saw huge mountains and glaciers for the first time in my life. I saw whole rivers frozen, and the crunching and colliding of two continents millions of years ago really is a geological show here in the Srinagar-Leh road. Greens, magenta, rust, copper, purples, reds - it was spectacular!

Ancient Tibetan monasteries in Ladakh were visited, and a new way of life showed itself to me. I wanted to leave the war behind. I was relieved to leave Srinagar and spend more time in Leh, where there was no war. It was here the first time I was asked by an Indian if I was a "buddh". Buddh means peaceful, awakened. It is the root word for Buddhism, those that practice the path of awakening.

Ladakh means the "land of high passes". It was also called "the last Shangri-La" and "moonland". It is barren, desert like in the middle of nowhere. Tibet is only a day's journey, and this area was threatened for invasion by the Chinese years ago. It is sandwiched between the Karakoram mountain range to the north and the Himalayas to the south.

"It was a paradox, these Tibetan Buddhist monks with contemporary watches and tennis shoes and their 300 year old bead rosaries for mantras. I went inside very old libraries with hand written books in Tibetan bounded by wood.

There was the Hemis festival and the music played as the monks joyfully shot the arrows unto a target. It was all comical, like a Robin Hood Buddhist style festival! I watched the monks in their maroon robes shoot arrows from a wooden bow and then skip to the beat of the drums laughing. It was like a Renaissance faire in Ladakh! I was one of the jury members, a guest of honor, with a cup of butter tea in front of me (my stomach churning). Then I was asked to shoot an arrow. As I stretched the bow, there was silence except the beating of the drum. Everyone looked at me and watched in anticipation. As I let go of the arrow thinking it would go straight for the target, it suddenly dropped to the ground. A roar of laugher followed! It was great!"

I wanted to stay in Ladakh, but the winter was coming quickly. I tried to get an airplane out of Leh into Delhi, but they were all booked. To my dismay, I took a bus back to Srinigar. I didn't want to go back to war. On the way back, all the vehicles (busses and lorries) passing through were stopped high up in the mountain. I was stuck in Drass, the second coldest place in the world. The first is Siberia. For two days now, Zogi La has been closed. It's not the weather. No one know what is happening. No vehicle was allowed to pass, civilian or army. We heard that some of the bridges had been blown up by the freedom fighters. There was hardly any accommodation and there was a cholera epidemic going on.

We didn't know when it would okay to move on again, until a loud banging woke us up. The driver drove like a maniac, overtaking the trucks as though we're raising to hell, down the slopes of Zogi La Pass. Many brakes that ended in just a few centimeters of near collisions. There were even more army checkpoints. Everything was checked. Our luggages and our bodies were searched. I was told I might have a gun between my breasts. Once we were allowed through, we saw the aftermath of a battle in Kangan. We realized that a public bus had been bombed, torpedoed by the Indian army because they thought there were terrorist in the bus. I heard that there were 4 militants and the rest of the crowded bus were innocent people. The bus was now only a burnt skeleton, and alongside it lay many dead people with white sheets covering them. That could have been our bus. We were all silent in this valley. How could beauty and ugliness occupy the same place? Yet this is true everywhere.

"When I arrived in Srinagar, there was a curfew. There was a crack down and army trucks have formed a convoy in front of Dal Lake. They have searched the houses and they are looking for the Islamic freedom fighters. It's past noon now and the Kashmiris are still being marched in the square straight ahead. The women and children stayed home wailing, but the men were lined and forced to walk up and down. It's really ironic because the mosque is calling its disciples for prayer yet there they are being forced against their will in the square. The lake is still and off limits to any boats. The only movement is the army vehicles."

It was horrifying. I wanted to leave and forget that war existed.

My hunger for living was so ravenous. Traveling continued to seduce me. I was invited by young Nepali friends to visit their village, Nepalghot. They were all young late teens, early twenties, who left the villages to work in the hotels in Kathmandu. Many had not been back in years. Everyone was excited to go home for a visit and bring gifts of their bounty to their families.

October 19, 1990

"Let me begin with the bus ride which begun at six in the morning. It was full so we had to sit on top of the local bus – about 50 of us cramped on top. It was quite cold. I felt such an exaltation being up there. Then all of a sudden, there were police and people yelling and pretty soon, people were banging on the bus and pointing their fingers at us. We were caught in a middle of a strike... again! The government of Nepal had increased the price of public transport due to the Gulf crisis. The people didn't understand the connection. To them, it's the government's fault, and thus the strike.

"We walked for two days, 100 kilometers. It was extremely hard. We passed through mountains, forged rivers, up and down, bent over rocky overhangs for long stretches of time. When we reached the first village, all the houses had candles burning on the doors and windows to welcome Lakshmi for the new year! The stars in the sky and the lights scattered in the mountains. Each day we walked 18 hours. There were no bicycles or cars. The Nepalese I met had very hard lives yet there was happiness emanating from their faces. The farmers in the mountains only ate what they grew. They didn't even drink tea and no sugar. I was the first foreigner to visit this village. They were very curious with me.

I took a bath and two young girls escorted me to the waterfall up in the mountain. I took my clothes off and they looked at me in bewilderment. They had never seen a bra before. I was self-conscious. Then I had to defecate. After I finished, the girls checked and scrutinized my feces and looked at their feces and then back again to mine to see if they were different!

Up the mountain, the villagers played the tablas and the men danced while red thikas were placed on their foreheads. I was struck by how happy and gentle the Nepalis were.

With such intense experiences of humanity, I felt pulled by life, yet puzzled at its changeability, and consequently my own instability. I yearned for something more. I was primed for the monastic life. Having seen a war, seen people die, been propositioned by men, met beggars pulling me from all direction (some even with typed cards explaining their circumstances in different languages), I felt that the full spectrum of manifestation of the primal and instinctual nature of man was overwhelming. I wanted solace, and space. I wanted to self-soothe. I was primed to enter the monastery. I could relate to Gautama Buddha's meeting the beggar, the aged sick man, dying person and sage outside the palace gates that sent him into solitude.

Practical Application for you:

1. What part of life has seduced you? How has this shaped you now?
2. What repels you in life? How did these preferences come to be in your beliefs? Who/what has influenced you?
3. Do you remember the first time you traveled to another land and how did you feel?
4. There are many wars that shape man's history.What is your relationship now to wars?
5. Understanding conflict outside means owning it. Where are the conflicts in your life now? How do you bring peace to these parts of yourself?

CHAPTER 8: WHO ARE YOU? MEETING MY SOUL BROTHER

In this first month long retreat, I met a man who also was spiritually committed to his path. Bonga was his name. Unbeknownst to either of us, he was to be an important part of my life, and in writing this book on spiritual emergence as well.

We had a playful meeting. Bonga was very funny, and he was good at disarming me. We sat next to each other in the dharma hall. We would exchange notes on our dharma notebooks between the Tibetan translations.

B: You want me as your bodyguard? __yes ___no ___crazy guy

K: What is a bodyguard?

B. Somebody who protects important people as Ronald Reagan, Albert Einstein, Karl Marx or Kasha for example.

K: Do you think I need protection? From whom?

B: From the KILLERS OF BEAUTY

K: How do I know you are not one of them?

B: Because I say so and I have taken the precept not to lie. I might be a killer, but only by accident, or ignorance…

K: Have you ever been a bodyguard before? What are your qualifications?

B: When I was a child, I had to look after the small body of my brother. I have a degree in Body-guarding from the University of Oulanbator, Mongolia. I, I, I, what about your bodyguard experience?

K: I am not a small-bodied brother. I think I am harder to handle.

B: You don't know my brother. I know both of you. My conclusion: Same same (he's just a little bit less pretty).

K: Tell me about your brother, besides the fact that he has big eyes!

B: When I was a child, we were in the same room At 4 or 5 a.m., he would come in my bed and I could feel his warm "brother-body" and his nice "brother smell." He has at least 15 different names that I gave him during all these years. I would like to love all human beings as I love him.

Anyways, this is how we got to know each other in that one month retreat...in the heart of the flower of dharma. It feels wonderful to write this dialog. Sometimes we forget those first meetings of seeing someone's essence. I feel grateful to have met Bonga.

B: life always flows, free
Only our minds try to catch it
In a smelling pond
Why?

K: a pond smells
Because death is stagnating
But even death
Nourishes the living.

B. Will my dead body
Only feed the worms
And my dead soul
A few memories?

K: why worry
What the dead can do?
Certainly the living is now

This exchange was written to each other in 1990. Little did I know that this would be the journey for me. I flew in the heavens with him, content at times admiring the sky and the birds that flew. I also spent time with him looking at the ground, my head bent from deep sorrow. Yet, even at those times, Great Spirit never once left. I saw the moon on the puddles on the ground, the feathers of birds caressed my feet as at times it was too hard to walk forward. The leaves now separated from the trees reminded of who is grieving, if any, the leaf or the tree? I learnt that passion wasn't just the color of bliss. And in that surrender, everything merged as one.

He invited me to work with 40 cows in the Swiss Alps for two summers. It was magical as I felt as Heidi with Peter, the cows making music with their bells. We yodeled to the cows to bring them in daily, rain or shine. Each cow had her personality and we gave them names as Kailash, Shakti, Helvetia, Shiva, etc. We could tell which cow had what color and shape of spot on what end of their body. We could tell who didn't feel well at the slightest mood change. I'd sing to the cows and brush their tails after we shampooed them. We loved the cows and they loved us!

The pine forests and fat cows along with the mountain thunderstorms and wild blueberries and picking mushrooms all created a simple and glorious life. The two cottages in the alpage had no electricity, water was available but there were no bathrooms, there was a stove with wood for both cooking and heating the place (and a little gas one too). There was no road and we walked 35 minutes to reach the place. We bought huge bags of rice, flour and lentils as our main staple for the four months we were up there. The farmers gave us milk, eggs and vegetables which we took turns fetching down the valley. We chopped wood and warmed ourselves with a wooden stove while we meditated in front on our woolen blankets. Many times, drying socks hung nearby.

I laughed as I shoveled cow shit and felt free as can be. We took it as a retreat time, just like in medieval times. Each day, we watched the sunset together, marveling of its beauty and grateful for the fortune we were bestowed. At times, the mountain was too small for both of us, especially the rare times when we spoke politics!!

Above the barn where the hay was stored was a hammock we had set up. It was a special place where we could say anything to each other, and the other listened. We repaired fences of old wire and wooden stakes when the cows crossed them thinking the grass was greener on the other side. We bathe quickly in the cold water where the cows drank from the spring. We'd get visitors too with their backpacks trudging up the mountain. They brought surprises of chocolate and cheese.

We came down in the autumn, four months later, and picked grapes along Lake Geneva. Most of the pickers came from France and Portugal. They also loved to drink and wine was plenty from morning onward. Neither Bonga and I drank alcohol. The alps stood over us as we crouched close to the ground snipping at the heavy grapes along the steep vineyards. In that week, we would make enough to pay for a plane ticket back to again live in a monastery in Asia.

Kalachakra

After one month retreat studying the Lam Rim (Graduated path to enlightenment), Bonga and I started a relationship that was to last 10 years. He had hair that went 10 directions, and had answers that stopped my mind. He was a wild and mischievous one, searching for his peace. People would ask him: What do you want? A half kilo of happiness. Do you like to eat so and so? Only on Tuesday mornings and Friday afternoons. What is your relationship with her (me)? She is my dentist. He just thought outside of the box, and people responded.

I remember going to Pokhara in a hotel by the lake surrounded by mountains after the retreat. We had arrived by an overnight bus from Kathmandu at three in the morning. I was very chatty and he motioned for us just to stop. We both peered into the silence and grandeur of the sky. The next morning, he requested I go to breakfast and he'd meet me soon after. Anyways, time passed quickly and he didn't arrive. By this point, I was getting a little concerned with his disappearance when a handsome, freshly shaven man suddenly came in and sat on my table. As I was about to ask him to leave because the seat was reserved for someone else, his eyes peered into mine with mirth. I felt surprised and extremely shy, and to my amazement, it was Bonga who had shaved his beard completely. I had not recognized him at all. Up to that point, I only knew his deep, penetrating blue eyes and the rest of his face had been covered with a really big beard!

Soon afterwards, we went to the Kalachakra teachings in Sarnath (just outside of Benares), where hundreds of thousands of Buddhist gathered in a huge tent. We all sat shoulder to shoulder on the dirt. There was a sea of maroon robes and the sonorous chanting of Tibetan sounds. The Dalai Lama presided over the group, and the respect and admiration everyone had for him was palpable. The devotion was simply magical! I felt so blessed to be receiving these teachings in the place where Gautama the Buddha had first turned the wheel of dharma over 2500 years ago.

Practical Application for you:

1. Do you have or have had a magic friend? What was that like?
2. When was the last time you were surprised by someone that your mind just stopped?
3. Do you have a sibling? What are the earliest memories you have of them? How did you show your affection to each other?
4. What sensations come to you when you think of touching the skin/hair of an animal? What is your relationship to animals?
5. When you think of someone you love, what feelings arise for you? How does your heart feel?

CHAPTER 9: MONASTICISM

"If you speak delusions, everything becomes a delusion.
If you speak the truth, everything becomes the truth.
Outside the truth there is no delusion,
But outside delusion there is no special truth.
Followers of Buddha's Way!
Why do you so earnestly seek the truth in distant places?
Look for delusion and truth in the bottom of your own hearts?
-Ryokan

Gospel of Thomas:
"They said to Him: Shall we then, being children, enter the Kingdom? Jesus said to them: When you make the two one, and when you make the inner as the outer and the outer as the inner and the above as the below, and when you make the male and the female into a single one, then shall enter the Kingdom."

As much as I loved the grandeur of Tibetan Buddhism, I was very much drawn to the simplicity of Theravada Buddhism, the elder's way. It was the path of simplicity and silence. I fell in love with Vipassana meditation. Goenka's teachings on the mindfulness of body sensations became a cornerstone in my life, beginning at the age of 22. To this day, this practice in anchored in my daily life. It was a simple abode in the desert in Rajasthan. There were peacocks that graced the grounds, and the accommodations were basic and clean. The mind and heart were so willing, and grace kept giving.

For the next years, the way of the elders took me under its wings as I studied with different teachers in Asia. I spent most of my time in the forest ascetic traditions following a path of austerity with training in virtue, concentration and wisdom. It is foundational for who I am right now. The cultivation there had proven tried and true in the most difficult times of my life. The four noble truths of the Buddha spoke directly to my heart.

1. The truth of suffering.

2. The cause of suffering
3. The cessation of suffering.
4. The Path leading to the end of suffering.

Because I knew deep inside dissatisfaction, it was easy to receive the teachings. I wasn't so interested in the cognitive study of Buddhism as most Americans do. The practicality of the actual practice of meditation caught me like a wildfire. It was easy for me to not read books for years. For once, I wanted to read the book that is me, and know what knowledge truly is.

The Buddhist teaching of dukkha is really about the nature of instability of life. Dukkha does not mean suffering. Dukkha is the point/place where the wheel lands/balances/attaches itself to the axle. In the olden days and still in many places of the world, wooden carts pulled by oxen or water buffalos have wooden wheels. That place where the spokes of the wheel connect to the axle is unstable, constantly moving. Not knowing the basic instability of life results in suffering. The fact is life is always moving, changing, fluid and flowing. This basic truth is what we forget and being veiled in this unknowing, we act out our suffering.

The Eightfold Noble Path is the core teachings of Buddhism. Simplified below are its tenets.

1. Right Understanding includes the knowledge of the four noble truths above.
2. Right Thought
   a. Thoughts free from:
      i. Lust, free from attachment
      ii. Free from ill will
      iii.Free from cruelty
3. Right Speech
   a. Refrain from
      i. Falsehood
      ii. Slander
      iii.Harsh words
      iv. Frivolous speech

4. Right Action
   a. Abstain from
      i. Killing
      ii. Stealing
      iii.Sexual misconduct
5. Right Livelihood
   a. Abstain from trading in
      i. arms
      ii. human beings (slavery, prostitution)
      iii.flesh (breeding animals for slaughter)
      iv. intoxicants
      v. poison
6. Right Effort
   a. To discard evil that has arisen
   b. To prevent the arising of the unrisen evil
   c. To develop unrisen good
   d. To promote the good which has already arisen
7. Right Mindfulness
   a. Mindfulness in regards to:
      i. Body
      ii. Feelings
      iii.Mental formations
      iv. Ideas, thoughts, conceptions, things
8. Right Concentration
   a. One pointedness of mind

This is the path to the end of suffering. At the moment when one is truly present, all these come together as one. Look at it like a flower. There are eight petals when taken apart. Yet a flower really is a flower because it is whole. Just like we can't take a flower petal by petal and call it a flower once you take it apart, the eightfold noble path is the same way. When all these qualities are present simultaneously, there is true seeing. Of course, we can take it one by one and use it as a guide to how to live one's life as well. There are many levels to the teachings, and as one practices, one's understandings deepen to reveal different layers. I was very fortunate to have wise teachers who deeply cared for my wellbeing, and were very generous with me as a student.

Shantivanam: Forest of Peace

I met Father Bede Griffith. He was a Benedictine monk who made Shantivanam flourish to welcome both Indians and westerners into the Christian faith with a Hindu twist. In the ten years I had known him, he definitely softened as his spirituality deepened into the feminine right after his stroke. He was kind mostly. He spent most of his time in his hut, except for prayers. He led a simple life. Some sternness came out though when one of the brothers let me ring the bell to call all for prayer. I remember saying goodbye to him one time when I was leaving for Pondicherry to visit the Aurobindo Ashram, and he smiled and said, "The brown bread is really good there." He knew how to come down to my level.

Many people were drawn to Shantivanam – Forest of Peace. It was built near the Cauvery River where we would meditate by the riverbank at dusk. I remember Bonga and I would hang out by the arching tree where they would cremate dead bodies. One time, he and I were mesmerized by one body in particular. It was covered in mud and the crackling dry elements kept us company long after the family had departed. The garland of marigold was laid aside, the dusk had turned into evening, the burning flesh between us. This too was life. It was evident.

Tea time was a great way to meet the pilgrims flocking to Shantivanam. An English physicist stopped me once and asked, "What have I gain being in the ashram?" I mischievously answered, "A few inches around my waist." I knew he wanted a profound reply speaking about the likes of Rupert Sheldrake's morphogenetic field that got read during lunchtime, or something about the Rig Veda or The Sermon on the Mount. The truth was meditation freed my joy and playfulness, and this time it came out this way.

Another time, a priest of 25 years requested a conversation with me after prayer. I obliged and yet he only stared silently at me. I was young, impatient, at times brutal. I said, "Stop drinking me!!" The next day, after breakfast, he had packed his suitcase, and said to me, "Would the Buddha have allowed himself to be drunk?" It became my koan for many years to come. Here was this opportunity that this elder priest had found something fresh and clear in the being of a meditator, who also happened to be physically beautiful. It aroused in him a desire he had not known his whole life as a priest. Looking back now, I realize that it was the inner beauty and those qualities of peace, presence, purity that drew parts of him and question something fundamental in his own spiritual journey. I was, however, very young and it took me years to understand this.

I came across a story by the Buddha. Ananda, one of his closest disciples, was doing his alms rounds in the village when one of the women fell in love with him and wanted him to be her husband. She beseeched her mother, who was into black magic, to cast a spell upon Ananda so that he would fall in love with her. Because the Buddha was clairvoyant, he saw what was happening and brought both this woman and Ananda in his presence. He then proceeded to ask the woman, "How did you fall in love with Ananda?" And the woman began to list all these qualities: presence, compassion, lightness, kindness, etc. as how he came to be in love with Ananda. The Buddha said, "You don't have to get married to Ananda. You can develop those qualities yourself." And so, this young woman, ordained as a nun and soon cultivated those very qualities that drew her to Ananda.

This story, though simple, made a profound impact on me. Over the course of my adult life, I began to frame attractions towards me in similar vein. Most of the time, I too pass on this conversation that it may further the development and cultivation of those same qualities people are attracted to in me. It's not simply about physical beauty alone, though I don't deny that at all.

Sister Mechtildes was a very close friend of mine. She was guest mistress at Shantivanam (Forest of Peace) when I met her in my early twenties. She was also 50 years my senior. I had a knack for making friends with octogenarians. At first, she was really more friends with Bonga. They shared the same birth language of French. But over the years, she and I became closer. She witnessed me grow from my early twenties into my thirties and early forties.

She was so generous, and I had grown to love and appreciate her in the two decades we were friends. She was originally from Belgium and became a nun in her early twenties. She had lived in the Congo, and had spent decades in India. It made sense that she thought she would die there too. As life had shown me, however, life is quite unpredictable. Even ashram life had its intrigues. She had to leave the ashram in her eighties and the only place to return to was a retirement community for nuns in Belgium. She had not been back in over 50 years.

I was with her during this dark night of the soul. We sat by the riverbank meditating. We watched the clouds in the sky and we smiled as they reminded us of the great Himalayas. I helped pack her books, and Bonga and I wrote sweet magical notes and secretly tucked them in the books that they may cheer her up back in the winters in Belgium. She was deeply disappointed, yet hoped for the best. She said not one bad word, and accepted her fate. In the temple, we'd pray in Sanskrit: Asatoma Sat Gamaya. Tamasoma Jyotir Gamaya. Mrityorma Anritam Gamaya. Lead me from the unreal to the real. Lead me from the darkness to the Light. Lead me from the temporary to the Eternal. –Brihadarnayaka Upanishad. In the afternoons, we'd sit underneath the old tamarind tree in our saffron clothes and listen to the wind - two souls that loved silence.

Once when we were mailing the books in the post office, Bonga and I got on a bicycle. He was pedaling and I was sidesitting with my long skirt on a metal shelf behind on this long, bumpy road. We had this wild idea to get a professional photo taken of us. After all, we didn't have a photo of us together and it would be so easy. So there we were in our best clothes in a photo studio in Kulitalai in the South of India. I wanted to send the photo to my mother in the US. I thought a picture with me sitting on a chair and Bonga standing next to me would be wonderful. Oh no, the photographer insisted, dismayed even!! The man had to sit down and the woman had to stand up, he demonstrated. Anyways, it was settled after much going back and forth, that Bonga and I would sit on two chairs next to each other so that equality was established! Sister Mechtildes laughed so much. It was wonderful seeing her have a reprieve.

She had two old statues: one of the sitting and still Buddha. The other was of the dancing Shiva. She gave the former to me, and the latter to Bonga. Of course, the path was to embrace both ends of the spectrum and to know deeply stillness in the dance and the dance in the stillness. This has been my journey – to accept my full manifestation as a human being, and consequently, all others. Once you know yourself deeply, it is like knowing others too. We really are all made of the same ingredients. We just think we are so different. The manifestation is unique yet the essence is a shared oneness.

She reminded me that part of Bonga's place in my life was to protect me, to act as a shield between the world and I. I silently smirked when she said that. She didn't know that when Bonga first met me at the monastery in that very first month long retreat, he verbally and in writing applied to be my bodyguard!! In the time between the Tibetan teachings and the English translations of the Lam Rim (The Graduated Path to Enlightenment), we sent notes to each other. "It was a geographical positioning on the cushion," we joked with each other. Back then, I enquired into what his qualifications were to be my bodyguard. He'd sent me a long list with boxes to check. I remembered he also said that he was a VIP – a very impermanent person!!!

Sister Mechtildes loved that we were together on the spiritual path. Perhaps, she understood us more than any. Shantivanam was the only spiritual community in Asia that truly embraced us a couple on the path. All the others tried to separate us and believed that the spiritual path was a solitary one. Many people liked getting to know me, though I was quite a hermit then. There was the sweetness of honey in me and I was also elusive. Bonga was the intervener and intercepter. He was also the socializer. I had my own little hut that looked into the fields and the horizon. At night the stars were very present! I loved being alone, but Bonga came to share books of interest with me or spiritual questions and enquiries. At times, we would read the same book, taking turns reading a page or two to each other until the book was finished.

After Bonga died, Sister Mechtildes and I wrote letters for another decade. She sent me hand made cards, or recycled cards with so much love and encouragement in them. They were always cheerful, much welcomed especially in the despairing years of difficulty. She'd asked me about my back injury and about Bonga's death, but I didn't want to write about that then. The drop into the sea that Kabir referred to was easier to speak of, while the sea in the drop was harder to find in the deep grief, not quite yet understood. She had bone cancer and it was very painful. Yet, amidst her pain, she found time to read to the nuns that had gone blind. She was such an inspiration. I called her one time because I wanted to visit her in Belgium. She was not happy and was very clear that I was not to visit her there. I understood. She was one of my last octogenarian friends to pass away.

Tiruvanamallai:

Ramana Maharashi's teachings on non-dualism are very close to my heart. Ramana simply ask the question, "Who am I?" That was the whole spiritual practice. Some of the wisdom of this great sage are as follows:

"What is illusion?
M.: To whom is the illusion? Find it out. Then illusion will vanish. Generally people want to know about illusion and do not examine to whom it is. It is foolish. Illusion is outside and unknown. But the seeker is considered to be known and is inside. Find out what is immediate, intimate, instead of trying to find out what is distant and unknown."

"Happiness is your nature. It is not wrong to desire it. What is wrong is seeking it outside when it is inside."

"God dwells in you, as you, and you don't have to 'do' anything to be God-realized or Self-realized, it is already your true and natural state." Just drop all seeking, turn your attention inward, and sacrifice your mind to the One Self radiating in the Heart of your very being. For this to be your own presently lived experience, Self-Inquiry is the one direct and immediate way."

Bonga and I spent a great deal of time there over the years. Mind you, Bonga had a look of a rebellious vagabond and some of the officers at the ashram's office had a thing about that so I'd go in first as I was a little bit more "presentable" in dress and demeanor to the likes of ashram eyes. Unbeknownst to them, my wildness is an inner one (and I was more of a Tasmanian devil than he!). We'd get a room that way in a much easier way! Even ashrams have these politics!

Once I was doing yoga early in the morning as was my routine on one of the roofs of a nearby ashram. There I was on the ground on all fours doing cat and cow asana, arching and rounding my spine. I was calm, following my breath, and simply going with the gentle and fluid movements. All of a sudden, I felt two hands on my hips from behind. I was surprised as I thought I was alone. While still crouched on all fours, I simply and quietly twisted to my left to see what was touching my pelvis. To my amazement, there was a huge male baboon with his hands on my hips, checking me out and ready to do his thing!!! I simply looked at him, he looked at me and opened his mouth with sharp teeth and walked away. I took this as my cue to roll my yoga mat and go quietly downstairs.

Part of the practice there was to do pradakshina (circumambulation) around the mountain. The legend states that Mt. Arunachala is Shiva himself. You see, there was a dispute between Brahma the creator, and Vishnu, the preserver as to who was more superior. Shiva showed up as a column of light in the form of Mt. Arunachala to settle this dispute! Once a year, there is a whole ritual of lighting the top of the mountain. Many sages are drawn to this holy site. Ramana Maharishi lived here from 1899-1916.

"All stones in that place [Arunachala] are lingams. It is indeed the abode of Lord Siva. All trees are the wish-granting trees of Indra's heaven. Its rippling waters are the Ganges, flowing through our Lord's matted locks. The food eaten there is the ambrosia of the Gods. To go round it in pradakshina is to perform pradakshina of the world. Words spoken there are holy scripture, and to fall asleep there is to be absorbed in samadhi, beyond the mind's delusion. Could there be any other place which is its equal?"

- Tamil Arunachala Puranam

81

Since we loved walking, Bonga and I had our share of pradakshinas. We wanted to offer something back, and since the inner path was hard to find, he and I bought limestone paint and painted the inner trail. We painted a few other walls in our time in different monasteries and centers. We didn't have to do it, but I must say, each time we finished the job, the rooms and the world looked a little lighter and brighter!!! It didn't take much to give, and the effects are so far reaching!

Sri Lanka: Nilambe and Kanduboda

We stayed for three months in Nilambe Meditation Center in Kandy where we met Godwin, a very gentle Singhalese teacher. His eyes were filled with loving kindness, and he moved with no rush. His words were punctuated with pauses. This was my first impression of him. I had arrived late in the evening after traveling the whole day. I was wet from the rain soaking through as we had the few miles with our backpacks up the hill planted with tea to the center.

It was a beautiful center perched on a hillside overlooking Adam's Peak in Sri Lanka, and the entire horizon gave one a sense of vastness, especially after meditating the whole day with eyes closed. I taught yoga twice a day to the meditators there. It was a time of healing, while sitting on the cushion or working in the garden. Every evening, an elderly Singhalese woman would collect plumerias for the altar. The walks were beautiful, but we had to watch for leeches and scorpions. The evenings were magical with the fireflies, and the clear sky shining with stars. It was a simple life, but very rich.

Once, the hillside was caught in a wild fire, and we feared the center would be burnt. The meditators came rushing out and we all began beating on the isolated fire clusters with grass brushes bundled together. There were no fire trucks, no water. It was sheer determination and the furious beatings. I think it was really prayer that made it possible for the center to escape the fire.

I then lived in a nunnery for 9 months in Sri Lanka, while Bonga lived in the monastery. Our lives were separated by a high wall surrounding the nunnery. There was a small hump on the path outside that allowed me to catch a peek of Bonga walking in a single file line, going to lunch with the monks, while I waited in line with the women in the enclosure. We shared a common white wardrobe, and our schedules were timed with the bells that called us to meditate or eat.

I wanted to see him more than a second peek at lunch, even if we didn't talk. I would go to the chanting in the main hall, and again, I would have a chance to spend non-verbal exchange with him. The Pali chanting and the sacred white thread that everyone touched were what connected us. Our bond became more the spiritual than the emotional or physical. That was to continue for the next eight years.

It was a year of turning inward. I became ill there, and had to be in a special diet. I asked for permission to remain given the circumstances. I continued to meditate. For the first time in my life, I viscerally sensed, observed, and remained with the emotion of anger. Most people know anger as an outburst at another. While in retreat, I had the opportunity to sense the heat of anger in my body. I felt the shame of my beliefs and upbringings around not allowing myself to fully express this emotion. I would close my window and door when these bouts of rage would burn my body because I didn't want to hurt anyone. It was the first time I faced my anger and separated it from violence.

I practiced Vipasana and loving kindness meditation. Vipasana is a Pali word meaning to see as it is. It is a practice of cultivating insight into seeing the true nature of reality: that it is impermanent, unsatisfactory and not self. In slowing down and observing the rhythms of thoughts, breath, feelings and everything else, we get to see what it really is. It is like looking at an electric fan moving, and then slowing it down. First it looks like one big whirl, then as it slows down, we see it as three different spokes moving. And so it is the components of what we think reality is. The insights garnered cuts through our conventional perception of reality, as we look at mind and matter separately and its relationship. My time at the nunnery was a period of bhavana, a mental cultivation like you would cultivate a garden. With faith and effort, my level of concentration deepened and silence pervaded in a different way. Wisdom arose with mindfulness training at times and in intervals. It was a very important time of my life.

Vipassana, of course, along with metta (loving kindness meditation) are like a sandwich. You need both. Sometimes the clarity and wisdom of Vipassana can be sharp like a sword, and so we need to meet it with the tenderness of loving kindness. I am so thankful for this combination. I definitely needed love at this time. I learnt that my experience of compassion lacked equanimity, and so there were many instances that I contemplated on my strengths and weaknesses while there.

There were a couple of times, snakes tried to climb on me while meditating, or fall from the ceiling. There were times of restlessness as I saw some women walked like tigers caught in a cage. I too at times wanted to scratch the walls. It was for the most part, a soothing time, a balm for my soul. I needed to be there at that time of my life. The material world had no allure to me. There was also a beauty of meditating with only women. Most of the time, I was the only Western woman there. I really appreciated the aged Sri Lankan women, and saw their beauty, regalness and dignity that came with a life led in peace and integrity. I saw women who taught me a trajectory of what I was to look forward to. Of course, there was also pettiness that I witnessed as an outsider. The monastery is a microcosm of the whole village after all.

There was not much words exchanged. We were mostly silent, and I enjoyed that. We woke up very early at dawn, before the sun rose. In the nunnery, there were no beautiful horizons like Nilambe. It was the opposite. There was a thick, high brick wall that was covered with moss. The focus was internal. When the tropical rain came, the jackfruit forests smelled ripe. And when the heat seared, the stickiness of sweat of white cloth on bare skin became just another sensation to be witnessed along with the buzzing mosquitoes and thoughts that came and went. I forgot the days, the months and the year. It was simply returning to the breath, one breath at a time.

The Sri Lankan people are a very generous group. Everyday, a family or a village came to offer alms of food to us. Some were wealthy with their silk sarees, and glistening gold. Others were very poor with their flat, calloused feet that spread and hugged the earth. The poorer the donors, the spicier the food was. The spicier the food, the redder it was. There was a lot of red food! The wealthier the donor meant fresher, less spicy assortment of offerings. There was plenty of fresh coconut drink and green herbal porridge at five o'clock in the morning. Along with food, we were offered medicine of tiger balm, toothbrush, bath soap for the body, and sometimes tobacco and beetle nut wrapped in a leaf. The latter was a special treat, and the donors loved giving them to me. I received them graciously and shared them with the older Sri Lankan women. Sometimes, I bathed in the big well dug deep in the earth. There the women would congregate in silence, each wearing a different batik sarong to bathe modestly.

It was a training in being equanimous no matter what was offered. There were many who bowed at our feet. It was not personal. They were honoring a tradition that was over 2500 years old. I was very fortunate to be supported wholeheartedly in the path of cultivating the heart. The confidence of the donors in the meditation was so profound for me. It really fed and nourished my faith and encouraged the effort necessary in the practice of mindfulness. I knew that I wasn't just doing this for myself. I was doing this for them as well. I was part of an unbroken living tradition of seeing truth clearly. I am so eternally grateful for this tradition that has lasted all this time, and that I have benefited even in this century.

Thailand: Forest Monastery

We had wanted to study in Burma for a while, but at that time, getting visas for meditation was very hard. We wrote our letters and it took a long time before we got responses. Anyways, we met the Sayadaw U Janaka in Bangkok, Thailand and sat a 10 day retreat with him in an air conditioned room. It was quite unusual for such luxurious arrangement of an air condition while in Asia. We were on our way to see him in Burma, so it was good fortune, to meet him first in Thailand. The Sayadaw was a very powerful teacher. He walked into the room, and his presence was palpable and strong. He didn't glide; he walked with a force towards the front. He invited me personally to study further in Burma with him during that 10 day retreat. I was elated.

In the meantime, he had to go to Singapore, and I decided to stay in Thailand to wait. I met Ajahn Poh in the south of Thailand in Wat Suan Mokkh in another retreat soon after the one in Bangkok. His demeanor was very different. He sat like a mountain. He glided with such humility and presence. He caught my attention in a very different way. I asked for an interview with him, and said, "Teach me how to be humble." He replied, through his thick glasses, "you haven't understood anything. There is no one to be humble." It was like an arrow that went straight into the core of my being. I knew I had met my teacher.

I stayed to study with Ajahn Poh, and let go of going to Burma at that time. He took personal interest in my spiritual development. I was aloof, yet very disciplined and committed to the practice. He took Bonga aside one day, and asked about me. Bonga narrated what he knew of my story with tears and sadness. When he shared this with me, I felt shy and vulnerable. I told Ajahn Poh that I didn't want a teacher. I wanted a friend. But even then, I had to test him. After all, you just don't accept a teacher like that. I hid behind coconut trees and rocks to watch him when he didn't see me. I watched him when he was with others, when he was along. I wanted to make sure I really wanted him in my life. He became my spiritual friend. He was very instrumental in my development as a person. He would remind me of "running away from the tiger just to meet the crocodile" when going from unpleasant attachment to pleasant attachment. He taught me that rocks are heavy, no matter if they are rubies or gold. You still got to carry them. We had walked by the sea in his home island, and he stopped Bonga and I, and taught us to look at mind like the waves of the sea. He kept establishing the right view, and encouraging me to gain stability and penetration of mindfulness and wisdom.

He believed in me so much, more than I believed in myself. He encouraged me to teach the dharma at a young age as my other teachers have. I was reluctant at first. I had dharma understanding, yet I also felt I needed to mature in other ways. I knew that teaching was like a sword. It cuts both ways. I've always felt that it was really not so much about teaching the dharma, but rather encouraging others on the path, through action and example, not just words. There is the seeing and realizing, yet this is moment to moment, and one has to stabilize in this.

The Buddha said before he died, "Beware bhikkus! We warn you thus: all concocted things disintegrate, you ought always to be carefully alert."

I was aware that the habit of "ownership" of me, my and mine was very deeply ingrained. This implicit ownership is what causes us to suffer. It is like touching a hot stove, and then blaming the hot stove. Pride in teaching can be a trap in the path.

As Evagrius, a Christian Desert Father, wrote, "Stay watchful of gluttony and desire and the demon of irritation and fear as well. The noonday demon of laziness and sleep will come after lunch each day, and the demon of pride will sneak up only when you have vanquished the other demons."

Being silent and in meditation appealed to me. Then one day, it was raining and there was a retreat. I saw people doing walking meditation back and forth between coconuts, the rain pouring, some under umbrellas, others just walking getting wet in the rain. I saw that they were trying to so hard. I noticed their dedication and perseverance. Compassion arose in my heart and my being. I walked to Ajahn Poh, and said, I will teach. That evening I turned the dharma wheel in teaching.

I was young, wild, impetuous, too smart for my own good at times. Once I felt that I may have said something in the teaching that left a saccharin taste, and I felt shame and remorse. The next morning, I paced back and forth awaiting Ajahn Poh to report my misdemeanor. He listened patiently, and said, "You can't do wrong. I trust and believe in you." I almost bawled right there. My heart felt so soft. Something deeply restorative happened. I was expecting to get reprimanded, and all he did was love me. It changed my life.

And so it was, he taught me in different ways by just the way he was. A solid, loving being that shared the dharma!! Sometimes, I would report to him that it was frustrating that some of the meditators broke the silence. He simply kindly said, "For someone to be silent even for one day is a huge deal. You need to develop more loving kindness." He encouraged me to cultivate mindfulness and discriminating wisdom. He also said, "Don't fix anything." "You can show/point the food to someone, but that person has to eat it. It is the same as teaching the dhamma." He said, "This body is the boat that will take across the river. Life is precious. These experiences of pain are also precious. They are treasures that make us want to be free of burden."

He saw that I loved being alone, and he gave me a place to go deep into meditation. For me, dhamma is the process of intimacy with one's heart, that which is full of creativity, of spontaneity, of humanness. It is the opening of the heart. I wasn't interested in religion memorialized and regurgitated as conceptual boxes, but rather the pulsating and vibrating lived experienced of it. Ajahn Poh said, "You can only know your mind, not other's minds." He just supported me wholeheartedly in the dharma. He said one time, "You wouldn't be able to stay this long here if your meditation wasn't benefiting you." Of course, it wasn't all bliss. There was the changing of the mind, the body and the feelings. But these were just phenomena to be observed. Just like the seasons in nature, they too change. And so it was, the first truth of impermanence got seen over and over again as a daily occurrence in life.

Life is like a river. It seems like it is one piece, but really when you look at a river, it is changing and flowing all the time. Life is the same, always flowing. It is not solid at all. It just appears so. Sometimes the river is clear, and you can see the debris underneath distinctly. You see a rock there, a piece of wood there, a fish moving here. This is a peaceful mind. You might even see a clear reflection of the moon on it, unwavering. You see water moons. Sometimes the reflection gets mistaken for the real moon. Sometimes, the river is muddy and you can't see what is in the bottom at all. It's boggy, and you can't move in it. This is a mind that is filled with the quality of sloth and torpor. Sometimes, the wind creates choppiness on the surface, and again, it colors what you see of the river. This is like a restless mind. So nature really is a very important teacher for how reality is.

I asked Ajahn Poh how long will I have to practice. He looked at me and said, "Until your last breath."

"Your worst enemy cannot harm you as much as your own thoughts, unguarded. But once mastered, no one can help as much, not even your father or your mother." -Dhammapada

"You may control a mad elephant.
You may shut the mouth of a bear and the tiger.
Ride the lion and play with the cobra.
By alchemy you may earn your livelihood.
You may wander through the universe incognito;
Make vassals of the Gods; be ever youthful;
You may walk on water and live in fire;
But control of the mind is better and more difficult."
                    -Thayumanavar

While in the monastery, I spent a lot of time by the ponds where I would watch the goldfish. One day as I sat next to it, this poem came:

A tear fell
On the lotus leaf

For all the children
Who haven't fed fishes

Another poem to describe my life there follows:

The hermit seeks to be lost with the gliding bats
To dance amongst the stars
And sing with the frogs when
The tender rain kisses the supple grass
To sit near the brook
Serenaded with its intimate tune
Steps unhurried
Pine needles prickling
Tender brown feet
Wind lover
Playing hide and seek
Tickling the leaves in fickle

Eyes like a mirror
A pond, the moon casting her gentle presence
Soft laughter
Nestled in the bosom
Of flowers in blossom

Another poem:

Meditation is not a battlefield
There is no warrior
There are no weapons
There is no enemy
Why do you make war in the name of peace
Why do you beat a child already beaten
Kiss the tears with love
Not with hatred
Embrace the broken heart with gentleness
Not with aggression
A head heavy, in vertigo
Tenderly placed on the Buddha's lap
His hands
One towards heaven
One towards earth
Both will meet and caress your troubled min
Soothing
Comforting
Another poem:

The monk without a robe
Longs for her friend solitude
To saunter in boundless time
Fairies dancing on their fingertips
Eyes stare towards that place
That doesn't exist
Only the silence between
The musical notes can understand
The breeze whispers behind the ears
Come to where I begun and to where I shall end

With eye lashes gently embracing
Who am I
Doesn't seem to matter
Suspended elsewhere
Like water without a container

Another poem:

Courageous little one
The full moon is there
But she is not yours
Her light shines
To illuminate all

Still another:

In the sanctity of silence
Slowly I bow down
Lids gently closed
Eyes remain open
Acceptance of what is
A tear, a laugher
A painful heart, a joyful toe
Each and all
Can show without
Feeling of shyness

Another yet:

Intoxication with beauty
It hurts

The candle
The ghekko

Sitting with the evening

It is so soft and tender
This heart
It wants to break free
Of its carapace

More poems on impermanence

Gentle drops glisten this dark hair
Flat feet
The shade of an old straw mat
Cling to the earth
The wind blows
A soft whisper behind the ears

Soon
The spine will be a curve
Like the bowing bamboo
And the shiny hair
Like white noodles in day old soup

Then the storm will quickly descend
The wind will then be a lover in rage
Its might so strong
These eyes which reflected the moon
Like the clear pond
Will be curtained with heavy drapes
Of her last monsoon

A poem about you and I and creation:

In the drops of rain
Passing from one leaf to another
Lies eternity

Does anyone really want to listen
To the serenade of the flowing brook?

Or to watch the fluttering butterfly
When it finally comes to a rest?

The clouds continuously change
The leaves move even in stillness

Does anyone have time for eternity?

true silence can not be disturbed
it holds everything

another poem:

crazy woman I am
stopping the brook from running
holding the pine's symphony in my hands
speaking to the fragrant flowers
bees and butterflies my accomplice
the clouds come and dance
the moon mirrors herself in my eyes
the rain, the fog, the dew drop
kiss the tips of blades of grass

CHAPTER 10: IN HUMILITY, THERE IS NO ONE

Ajahn Poh was not a craftsman of meditation. He is meditation.

What was I learning in this long retreat?

1. Aversion from unpleasant
2. Desire for pleasant
3. Change is feared
4. Mind that has an opinion on everything
5. "It should be this way" "it shouldn't be this way"
6. Attachment to peace
7. Silence is scary
8. Suffering of being alone
9. Suffering of being with others
10. Constant grasping to formation of ideas such as truth, retreat, progress
11. Thinking something has to be going on for something to be happening
12. Nothing's worth anything. It is just a passing show.
13. Truth can only be found in the moment. It cannot be grasped; only the concept of truth can be grasped.
14. In criticizing others, there's a simultaneous feeling of superiority and inferiority – a lack of self confidence in proving one is better than others.
15. One can use meditation and spirituality not to take care of one's self
16. How little self-love is present
17. We are all the frog in the well imprisoned by our limited vision of reality
18. I must be willing to be uncomfortable to truly see what is discomfort
19. In an open room, one can see many things distinctly; in a crowded room, one can't see anything. It is the same with the mind.
20. I have no control.

21. I spend so much energy trying to create external silence instead of devoting that energy in meeting what is here, and thus devoting internal silence.
22. How many times must I run away?
23. Look out for the ways I create internal battles in spirituality.
24. Notice if meditation becomes a means to an end, rather than moment to moment being
25. In the spring of silence, duality of creation and destruction ceases.
26. It is a big relief that the sky changes
27. It's a bigger relief and comfort that the sky is always blue even if it is covered with clouds.
28. Every action has an intention prior to it so if one is mindful, one has the freedom to know a thought for a thought and drop it or get carried into action.
29. It is humbling to see that we think we know might not be the reality or even close to it
30. Everything is just right the way it is. But like a fool, I want to change all to make me happy.
31. Thoughts are interlinked unto each other, and then we believe it to be solid!
32. To endure is to have this quality of flexibility, and essentially, an emptiness open to be filled with anything and then only to be empty again.
33. Basically empty and form are no different.
34. The greed, hatred and ignorance in my thoughts, words and actions are the blueprint of the greed, hatred and delusion of all of humanity.
35. When there is space for the cultivation of love and compassion in the garden of my heart, then truly it is so that humanity can reap its harvest.
36. When one has a quiet mind, one sees a situation from many points of view. One can see not only one's suffering, but also the suffering of the others.
37. One sees how this suffering leads to careless behavior which in turn hurts/harms others.

38. When one sees this chain, then there is understanding, forgiveness. There is a surrender of blame, a laying down of swords.

39. There are fewer and fewer "why"s and more of being with what is.

40. Mindfulness is not only to be aware of the minute mind-body processes, but also the desire behind to be mindful, to have control, to catch thought at moments of contact, the desire not to daydream or feel restless, desire not to desire.

41. There is a quality of softness, non-violence in letting things be just the way they are.

42. There is an absence of manipulation, interference, expectation. There is a presence filled with no desire to acquire or to change or to disrepute.

43. Mindfulness is this presence that is joy, compassion, love and equanimity all rolled into one, but radiates into all directions.

44. When the eye sees a blooming flower, we don't shut and blame the eye for seeing.

45. When the ear hears the song of a bird, we don't plug the ears.

46. When the tongue tastes the sweetness of a cabbage leaf, we don't cut the tongue.

47. When the nose smells the fragrance of freshly cut grass, we don't put a mask on

48. When the skin feels the gust of wind during a thunderstorm, we don't run into an atomic shelter. Then why does a meditator flagellate himself when a thought makes friends with the mind?

49. To be present, one must drop the idea of what present is or is not.

50. It is this quality of unhurriedness, which is not related to speed. It is a state of being which rests in being in the here and now as an end of itself.

51. The times I need to be kinder to myself are usually the times when I am harsher.

52. Body sweeping during meditation is more intimate than sex. I am more in touch with my body.

53. Everyday, the frog tries to jump out of the pond. Ah, he knows there's something else besides the circular sky he sees passing by. Thank you frog for inspiring me to see beyond my own reality.
54. Look at the spider who is busy building his web. His web is his home as well a means to catch his food, but when danger threatens his life, he does not hesitate to leave his web.
55. The idea that there is something, somewhere, someone else in time and space that is better is just a thought.
56. Fear and hope are the same thing.

As much as I loved and benefited there, it was also difficult to be in a highly patriarchal system. There was such austerity. We ate two meals a day. I slept on a concrete bed. I had three changes of clothing. What I valued was the time and opportunity to truly practice. I didn't mind the simplicity at all.

What I did mind was the clear division of the sexes, and the power differential inherent in the culture of Thailand, and of the monastic order. I couldn't speak to any man, monk or otherwise, unless it was in a public place and there was a chaperone. There had to be a certain physical distance between myself and them. I couldn't touch the same object at the same time as a monk. Many of the young monks, when they saw me coming, turned and walked the other way when they met me. I longed to have my incarnation be also part of the understanding of essence. I longed for my juiciness as a woman be part of the acceptance of true nature.

My deep love for Bonga fed some of these parts. We both were poets and wrote poems to each other.

Sweet Kasha by Bonga
Eleven o'clock
As you sleep
With your eyelids
As vast and peaceful
As a mountain lake
I know now
Why these feet of
Yours are so attractive to me

These feet
Are the feet
Of a wild child
One
Who spends her time
Running half naked
In the mud of the forest
One whose color is
The color of earth
As you sleep
With your eyelids
As vast and peaceful
As a mountain lake
I would like to take a dip
In its purple water

We shared dharma notes, poetry, sketches, learned Gothic calligraphy on shared notebooks. Once I was so elated to read Suzuki's book on Beginner's Mind that Bonga took three months to handwrite the whole book in calligraphy to give me as a surprise present.

There was so much magic at times. "If Kasha had a sister, there would be one more happy man on earth," Bonga would say.

"As stars, a fault of vision, as a lamp,
A mock show, dew drops, or a bubble,
A dream, a lightning flash, or cloud.
So should one view what is conditioned."
-Diamond Sutra

So we traveled in conditioned reality (knowing that it is perishable by nature) and also touched unconditioned non-doing at times. We shared our aspirations to live happily and practice to deepened these realizations. We studied Vedanta, Taoism, mystical Christianity along with Buddhism. Basho, Patanjali, Han Shan, Ramana Maharishi, Krishnamurti (both UG and J), Thich Nhat Hanhn became regular reads. The places we went and lived required separation of the sexes, even in sitting meditation. We practiced so diligently that people would comment on how Bonga held one wall up (men's side), while I held the other up (women's side). I smile as I write about these times. It was almost a preparation and reminder that we are all butterflies visiting for a short time. Little did I know that my "papilion" (butterfly) would only visit for a really short time. In reflection, all the times we observed corpses burning in India have been preparations for me to see through all my attachments to him, to life, to death, to myself. In that short time, we climbed Mt. Fuji, walked parts of the Himalayas, frolicked in the Swiss Alps, walked across land mines in Cambodia, faced the worst parts of each other and bathed in unconditional love in each other's others' presence.

I vividly remember sharing slices of watermelon in hot Madras just outside the Theosophical Society. Quenched, we then would saunter the old pathways near the banyan tree and think of Anne Besant and Madame Blavatsky before we'd go to the ocean on the other side of the gate. We walked everywhere. Sometimes we wore big boots. Other times, we wore slippers that quickly got thinner with the miles. There were so many pilgrimages we undertook. Some in the middle of the night up mountains so we could catch the first ray of sunrise as it hit inner chambers of temples or valleys. At times, we just wanted to witness the night sky unobstructed. We walked to the source of the Ganges and marveled at this beautiful water coming out of its glacier, other pilgrims poorly dressed for the cold mountains yet their hearts were so hot for God! Bonga once invited me to Ginza in Tokyo, and we went garbage shopping one evening. Ginza was the richest part of Tokyo and boxes are thrown out unopened!!! Like queen and king, we gathered and gave away boxes of chocolates to peddlers on the streets. We saw the homeless situation in Japan as we meandered down dark alleys. We also helped many people along the way, bringing one man who was dying on the street to the hospital or distributing food and clothing to those in need, whether in disaster or group homes.

The magic of romance and lover ship wore thin after the first two years as it was replaced by the drive of two ascetics in search of freedom. We became more as siblings, and I began to live more like a hermit.

Practical Application for you:

1. Who is the person in your life that when the thought of him/her arises, your heart dances?
2. Was there a time of prolonged silence for you? What did you most vividly remember about this time?
3. What is more predominant in your inner scape: a battle field or a love field? What is that like?
4. What are you sensing in your body right now? How does your belly feel? Is your mouth dry or juicy?
5. Do you remember an elder, a teacher, or someone who inspired you to be a better version of yourself? Or just accepted you fully for who are?

CHAPTER 11: PILGRIMAGE FOR TRUTH WITH MAHA GHOSANANDA

In my mid twenties, I joined a "dhammayietra" – a pilgrimage for truth. It was a month long walk across Cambodia. We started at the Thai border and ended in the Vietnamese border. When I arrived that day, there were 600 Buddhist monks and nuns waiting for us. They were already on a line on the road – double filed. Maha Ghosananda, the supreme patriarch, means the leader of the Buddhist religion in Cambodia was smiling, warm and dressed like a pumpkin. He was very beautiful, humble and loving. We were joining him. It was such a blessing and privilege to join for this walk.

But let me back off a little bit first. You see, I lived in a forest monastery in southern Thailand and lived a life mostly in silence – waking up at 4 in the morning and meditating most of the day in formal practice until 9 or 10 at night. I also taught meditation and Buddhism to those who came for retreats. I had a wonderful teacher, Ajahn Poh, whom I loved and respected dearly.

When he found out what I was planning to do, he was very concerned and tried to persuade me to stay. And I would say, it's only for a month. And it would be good for me. Then he replied, "It's dangerous there. A war. Landmines. People got killed in last year's walk." So I kept insisting in my stubborn way.

One day, this group of westerners arrived there and several months earlier, they had started a walk from Auschwitz, Poland in a concentration camp, across Iraq, the Middle East, India and now Thailand. They were walking to commemorate the 50th anniversary of the end of WWII and the walk would continue ending in Hiroshima, Japan where the atomic bomb was dropped. Well, my impression of this crowd was of rowdiness. You see, many were very political and angry. And the peace walk is about peace and compassion. But sometimes, people come to a cause from many directions. So my friend asked me, "Why are you going with this?" And I replied, "This is why I'm going." I felt that I wanted to have and be peace even when others were angry and rowdy. I wanted the walk for a month to be a walking meditation just as I walked silently on my forest path.

So the day arrived and I snuck out of the monastery without telling my teacher. I didn't want him to stop me. My friend Bonga insisted to accompany me, "I'll come with you because you need a bodyguard." Very few westerners were selected to join in.

And so back to the Thai border with this beautiful elderly monk that looked like a pumpkin. He was also called the "Mahatma Gandhi of Indochina." Maha Ghosananda's relatives were mostly killed in the war in Cambodia. He was meditating in a Thai monastery then and he would tell his teacher, Ajahn Dhammadaro, that he had to go and help his people. And his teacher would say, "Not yet. You are not ready yet." He then would return to his hut and cry and cry. This happened many times until he was ready to go.

There was a lot of excitement and nervousness too. You see, when I was there, the war was still raging and people were dying all the time. There were lots of land mines and many people lost their legs or arms when a land mine exploded. And the land mines were everywhere. They looked like toys even dropped from airplanes or planted everywhere. It was a war that tore a nation. Land mines were cheap-like toys- and very costly in terms of its effects. There were so many land mines that we walked for three to five days and we could only stay on the main road because all the land had red signs with skulls and bones. They meant – "Deadly – stay out – land mines everywhere."

We'd walk 30 kilometers a day on one side of the road double file in silence or chanting. One morning, we were on one side walking for and in peace, and the other side was filled with soldiers with bazookas and missiles heading the other way. I was scared and angry and confused and I knew I was walking there for a good reason. I also understood that soldiers were people too in green clothes. And they too wanted peace. I just kept going back to what it means to be at peace each moment, each step. I kept going back to my breath, my heart. During the walk, if I peed, it had to be on the road itself.

I will kid you not. It was very hard. The first week, I heard gun fires and bombs at night while I slept under a tree or a small room crammed with everyone. And there were so few bathrooms and toilets for all of us in the monasteries. The food was poor, rice and lots of mangoes with little vegetables that the villagers donated. The food didn't matter really that much because they gave it with so much love and blessings and hope and belief and gratitude. You see our walk was inspiring people to go back to love and kindness, that hatred cannot stop with hatred. Only with loving kindness can hatred cease. These were the words of the Buddha. And when Maha Ghosananda was ready, he printed thousands of these and spread them in the refugee camps. And this was the message of the peace walk.

During the war, Pol Pot killed all the monks and had them disrobed and forced to get married. He forbid Buddhism or any religion in Cambodia. He killed anyone who read and was intelligent or had glasses. And he made people hate with his hate. He let children turned their parents in. It was really terror ridden and friends couldn't trust friends, brothers and sisters did not share secrets even.

That first week of the walk, we waited until it was daylight before we stepped out of the monastery, even though we were already up and meditating before dawn broke. I understood why one morning as each of us silently stepped over a string on the road attached to a land mine – ready, waiting to explode. Everyone was setting them up to protect themselves.

So when I saw kids with no arms or legs on the street waiting for us to bless them, I understood. My heart cried. The peace walk called for peace and an end to land mines. Each day I would walk and knew why I had come and why I stayed even though it was so hard. Maha Ghosananda taught me that each step is a prayer.

We walked day after day for one month. Thankfully the land mines were only the first few days. There were lots of other excitement too besides. Once we were walking just in prayer and then these tanks started rolling towards us from the other side. We all just stopped and I was towards the front so I saw all the action. I still remember to this day the quickening of my heart and swallowing my breath and thinking that I might die then and could I die in peace. And was ready, still, holding my ground as all the monks and nuns were.

I knew when I joined the walk that there might be casualties, my life included. The year before, the peace walkers were caught in the line of fire and several died. This year, we were warned that our foreign blood (around 20 of us) was threatened for kidnapping to be held as hostage. It was risky, dangerous and I didn't know that full extent until I was walking there.

The people's love and devotion were astonishing to me. They would line the streets wherever we went with containers, pots/pans, cans, anything that can hold water. They had formed sticks and branches/leaves so we can dip them in the water and bless them. We also dipped lit incense into the water extinguishing the fire of war. It was auspicious this pilgrimage for truth and what it stood was everyone's deepest hopes in their hearts for the future and a forgiveness of the past. It was the honoring of their deceased relatives who perished in the war, and the future of their children and grandchildren. And I felt so privileged and honored and blessed to be part of all of these.

While in Batambang and Phnom Penh, so many lay people came to join the walk – swelling to thousands on the street. I also went to the "reeducation camp" there and my soul kept tearing apart to witness how much hatred in our hearts can lead us to torture others this way. We as human beings are capable of so much love, and at the same time, of so much hatred. I felt so sick and knew that this too is part of the human story. I've witnessed this in Auschwitz seven years earlier. I knew then that I will want to choose love over ad over and over again in my heart and it wasn't necessarily going to be easy either.

Along the walk, I slept in crematoriums, in places that kept skulls that were buried in mass graves, saw schools where old undetonated bombs from the Vietnam war were still alive and waiting to explode and maim children. I saw illegal logging of old-growth trees for consumption in the industrialized nations. I saw big cigarette multinational companies giving free tobacco to children as young as four or five so they will get addicted and be a customer for life. I saw so many things that broke my heart and I felt angry, helpless, confused and did not understand the way the world is. And I wondered too. How could I make a difference? How can my life affect the lives of those I touch in positive ways that make this world a better place to live. And that's what I've been doing with intention in each day I breathe. Making life a little happier for each of us. Showing those nearby that I care and they matter and are loved.

Practical Application for you:

1. When you feel free, what qualities arise for you?
2. What or who inspires you in your life? How does inspiration serve you? Do you inspire others in your life?
3. Love and hatred are twins. What do you think? How is this true in your life?
4. If you are to make a physical movement now, what is the movement of inspiration and freedom?
5. What do you want to pass on to the next generation of your life's learnings?

CHAPTER 12: LEAVING THE MONASTIC PATRIARCHY IN THE FORM OF MALE TEACHERS

My friendship with Bonga blossomed in deep ways. The monastic life though did not encourage it, rather the opposite. There were lots of projections upon me and us. I withdrew more internally. At times, we rented a hotel room for an hour or two just so I could cry and share with him what was my internal experience. Buddhist scriptures in the past as well as what is taught currently in traditional ascetic monasteries did not think highly of women. In fact, women were seen as Maras (evil) that tempt men sexually out of their aspirations for a pure life. There is a belief in some countries that women are born as women this life time because they did something wrong last life. I didn't believe this at all.

I felt the immense support Bonga and I gave each other all those years of meditating. I missed looking up and seeing that he's right there sitting or walking not so far away watching body-mind. Our journey was really that.

As much as I had benefited for years from the profound generosity and benevolence of monastic life, there came a time that the flower that was me needed a different garden. I yearned to be met in other ways that included my manifestations as a woman of the twentieth and twenty-first century.

Bonga was very helpful and generous with everyone. When he saw a bag of a friend who had a broken zipper, he would volunteer to fix it. He painted mandalas and embroidered his handmade bag. In the monastery, he would cover all the books (thousands) in the library with plastic covers so that they would last longer in the tropics. So I helped him in some of these tasks, and it was time we could spend together. I remembered him excitedly riding his borrowed bicycle across the red road, its basket filled with so many dharma books. I lived in a different part of the monastery, and he had to bring the books a few miles to me. We then would cover them in one of the open huts where everyone could see us. It wasn't allowed for men and women to speak privately. We were no exception. It was our time to share the experiences and insights we were having in meditation. We also asked questions and enquired into areas that were tender or unclear to deepen the sharpness of seeing and sensing. There was a deep appreciation and love of each other that we were walking the path together.

Once I was given a really wonderful retreat room called affectionately by the yogis "the penthouse." There was joy for me, but also some jealousy. Bonga wanted the other penthouse, and requested for it. The abbot, however, felt it was too close to me, so he gave Bonga a hut in the muddy forest. It was really funny, especially his reactions. Anyways, another yogi and I helped him gather boulders of rocks to create a path without mud into his hut. The three of us, laughing, would push the wooden cart laden with boulders. Then Bonga yearned for a meditation path that was drier. I so wanted him to be happy and support his practice. I snuck and helped him create a path in the bamboo forest. I carried trays of sand on my head and dump them on the path. It brings me joy right now to be of service that way. We both were so happy that we could support each other on the path. We were like Ryokan and Teishin.

I longed for female teachers as well. The patriarchal system I inhabited left me dehydrated.

When I left the forest ascetic tradition and male patriarchy, I searched for female teachers. I read a book on Buddhist Women Teachers that were trailblazers. Each chapter was dedicated to the history of each woman teacher. I was drawn to five women in this book. Within one month, I met three and studied with them: Roshi Prabhasa Dharma, Ruth Denison and Charlotte Joko Beck.

Charlotte Joko Beck's zendo was an actual normal suburban house in San Diego. The living room and the dining room was L shaped and that was the zendo. It was simple, effective, right to the point. Walking meditation was out in the neighborhood. I loved that it didn't separate ordinary urban home life with spirituality. This was very important as there is a great division for many new practitioners of this in their lives. I have seen for many meditators, integration becomes an issue. This is especially true with practitioners with very strong concentration practices who predominantly do long intensive retreats, yet daily living insights are off. The reversed can also be said with practitioners who have strong daily life practice but don't have strong concentration practices. The sharpness to cut through deep truths is not as available.

She was already in her senior years when I met Joko Beck in the early 1990s. She was a renowned Zen teacher. She was the dharma heir of Hakuyu Maezumi Roshi and was the founder of the Ordinary Mind Zen School.

These are some of her teachings:

"Practice is the slow reversal of our self-centered dream. For most students this reversal is the work of a lifetime. The change is often painful, especially at first. We don't want to allow fresh currents into awareness.

The measure of our practice is that we see life less as a burden and more of a joy. We begin to have a sense of humor about our burden.

Whatever we do in our sitting (fantasies/worry) is like a microcosm of the rest of our lives. Our sitting shows us what we are doing with our lives.

Sitting is not about finding a happy blissful state. Opening into something fresh and new is the consequence of experiencing pain, not a consequence of finding a place where we can shut pain out.

Many suppose that within the first two years they understand the practice. In fact, if we get practice straight in ten years we are doing well. For most twenty years is what it takes.

When we realize that nothing external is ever going to satisfy our thirst, then we are more likely to begin serious practice. Practice has to be a process of endless disappointments. We have to see that everything we demand eventually disappoints us. This discovery is our teacher.

The pull of our self-centered thoughts is like walking through molasses, our feet come out with difficulty and get stuck again. We can slowly liberate ourselves, but if we think it is easy we are kidding ourselves. The key is attention.

There are two parts to practice. One is endless disappointment – if we are not disappointed we never wear out our desire to think. The other is to wear out the illusion that other people are going to make us happy. Other people are part of the wonder that life is; they are not here to do something for us. Life is wonderful because it doesn't give us what we want. To go down this path takes courage. Only a very few, who are enormously persistent and who take everything in life as an opportunity and not as an insult, will understand.

If we practice then in time we are more willing for things to be as they are. We continue to have personal preferences but not demands.

The point of our lives is to fulfill that which we were born for, to heal into life. To heal out of the pain our separate 'I' into openness."

Ruth Denison

Ruth Denison lived in the desert not too far from where I grew up as a teenager. With her long skirt blowing and her head tied in a colorful scarf, she called out one morning into the wide desert, "Karma, where are you?" It stopped me on my tracks and I paid attention. She was calling her dog, but I didn't know that at that moment.

Ruth was full of life even in her later years. She had studied in Burma with U Ba Khin, the same teacher as Goenka. When she came back to the west to teach, she realized that westerners need a slightly different way of grocking it. She brought her creativity in the skillful means department that the meditators could really own the practice and integrate it into their daily lives. She brought play into meditation. When we did walking meditation, she would vary it with different movements. She saw that too focused concentration during walking meditation made a very tensed body. So she introduced different ways to have both concentration and ease and relaxation. I really got it because I had witnessed these same patterns while I taught meditation to hundreds of people. She also made sure people smiled too, and that it was a joyful path.

I feel that Ruth has been very much misunderstood in the dharma community. I believe she deserves much more respect that is given her way.

I lived with Ruth for more than one month in the desert. She was mischievous. I cooked in the kitchen, and one day, I was so pleased with myself for preparing a very subtle pumpkin soup for the meditators. My co-cook and I were grinning from ear to ear when Ruth sauntered in the kitchen. She tasted the soup, then added that it needed just a little bit more spice. She took a jar of turmeric curry and poured so much of it and then gave us a big smile, to both our dismay as cooks. It was a huge lesson on attachment.

Her center was rugged. Water was scarce. It had to be trucked in. We recycled water. After washing the dishes, we used the bucket of water to water the plants. The same went for taking a shower. The used water gets collected to water the plants. The toilets were pits. You have no choice but to meditate on the sense of smell.

In the late evening after a full day of work and sitting meditation, Ruth would take out Bhikkhu Bodhi's thick book on the middle discourses of the Buddha. It had just been published. She would then read it aloud to me and we would discuss it in her living room. She didn't know that I had met Bhikku Bodhi in Sri Lanka. I had to work with my own personality preferences and separating it from Buddha's discourses. At midnight, I would walk in the desert, hear the howling coyotes and enjoy the crispy evening and the stars. The next morning, I would awake really early to prepare breakfast for the meditators.

Towards an end of one women's retreat, Ruth sent me to retrieve a box of chocolates for the women. I searched and searched and saw a box. I saw a box with heart shaped, individually wrapped chocolates, but they weren't enough chocolates for everyone. So I thought, I'd better break the hearts into two so everyone can have half a heart. And then with eagerness I brought them to her. Ah, the look in her face as I delivered the half hearts...To make a long story short, I felt so bad, I went back to her house and began to piece together the broken hearts, ironing the foil wrappers with my fingers, and then rewrapping them again making sure they looked close enough to untouched. Thankfully, my concentration and agility in breaking chocolates was so precise that it was easy to match the broken hearts back!!!

I loved Ruth. Once I came to her with a gift of sand in the desert. I said while looking into her eyes and palms open, "Ruth, I offer you the mountain." We both smiled. The teacher and the student were one. It was only dhamma (truth).

Ruth wanted me to stay in the desert to study and live there with her. I would have, but it was my time to be with Roshi Prabhasa Dharma.

Roshi Prabhasa Dharma

My disappointment with the highly patriarchal and sexually one sided Theravada monastic tradition encouraged me to seek a woman teacher. I met Roshi Prabhasa Dharma while visiting my family in the US. I was an assistant cook at a retreat in the desert and I requested an audience with her. Since I wasn't part of the paying retreat, the staff dissuaded me. However, the Roshi, came into the office one morning and I asked for an interview with her. I was tenacious that way. While in an apron preparing the dinner one day, I was summoned into her bedroom. She was regal in her golden robes, definitely not ascetic as my monk teachers in Asia. There were no hellos or polite greetings. Her gaze penetrated me and she asked, "What have you realized?" The teacher, the student and the teaching were one at that moment.

Roshi and I had a complicated relationship. I admired and loved her. I also questioned her. I undertook a study of koans with her as our teacher-student relationship blossomed. I began to deeply understand insight and creativity and life and fullness together. I worked very hard, like a samurai. Yet at the moment of each relationship with a koan, there was simply freedom. Koans are to be carried like one carries a lover. You never let it down. An example of a koan is: What is the sound of one hand clapping?

When the bell rang, the students raced, running to be the first to declare their realization to the teacher. This was not slow-motion mindfulness walking meditation. People sprinted! And often, just as students are ready to sit to declare their whatever, the Roshi would already have rung the bell for them to leave. She can see just by the students entering the level of their presence. In fact, students had to wait in a waiting area, a mini zendo to wait for

114

their turn. It was their turn, they would ring the bell with a small hammer. There is a spot that one hit perfectly, otherwise, the sound would be off. The Roshi's ears were very tuned in to this sound. So even before the students enter her door, she already knows a lot.

I loved these times of koans with her. They were very playful for both of us.

The other students spoke of times when the Roshi would ask everyone to pack a bag for three days and get in the cars. They didn't know where they were being led to. Then of all a sudden, the Grand Canyon was in front of them! Another time, she would again packed everyone in cars while in sesshin and drive into rushed hour traffic in Los Angeles.

The Roshi taught very creatively. She broke any distinctions and preferences around external silence. Roshi had her own path.

Once we were in Germany and her way of teaching me was to take me in a wine tour along the Rhine. I didn't drink alcohol. We stayed at a nice hotel and while the television was on and I was ruminating and agitated as to this trip being spiritual or not, she said to me something about the noise being in my mind, and not on the TV. Soon afterwards, she took me to a casino and placed a handful of coins in my hand and ordered me to play the slot machines. As I sat there, I thought, what's next. She will ask me to have sex with someone! So I came from a very strict, ascetic monastic Theravadin Buddhist training and now I was in Zen training. The skillful means were very different. The aim, however, is the same: to cut through and see reality as it is.

When I met her, she already had cancer. I would cook special meals for her lovingly, then I would join the rest of the students for meals. Once the Roshi took the plate I cooked, and in front of everyone proclaimed in a very upset way that how could I leave a hair in the food. I felt a surge of shame and humiliation. It was the way she taught. I had to keep facing these parts of myself, and see how thick were the identifications within me.

She did everything to break me down, to break down any attachment to anything. When I arranged flowers for her, I would find them outside the door to be rearranged again. Even photos of us together were cut in halves by her. It came to the point where I didn't want to go for an interview. And just like the classic Rinzai Zen stories of old, the officers were sent to the kitchen asking me to report for an interview. You see I was the head cook, a tenzo. I marched with my apron to her and expressed my anger at her. She was very strict with me. When food was brought to her and she saw that the vegetables were not uniformly cut by the students, I would be reprimanded. The tenzo had to run the kitchen as a meditation hall. I had to watch that the level of concentration was equitable to their practice while sitting. I was being trained to teach meditation in action.

Good enough wasn't what it was about. It was about what identity I had invested with everything I did. That was the pact between Zen teacher and student. Her job was to make me see through reality. To break through whatever hides the gem inside. You just hope that you break through and not break down in the process.

It was very difficult for me and very lonely. After a time traveling as an attendant in Europe with her, I gave my resignation. We both were sad. I said I was going on a solitary retreat in the mountains in Norway. She asked me to return afterwards and help her teach the dharma.

The Roshi trained many students in both the United States and Europe. Although she trained under the Japanese and Vietnamese Rinzai traditions, she had her own way of teaching the way of "kensho" (seeing one's true nature). When I met her, I already had a very strong stillness practice having had meditated for many years. My training with her was about embodying wisdom within the activities of daily living, fast or slow, no matter where I was. The training included zazen, koan and samu (physical work done with mindfulness). Rinzai training is sharper than Soto Zen training. There is a saying: "Rinzai for the Shogun, Soto for the peasants."

She asked that I ordained as a nun as my previous teachers had done before. I knew already that I didn't have to take the outer robes to have the commitment of a contemplative. I became her attendant and we traveled in Europe together while she trained me in the Rinzai Zen tradition. We made an agreement of one year before ordination to give each other a trial. My daily bread were koan studies and tough love. But the fire was hot and I was her attendant. It is said that one's relationship with one's spiritual teacher is like a moth's relationship to the fire. You want to be not too far from your teacher that you will not feel the warmth of the fire, but not too close to the fire that you get burnt and eaten up by it.

She promised to treat me hard in my tutelage. The Roshi trained me ruthlessly and tried to break me down so I could have a breakthrough. There were brutal times as well as the love that binds a teacher and student. In this process, I saw that the early years in the forest monastery of loving-kindness for myself was getting thawed into a cold hardness of the way she was training me. I left the Roshi and went alone in my spiritual journey.

My first exposure to Buddhism was the path of Vajrayana with Kirti Tsenshab Rinpoche, yet I was drawn to the silence and simplicity of the Theravadin path. It taught me that form is emptiness. And when the ascetic path denied my manifestation as a woman, I felt I needed to have my form be included in my spiritual path. I met Roshi Prabhasa Dharma in the Rinzai Zen tradition where my study with her was precisely about the second half of the Heart Sutra – emptiness is form. Then I studied Vajrayana again, where everything in existence is nectar. And now, they are all skillful means. There is just the here and now. I am grateful for all of them in my life.

The teachings of the Roshi focused on the Heart Sutra. "Form is emptiness. Emptiness if form. Form is form. Emptiness is emptiness."

The maturation of the heart sutra in my life kept developing in the market place daily. It will be my whole life this stabilization and cultivating confidence that is unwavering. I saw emptiness in form, understood that form is a display of emptiness. That form is no other than emptiness. No wonder the realized ones have so much compassion for us all in our ignorance and mistaking this for a reality and not seeing it for what it is. I felt great gratitude for the compassion of all my teachers for waking me up. I was given this jewel and after all these years of unraveling, kaboom! I can see the face of my first teacher smiling at me now and his benevolent heart with so much kindness guiding. And the Roshi had one of the hardest jobs to break me through illusions of stillness and silence. It was never about the external. I have come to appreciate her more and more as I get older and mature in the practice. All my teachers stand by the birth canal, all the spiritual midwives to my birthing. I understood in a very different way appearance is emptiness, understood the teachings from new eyes and a different heart and bodhicitta was born anew in a way I haven't grasped before. The good and bad are both displays of the same emptiness. That emptiness contains everything. It is as the mist being born out of space, and then disappearing into space. The mist is space itself. How can it not be?

Norway Solitary Retreat: Tasting Snow

After I left the Roshi, I needed to go into silence to collect myself. I was confounded with so many questions around the student-teacher relationship. Organized religion and spirituality left a funny taste on my tongue. I needed to recollect myself anew and clearly see what was emerging for me. I had left the patriarchy of Asian Buddhism for the promise of more forward thinking of female teachers in the lineage in the west, yet it wasn't any different. Part of the wall I found myself facing was it didn't matter whether it was east or west, male or female. Essentially I had to face what was my true face before I was born. I was caught in the identities I didn't even know were pulling the strings of my self, and yet simultaneously were inviting me to a fuller, deeper penetration of my individuation here as a form. I was straddling multiple facets of waking up.

I was in Holland at the time and reached out to a new friend who had offered his home in the mountains of Norway. I met Sugata that same year and the deep connection and respect he had for my dedication to the spiritual path propelled him to offer his assistance anytime I might need it. Sugata was the first Western Theravadin monk in Nepal in 1953. He had two homes in the mountains in Norway. As soon as he received my message, Sugata sent me a train ticket from Amsterdam to Oslo in Norway. I was surprised that he didn't ask any questions in the beginning. As I packed my few belongings, I took a few of my most precious possessions in my back pack and gifted them to the people who hosted me. I took the brown robes the Roshi had given me and passed them on to one of her beloved disciples. I took the silent Buddha Sister Mechtildes bequeath me and gave it to another. In turn, I welcomed the gifts the monks and nuns have given me to keep me company in my winter retreat: a small bell, eating bowls, fleece sweater in deep violet. They were to remind me of the spiritual friendships as well as the discipline, warmth and beauty in the cold and aloneness of winter.

It was a long, drawn-out journey as I left the autumn leaves blowing on the streets just outside of Amsterdam. I felt alone yet strong. I was traveling into the direction of the land of my paternal ancestors. I had not been there before. I had not seen frozen lakes or harsh blizzards. I had never been in the dark of winter where light barely shone. The train stopped in Copenhagen and I looked around the passengers. I couldn't believe that I was a quarter Dane. They looked so different than I. The snow fell in Denmark as the train rapidly sped up north. I crossed the ferry into Sweden and then arrived in Oslo where Sugata eagerly met me. We barely knew each other, yet somehow there was bond that was deep. He welcomed me and visited Oslo. We even watched the movie "Evita" in a movie theatre. We took another train to the middle of Norway and I watched the icicles on the trees and rivers in wonder. And when we arrived at our final destination, there was so much snow on the ground! I had no idea what was in store for me. His car was waiting and there was still a distance to go - across the frozen lake.

As we entered the last bridge, Sugata stopped his car and said, "It's your last chance to turn back." I gulped, noted my fear, and overrode it. He gave me one of the houses half buried in snow, showed me how to turn on the heater, gave a tour of the pantry and I began my winter retreat. It was a beautifully crafted wooden cottage with rose paintings of a double vajra (Tibetan for thunderbolt) on its ceiling. Its simplicity framed the depth of blizzards and the ever changing snowy landscape that engulfed me. I burnt many candles that winter. I had shelter, food and all I had to do was watch the mind! I grounded oat seeds by hand and soaked them overnight. That was breakfast. Lunch was rice, sprouted mung

119

beans, maybe grated carrots. Dinner was same or soup with rye bread and homemade cranberry jam. Once a month or so, I would have frozen spinach as a treat. It was harder to cook for myself than to cook for the whole monastery with the Roshi.

Sprouting the mung beans was essential for me that retreat. The seeds reminded me of the mystery of life and no never underestimate it. The power of life force breaking through into its next manifestation is simply immense, powerful and mysterious. The changing snow landscape was my constant teacher. I could not predict anything. I surrendered.

Initially, I took down the bathroom mirror at the beginning of the retreat and hid it. Though as winter progressed, I would peek at it just to remind myself that I was still there. The sun did not touch my side of the valley for the whole three months except the last two days. The first week in Shangri-La, I could still walk with my regular shoes outside, but then it kept snowing and my legs got swallowed up by the snow. I didn't know how to ski. Sugata gave me a very quick lesson and bought me skis and a red anorak. Red so if I get lost in the countryside, I can be seen and found quickly in the landscape of snow. He took me on top of a hill, and said to bend my knees and let the poles swing behind me, and I flew in the air down the hill so fast. He hadn't taught me how to stop yet. The fall on the bottom was cushioned by laughter as I saw Sugata, this generous man in his late eighties, running down the hill towards me to make sure that I was all right!

I went out everyday when the light was out. It was so cold that even the hair in my nose froze. Once, I cried and asked loudly, "Why?" and there wasn't even an echo back. The tears rapidly turn to ice as it glided down my cheek. It was all such a cosmic joke!

At times, I just sat by the frozen lake and listened to its grumbles and murmurs as it fell underneath itself. I felt as ancient as time and young as forever.

I would go outside while the snow fell. I would catch the humungous snowflakes and marveled at each unique design that fell unto my red jacket. I would stretched my tongue out and taste the snowflakes by the frozen lake. The visibility at times was nil. I would look behind me, and even my footsteps rapidly disappeared.

I left no trace, backwards or forwards. Only the moment existed, and even that could not be caught. Who am I? Only the vastness.

On one side was the dire loneliness, yet at the same time there was the palpable interconnectedness with the whole of creation. I felt the mountains were my brothers, the snow my sisters, the sky my cousin. I was overjoyed to see the elks' tracks or to sneak a peak at the rabbits eating the carrots I had left outside. I felt one with the air and euphoric with the shooting stars. The dawns and dusks that winter were eternal. I am so grateful for that winter retreat. Confidence that was beyond what I knew was planted by the winter storms that kept changing their form right before my eyes!!

Seeing I was a natural hermit, my friend Sugata offered me the home up there. I, however, felt that there were other ways I still needed to grow and know the other facets of the diamond that I was. I was still in my twenties. There is something about accepting the full expression of me and the full expression of creation and manifestation. True tantra.

Sri Lanka with Bonga after Norwegian winter

Sugata wanted me to stay, but I knew that Bonga and I needed to meet again. Overnight I flew from the Scandinavian winter to the tropics of Sri Lanka. The sound of the insects was deafening!! Bonga wasn't happy to see me. He didn't trust me because I left to become a nun. While I was away, Bonga's kundalini had awakened. On one hand he didn't trust me, but he also needed my help. We lived in a very strict gender separated meditation center. Bonga would "lose" his sense of self and enter different dimensions. His "I" left intermittently during this time. It was so difficult – a double bind. I would help him to his room but I couldn't speak too loudly because I was in the men's section, and I wasn't supposed to be there. I was rebelling against this particular form of religiosity. I didn't want to be there, yet Bonga needed my help. He was afraid to leave that life behind. And I was setting my terms. Finally he agreed to leave, but our life revolved around the kundalini. He blamed me for abandoning him, the kundalini rising, then coming to his life again and disrupting it. The emotional outburst came with the kundalini journey for him. I too felt hurt, misunderstood and wanted to run away, yet felt too guilty to leave him in his situation. This activated my patterns and hooks of "being responsible" for another person.

Practical Application for you:

1. How do you recognize satisfaction? What is the color of disappointment for you? What is the taste in your mouth right now?
2. What is the journey in your relationships between closeness and distance? How do you dance with your masculine and feminine aspects?
3. Is there a difference between the teachings coming from a woman as opposed to a man? What are the similarities? How do they personally touch you as a man or a woman?
4. Has nature been a teacher to you? What was that like? How often to go out in nature to receive teachings?
5. Put your hands on your ribs, one over the liver on the right, the other on the left. Breathe three times. Now put your hands on your ribs just under your collar bones. Breathe three times. Leave left hand just above your heart and place the right one back on the liver. Breathe three times. Place right hand under the collar bones and the left on the diaphragm. Breathe three times.

Part II: Emergence switches gears and enters emergency

CHAPTER 13: SHEDDING THE OLD SKIN

Deep yearnings to pursue my wholeness beckoned me out of the path of holiness, and into the streets of San Francisco. Even with all the blessings and charm of my life, a part of my soul yearned to be met in other ways. I left the monastic life in Asia to pursue graduate studies in California, as a response to this call. The basements of my soul were whispering.

Leaving Bonga was a necessary part of my journey. We had known each other for nine years at that time. We've been through heaven and hell together. He was my magic friend and my soul brother. Yet, my journey beckoned me another way. We said goodbye at the bus station in Tiruvanamallai in India. It was the first time I cried so much in a goodbye. I didn't know why. My soul felt it was the last time I was going to see him. He died a year later.

With only a backpack, I arrived in San Francisco and entered grad school studying psychology. Deeper waters though promised to lure me into that which was unknown to me. My psyche was ripped open and all the spectrum of consciousness flooded. The serpent kundalini danced wildly as I entered a dark night of the soul.

Deep in the psyche, images dance and present themselves to be called attention to. It may come in many forms. Some through painting, poetry, meditations, dance, song, prayer, guided imagery, focusing, syncronicities, and of course dreams, amongst a number of other possibilities. I have and continually use all of these in addition to other avenues of explorations. I invite you to join this humble journey which can in no way be contained in these pages. What will unfold is a story of a fragile and strong being who will blossom as the high mountain flowers continue to weather the drastic changing seasons that are especially characteristic of high altitude life.

A dream emerges in mid-spring the year 1999 along the bay of San Francisco. In an office, a detective speaks to a woman. There has been a series of theft and he insists that the motives or appearance is not as obvious as it may seemed. There is definitely something else going on underneath the surface. The theft is an alibi for something bigger that is happening.

The detective proceeds to go to the bottom of a huge battleship where the theft had occurred. It is a huge aircraft carrier that navigates across the Pacific. He descends to the basement where the crime had occurred: a dusty room with an cream colored curtains that looked more like rags hanging against the missing bars on the tiny window. It looks like a cheap hotel room in Bangkok. The detective upon investigation assumes that this theft is really a ploy to divert his attention away from the real intention. As he finishes searching the room and began to move tot he doorway, a shabby man with stables and a potbelly nervously appears. He emerges from a secret door suddenly appearing on the corridor where none had been before. He is carrying a box that is half white and half blue. The thief runs in fear as the detective pursues him on the stairs with a silver magnum gun. But to no avail as the thief disappears on the spiral steel staircase. A group of non-white extroverted men and women descend blocking the passageway for the frantic detective. It appears that they've just been at a party so they look strangely at the sweating searcher. In any case, he continues his pursuit and upon hearing noises began shooting. It was suddenly dark and the sound of helicopters landed on the deck. The SWAT team along with the police force arrive. There is much confusion as the detective is not identifiable from the thief in the big commotion in the dark. The detective gets shot and blood begins to drip. He takes off his shoes as not to make any sound, but his footsteps are bloody. He ascends to the deck of the battleship in the middle of the tumultuous ocean. The SWAT team recognized him and embraces him. "You're on safe ground..."

This dream is symbolic of the journey that unfolds me. As I descended to the different levels of the battleship, questions emerge: who is the thief and what is being stolen? Why is it such a secret? The thieves' headquarter was below what the detective thought to be the lowest floor. In what areas of life is conscious? Where is she fearful and unfree? Where is she awake and what is she avoiding? How is she being led by what she doesn't know? Is it possible to se the difference between what is actually happening and the way she is describing it?

While waiting for the traffic light to change, a Lakota Indian approached me. He asked, "Have you ever slept with a rattlesnake?" I said that I don't remember. He proceeded to draw a snake on my third eye and began to do a ritual right there. That evening, I dreamt that a huge snake was watching me on my bed. The next day I saw many snakes in the park. Truly I delved deeper into transformation where the old skin sheds and the new skin emerges.

According to Animal Speak, the snake "is a symbol of transformation and healing. Snake ceremonies involved learning to transmute the poisons within the body after being bitten multiple times. Survival of this would then enable the individual to transmute all poisons – physical or otherwise. It activated the energy of kill or cure, ultimately leading to dramatic healing.

Learning to use the eyes to mesmerize and look into the hearts and souls of others directly is part of what traditional snake medicine can teach. It may even indicate a need to look more closely into your own heart and soul.

Snakes are symbols of change and healing. They have speed and agility, so those who have snakes come into their life usually find the changes and shifts occur quickly and are soon recognized and defined. When snake comes into your life you can look for a rebirth into new powers of creativity and wisdom."

Below are exchanges of letters between Bonga and I as we speak about the kundalini and its effects on our lives.

K: may 1999
    Dearest Mahal (love),
It is with tears that I read your letters. I miss you and I wish just this much would lessen your pain. I am so sorry that my being here hurts you so much. I don't know why I am here, only that I need to be here now. It is not easy by any means, but somehow heart accommodates all of it, with all its perplexities, apprehension, sadness, paradoxes. Being and walking around the city breaks my heart so and I see so much, and I just want to hide and pretend that the world is not so....maybe we can meet in Canada... I can drive Roxinante up there and we will be Starsky and Hutch!

Take it easy Mahal. Don't let this kundalini take over your life again. I love you. I love you. I love you. The nutty Cacahuete (peanut)

B: may, 1999

You are really a kind of Don Quixote trying to attack all the windmills of human darkness. But where is Roxinante? Where is Sancho Panza?....

I pray that you discover more and more this softness and vulnerability you are talking about and hope that the Don Quixote in you will take it lightly.

Be kind to yourself, do not overdo. Do not be like the hamster running more and more wildly in its wheel and then being surprised that it is so intense. I'm with you.

K:

I walked down the street and two women with long hair that looked like Mary Magdalene passed me by. They turned around and looked me in the eye and said, "Don't forget God." How could I?

My inner middle belly is really taking in the whole city. I want to vomit. It's cellularly too much for me. The frequency of my being is radically being altered. I feel like I have been placed in a big blender.

B: may 25, 1999

Dearest you,

Your latest email broke my heart. I wish I could hold you in my arms and reassure you. What you are going through is of course very familiar to me, but I am concerned that your situation in San Francisco might not allow this most precious and terrible phase of your life to unfold gracefully.

I pray that find very soon, a safe place where to retire and be with good people. You must understand that all your life has brought you to this point and now there is no going back to the old.

You are sitting on a volcano and now it is very important not to add fuel to it. Yes, my dear jisan, it is time to switch off the striving, the intensive search. You have done your homework, Mahal, and of course, you have been doing it very well, thoroughly.

It is time to let the energies do their work and I think that both traditional meditation and therapy do not meet the intensity of the process you are going through. I think it is important that you leave the city and although I want to be respectful of your choices, know that I would meet you in Asia and find a place to rest and to be in nature. This is an invitation, Mahal, and consider it....

Dear Kasha, you are really blessed and no matter how dark and painful this phase of your life may be, believe me that each moment is worth the price. At times, I cannot help but rejoice in what you are going through because I know that it surely will lead towards more joy, more space, more love. Above all, the forces of the universe are going to work for you and I pray that you might relax in the midst of it all.

God's grace is overflowing and you are such a worthy recipient for it all.

Please consider what happened to me and what price my body has to pay for my stubborn attitude. This is a very crucial point in your life and whatever you do now is magnified, multiplied by these tremendous energies.

Your poetry is beautiful, especially the one about the whale. Keep a journal. It will help you to keep some distance in the midst of it all.

A very potent tool I have discovered recently is to speak to these energies and to acknowledge her presence and to let her do her work. The more the resistance, the more devastating it might become.

You have fought the battle, oh you beautiful and daring Don Quixote. Now it is time to leave the driver's seat and to enjoy the ride. I feel for you and send you much energy, smooth and healing ones. You are in touch with raw, naked life and it is such a bloody blessing.

If I had to describe you in one word, it would be IMMENSE IMMENSE....The feeling of timelessness and spacelessness that you describe are very familiar to me, even now after three years in the process. It is groundless, it is scary, but it is also free. You have applied to the faculty of transformation and consciousness, so there you are Mahal...one day you will look back at this time with wonder and deep gratitude. It is a GIFT GIFT GIFT.

If you are fed up with psychologists and Buddhists, I know a messy guy from Switzerland who knows about what you are going through and who will share this time with you, maybe on a beach in Thailand, maybe in the mountains. So think about it Mahal and take very good care. Remember that we share more than a bank of America card together.

B: june 29, 1999

It feels like an endless exodus without the rewards of a promised land. Drifting away, further and further, the spring of will has been broken a long time ago and now life is doing here dance, pulling the invisible strings of this broken doll.

The radiance of this power is slowly eating the flesh away, but even in the deepest tiredness, where the body feels totally exposed and vulnerable, deep bliss and profound relaxation are present, making it possible to stretch one's boundaries and to encompass whatever is present in the field of awareness.

The terrors and paralyzing fears seem to have never taken place but these monsters have very light sleep and the sound of a feather touching the ground, the slightest emotional imbalance can bring them back to life and power. These energies look like those wrathful deities dancing in a magma of fire, wearing severed heads and tramping over corpses. There is so much dynamism, a mad precision, a control folly in the work they are doing. The least of their concern is what I feel to be myself, this bundle of thoughts and emotions, an endless succession of expansion and contraction, a pitiful attempt to give a shape and solidity to what by nature is fluid and without substance...

When the current of a river meets with a stone, it gently finds its way around the obstacle and resumes its journey. The tao way, softness, flexibility. But when these energies meet any knot, any resistance in the body, it just burns them up, crush them, squeeze them, smash them. Where is the gentleness, where is the compassion? The fire of this love is no cotton candy, no gently breeze or Chinese landscape inundated by silver moonlight. Sorry.

Spirituality is not a soft and warm cocoon where one can curl up and take a nap. It is not a Mickey Mouse band aid on a wooden leg or a perfumed Kleenex to fix your tears up. The smile on the Buddha face is fine, but how much agony, doubt, uncertainty, terror was its crucible? And yet we sit with quiet desperation with this half smile pasted on a most horrible mask. You may go deeper and deeper, but there will always be a point, at the border of insanity, where you will be asked to go back to the safety of your breath, your tradition, your practice. You are asked to gnaw at the rope, but don't you touch the live wire.

The screams and tears of countless truth seekers are bursting in my chest and the dedication and discipline of those who abuse themselves in order to find peace make me feel like puking...

B: 1999

Your very body
Is her temple
A very shaky temple

You might look
Like the little ugly duck today
Only to find out later
That you are a majestic swan

Do not jump on conclusions
The christ's victory
Took place in the deepest humiliation
Take it one ant's step at a time
No one knows what is coming next
A laughing Mickey Mouse
Or a terrible Tasmanian devil

You've gone through countless battles
And yet your skin is so smooth

And the soles of your feet tender
Who would believe
That you are a war veteran
That fought his battles for peace

I love you so
I kiss your wounds
And your scars too
And my healing hands
On your aching heart
Listen in awe
To the half-buried memories
The shameful secrets
There is this endless
Source of energy
Sacred atomic power
In each one of your cells
But only with utmost tenderness
The caress of a soft feather
Will you unleash
The Goddess

I drink your tears
And hold you against my heart

K journal:

Of course, I ask myself, am I just so damn messed up? What's wrong with me? What I would like most of all right now is someone to hold me tight when I'm so frightened. I want my feelings to matter too! I'm beating the pillows, crying and all these images of bright, white lights and deities with huge jewels above their heads and the fire raging.

I must not forget that place which holds all these emerging and disappearing. Being here in the school of psychology, there is so much focus on the "I", the self. It is important for me especially now to see the "I" that tenaciously holds, that competes with one's self and its ideas about one's self, while simultaneously respecting that place that is hurting. What are my biases? My beliefs?

B: 1999

I'm just back from another expedition in Kandy and the email place there is the equivalent of the municipal library in Victorville. Today's reading of your email was a most beautiful gift. Its beauty and depth is haunting me and I feel so connected with this big heart that is beating in each living creature. I found myself in every character. It is really mesmerizing. Thank you for such a gift.

I find myself practicing what Da Free John calls the wound of love and I feel so open and my heart is spilling out and I find everybody so beautiful and worthy of love.

I feel so grateful to know you and to have a taste of your depth and immensity. I see you as a doorway to my own heart, a bottomless well of unspoilt life...

Do not expect to be fully understood, dear one, for your process is unique. Just surrender to the force and she will take care of you in such unexpected and beautiful ways. No need to run here and there and let people spill their stuff on your raw and tender wounded heart.

There is such a big place for you in my heart so please, make yourself comfortable there and feel free to visit as often as you wish. The tips of the iceberg are miles away, but the roots are really one.

How I long to look at you, at your beautiful eyes and your open, questioning face...

How could you stop blossoming and be a light so bright? Just trust and surrender as I do and let the universe play with Kasha and Bonga.

I love you like I have never dared loved before. Be well and know that I am here, just right at your side.

K:

Through this process, I'm seeing how scared I am. It's okay not to feel well. I do have permission to be unwell and sick. I don't have to prove my worth by what I do, what I produce, by how others see me or expect from me. That it is okay to ditch classes, go to the beach and watch a movie and the world actually moves on without my sense of order or control.

In class today we did an exercise of moving to protect ourselves, make boundaries and make a stand. I did the movement and I just cried and cried. My posture to protect myself only exposed myself more and it hurt physically and emotionally. It hurt that I didn't know how to protect myself, and inside me said, please don't be hard to myself.

B: 1999
You are an old soul
Older than the sand and the stones
You know the movements of the universe
And feel the pain of her labour
Let us meet soon
Me the green horn
The tenderfoot
I'll teach you
The art of stupidity
And the childlike wonders
Of being carefree
Let us meet soon
And mix our souls
Let your hand rest in my hand
And our fingers
Dance in pairs
You'll be the noble elephant
I'll be the mischievous mouse

K:
I was laughing, then I was crying. Then the energies begin to whip my spine and the speaking in tongues and burping and throwing up. I want to move, to sing loud, to dance, to explode this energy so strong that wants to go out. I feel like a kite and I want to cut the string and fly high up in the universe and never come back. I feel afraid because who will watch and make sure that I

come back if things don't go quite right. I feel sad that I am here trying to wrap my wings so tightly.

I want to scream. Jesus, take care of me, don't leave me alone. I want this toxic to go out.

B: July 17, 1999

Be like a dignified Pharaoh
Deeply buried
In a magnificent pyramid
Your throbbing heart
In the dark chamber of your body of stone

Be like the mythical phoenix
Raising back to life
From the deadest ashes

Be like a newborn child
With a soft brain
Of virgin wax

Be like a few lines
Written on the sea shore
By a desperate lover

Go and take a nap
And fall asleep
Like an old, grey woman
Only to wake up
Fresh and radiant
Like the first morning of spring

Unload yourself
From the burden of time
The thick leather
Of a thousand sheets
Of dead memories

Rise up roaring
In the vast and exhilarating
Unlimited and frightening
Expanse of your mad mind

Do you know that all of my fears
All your fears
Of wool and iron
Where a most beautiful butterfly
Awaits its birth?

Now is the time of deep rest
Now is the time of gestation
Now is the time for the deepest respect

K:

I was being whipped on my spine as I did the child pose. The kriyas (spontaneous movements) keep happening. There are so many different languages coming out of my mouth. I feel so wired and electrocuted.

I was so disconcerted. I knew that it wasn't safe. My short term memory begins to fade. I have to check at least twice if I locked the door or tuned off the stove because the moment before didn't seem to have happen.

What if I am going crazy? It's so lonely not to be able to share what is happening to me. How can I share that I feel that there are so many snakes moving in my head? All these visions won't stop. Who will take care of me? What if I get sick? I am so exhausted. Who will hold me?

I am confronted with so many self-worth issues. Giving up control over that which I consider as my structure. It's happening so fast. The structures I "need" to hold unto are collapsing. I am afraid that I may lose myself. I am afraid that I will be found out. I am afraid that I will fall apart. I am falling apart and I'm desperately trying to give the impression that I'm not. My will is so strong. Too strong. It is a war. I am being broken. Broken to surrender.

I am burning. The inner fire is raging. I cool myself in the freezing ocean in San Francisco. The waves are tumultuous. There is a storm in the sea. It feels good to have intensity outside because it matches or comes closer to the intensity inside. I don't feel so alone.

I'm learning a lot, mostly about letting go of control. I feel ashamed that I'm not in control. It's like this energy is forcing me to submit to humility. It's a hard lesson.

B: oct 1, 1999

This little vibration might be a euphemism for you these days…yes dear sister soul, that is the treasure that is you, the aliveness, the dance of Shiva in your cells, the vibrancy that permeates even the cold and dry universe of the virtual messages sent these past months.

K:

My nerves feel fried! I feel like someone had operated an incision on my front side and took all my internal organs out and didn't sew me back up, so I have to hold myself together. The old structures are falling apart and the new ones haven't quite emerged yet. I'm calling for help. I knew people loved me when I was strong, but I didn't know that people could love me when I'm not strong. It is a revelation.

It happened again at school. The heated energy shot up and I hurried to the disabled stall in the bathroom to allow the kriyas and shaking. I feel so exhausted from all these energetic risings. I have a bump on my lower back, warm and pulsating. I have two bumps on my skull like two horns. How can I be open and not feel so raw and exposed?

There is this rage for the society for abandoning its daughters, for ignoring, setting them up to fail, knowing full well that they'd be alone with their babies, not educating them, giving them skills, preparing them, instead throwing them in the lion's den to be eaten alive. Rage for the men. Rage that I don't want this to happen to me. Rage for my grandmother's helplessness, my mother's helplessness, all women's helplessness, for my helplessness…

Looking back now as a healer to myself 16 years ago, I understand more fully what was happening to me. Patterns of contraction and tension are deeply embedded in the physical structure. Often people have become habituated to their shape that it goes unnoticed, except when there is that low-grade feeling of nervousness, ants crawling on the skin, or the little tremors or twitches, or the sense of pressure pushing in, or just the feeling of not being right somehow. I was no different. Usually this pattern is the way our nervous system has arranged itself to negotiate trauma in own lives. We have learnt patterns of how to use our life-force to hold down anxiety, terror, rage and fear. Similarly, the patterns of life force movement shifts when there is joy, relaxation and connectedness. The patterns of how we negotiate our sense of safety and manageability of life result in the quality of optimal organization as a whole system. With the kundalini process, I was unwinding at very deep levels. These spontaneous unwindings continued for many years.

CHAPTER 14: COMING BACK TO SHARE THE STORY

The spiritual emergence that blossomed gently over the years now exploded into a spiritual emergency after taking the holotrophic breath work with Stan Grof, an experiential psychotherapy class in my graduate program. This practice uses particular breathing techniques with music to allow access to non-ordinary states for the purpose of self-exploration and therapeutic benefits. Much to my dismay, I found myself raw and vulnerable in an environment that could not contain the "soft dynamism" and "pain" of spiritual transformation.

I lived in San Francisco close to 16th and Mission Street. It was called Crack prostitute street. I'd wake up in the morning and the street would be littered with drunken and drugged bodies, sometimes with used needles at their side. The sight of deeply lost and wounded souls was very difficult, especially in a place of openness. There were times in the evening that I would call friends to remind me not to run the streets at night because the internal energies were very strong. I knew enough the external environment was dangerous to me at that time. Yet, it was the fodder for compassion. I lived there for a year at the most intense time of my opening.

"I dive down into the depth of the ocean of forms to gain the perfect pearl of the formless. No more sailing from harbour to harbour with this my weather-beaten boat. The days are long passed when my sport was to be tossed by the waves. And now I am eager to die into the deathless. Into the audience hall by the fathomless abyss where swells up the music of toneless strings I shall take this harp of my life.

I shall tune it to he notes of forever, and when it has sobbed out its last utterance, lay down my silent harp at the feet of the silence."   -Rabindranath Tagore "Gitanjali"

"With this little vibration within, we are no longer alone. It is there all the time, everywhere. It is warm, intimate and strong. And strangely enough, once we have found it, we find the same thing everywhere, in all beings and all things. We communicate directly, as if everything were the same, without any partitions. We have touched something within us that is not the puppet of universal forces, not the rather thin and dry 'I think therefore I am', but the fundamental reality of our being, our self, our true self, our true center, the warmth and being, the consciousness and force." -
by Satprem, Aurobindo, the Adventure of Consciousness.

The first holotrophic breathwork: description of the journey of non-ordinary states

Immediately as the evocative music began her beating, my body responded and synchronized her movements to the changing tunes. I was ecstatic – my movement not fast enough to what my inner rhythm wanted. I writhed, crawled, kicked, twisted, moved in circles. I found myself all over the floor. Something wanted to come out – to express itself, not softly but explosively. The foreign languages (unknown to me) began to roll out of my tongue. I screamed, cajoled, begged, pleaded, lamented. I was angry, lonely, afraid, confused, abandoned, misunderstood. As though vocalizing these emotions was not enough, my body wanted to get rid of this poison in the pit of my stomach. I spitted and vomited and still it was not enough. It was as though I wanted to run amok. The facilitators held me down but the rage was so intense as well as immense. The bodywork stimulated more poison to come out. But little did we know – we had had just begun.

There were many images. I felt that I was not there in the room nor in this time. Once scene found me as an African (South of the Sahara) dancing frantically with other young men in a circle. Our upper bodies bare, grass skirts hugging our hips while a a clothe with circular bells adorned our ankles. There were drums and there was fire scorching right in the midst of the circle. I danced with a spear in my hand. My body agile and vital – turning round and round, perspiration drenching down my torso. The feeling was very high and trance like. It was clear that it was an initiation. Suddenly, I was left in the jungle – all alone. I was scared. So frightened that I ran crazily between the trees in the dark forest. My eyes bloodshot. My mouth screaming to be found.

Then suddenly I was a young woman with long dark hair, a beautiful fleshy dress dancing joyfully around the fire. It was in Central Asia up in a plateau. It was my wedding. My groom was a strong dignified young man with long hair tied in a ponytail. It was clear that he wan not a commoner since he carried himself with such an air. We laughed a lot. I was full of life. The next frame in the scene was haunting as I was tied with light-colored clothe (as in a bandage) to a wooden stretcher and carried up to the mountains. They had draped a brown blanket with designs over my body and a red banded jewelry adorned my forehead. They brought me to this barren meadow with no grass or trees or even shrubbery – only rocks and the cold wind. I was brought there to be left alone to die. My husband sat beside my bounded body. He looked deeply saddened by the turn of events. I begged him not to leave me. We were just recently married, and why was I being abandoned to die? I felt confused. I knew that the old people were brought in the mountains to die, but I was not old and why had they bounded me? Did I do something wrong? Was I crazy? I swore at him. Pleaded to him. Spat at him. But to no avail. He left along with the two others.

I clawed the hard, dehydrated earth begging them to return. Te evening came and I was alone. I saw the stars so clear above and it became even colder. I knew very soon that I would die. I was angry, afraid. I couldn't accept that it would soon end. As I began to accept death's inevitability, I began my prayers. First, I thanked the mother earth, then the sky, the moon, the stars, the wind and so forth for care of me and my people. I acknowledged that I was born from her and now I shall return to her once again. I became quiet and peaceful. Then the snow began to fall, and I felt and asked, "Can it be true?" Snow falling was a good omen, but I will die freezing. I became frightened again as slowly, slowly I began dying.

For the third time, the scenery shifted to ranges of mountains covered with a thin blanket of mist. It was not as barren as the previous scene, but it was not a tropical forest either. I was now a young man in very dirty, smelly woolen and leather clothing. My hair unwashed and my skin hard as callused feet. I carried a stick on my shoulder with a pouch on its end. I felt alone and lonely – not belonging to anything. I was a nomad. The same feelings as the two previous stories kept repeating themselves as physically, I grieved, cried, puked and pounded on the ground.

My sitter cradled me and Stan along with the other facilitators supported and nurtured me as well. It was a new experience to be held and allowed to cry my heart out in such a way. I felt uneasy to paint a mandala. I was still shaky. There was a deep need to touch this place within my being that was so much wounded. I longed to be nurtured, cuddled and held...I kept to myself that week.

The second time:

I was apprehensive as I sensed that more would come but I didn't know what. Just as the previous session, I entered the music fully and wholeheartedly. I danced so much, but this time, they were mostly dances of joy and celebration. The drums started beating and I sprang to my knees and began movements that were vigorous, vital, sensual even sexual in nature. I kept falling down, losing my balance as I was dizzy. These big fluffy pillows and supportive hands kept catching me. I was exhausted but he body wanted to move so I'd get up again, fall and get up once more and so on. It felt good. I felt I could be just me and it's okay.

Then suddenly the image changed. It was evening and the only light was the fire that was burning the village. There were many houses made of grass, circular indesign with a cone for a roof. I screamed "Fire" but it was too late. I went inside the burning houses and carried babies and children out in my arms. To no avail as everyone was burnt and bloody- burning flesh the scent of the evening. Everyone except me had died. The entire village had burnt and only the embers on the corpses everywhere.

I wailed and wailed and couldn't understand what/why all this had happened. I felt alone. Again. And even my home was gone. Where would I go? Who would I be with ? It was dark all around. Where is the light that would lead me where, when, how, who? I grieved and wailed some more. This soothing music was playing and the Great Spirit sang a beautiful song healing my ailing heart. All these images came: images of mass corpses, all scattered or in big trenches/holes and line after line of coffins. All the scenes of mass death kept coming and I just kept crying. Each time, I was left all alone.

I was back in the village where fire had massacred all. I bowed to each dead body, crying,saying good bye. Each time that I bowed, the pouch around my neck would touch each dead body. This pouch moved as though an offertory/blessing like the big incense burner in the Catholic church. I knew that in this pouch was my spirit, my people, my home – all of creation. After the benediction of all dead bodies, I took a staff and walked alone into the darkness knowing it was al right. I knew it was within me, within this pouch. It felt liberating to go, to start, to be born again.

My presence returned to the physical body lying in the workshop room. When this beautiful piece of Asian music played, I began to make very small, delicate gestures with my toes. My arms and legs joined in this graceful dance that appeared to me as an offering to the Gods. There was so much precision in the fragile but powerful movements. I danced in the air balanced only on the small of my lower back. It felt fluid – as though kelp dancing in water. It was very calming and life giving.

Suddenly I began to laugh. I was now a young European lady running in the prairies and the forests. My lover (Gaston) was chasing after me playfully. I danced in big ballrooms with my blonde hair high atop my head and my buxom cleavage pushed up to the heights. Then I growled like an animal and clawed the ground. Quickly, I was transposed as middle-aged man in a long black coat, a gun in my hand. I was in a wet, dark tunnel speaking in a guttural language oppressing a group of scared captives. I was angry, threatening and violent.

Stan and the others did bodywork with me as before. More vomit, screams, tears, etc. This time, they pulled my legs apart and I felt so vulnerable, forced. Images of sex and of giving birth were predominant. I screamed. I felt that I died and this womb of mine had closed and when I tried to open it, it was extremely painful. I screamed for all the screams I never screamed before. I knew it had to come out. This time I was not alone. There were others nurturing me and saying it was all right.

I felt that these two workshops had ripped open someone who was already open to begin with. My unconscious terrain laid bare without its armor. The presence of others that really cared and nurtured me made me realize that I can trust and allow others to see my tears and hold me. I can actually allow myself not to be strong. This support encouraged me to open further and explore more deeply the issues of mistrust in my life. Even the times when I felt weak and scared, I'd still take the role of the one supporting. I'm the one who usually catch others when they fall. I experienced being caught and held in a positive way.

My hyper-independence became a mechanism for self-sabotage. I had many loving and caring friends, yet there was a place of me that couldn't receive that care. There was a part of me that was not okay with me feeling weak, sick and dependent. Crying was a rare occurrence in my life up until I was 24-years- old. Crying was a private affair, done at night when alone. Crying now felt liberating.

The process of opening did not close for me as it did for others in the workshop, but continued even more pronouncedly. This time, I was alone and there was no support. I felt like a derailed train, not knowing where I was going. Spontaneously, the different dimensions would erupt like a volcano no matter where I was: biographical, perinatal and transpersonal. I'd shake, speak in tongues/foreign languages, vomit, cry, laugh, etc. A wide spectrum of emotion, repressed and suppressed memories emerged into consciousness. Evenings of being born and giving birth became daily bread. Images of destruction, torture, desecration, vomit, blood, pus, feces were common. Dances with cobras bigger than myself and other archetypal scenes were normal occurrences. Vivid symbolic dreams continued in my waking hour. Synchronicities appeared.

This death/rebirth process was definitely a transformative part of my life. It was sacred. I finger painted hundreds of canvases: ugly, shocking, painful images. A dam broke lose and I was scared with the sacred!!! My daily functionality was challenged by the multitude impressions gushing my psyche.

I felt raw, naked, and I felt everyone and everything. I had no skin. Remember I lived in one of the worst part of the city, not a quaint idyllic countryside. I felt everything and it wasn't pretty! What I knew of myself was falling apart, and I tried to keep a semblance of everything going all right. When I reached out, people responded well at first. I was sweet after all. But then, I began to be pathologized and boxed in. Their helplessness in the situation was not accepted as such and rather projected unto me. People tried to "fix" me as well as deny my reality. There were gems of friends who held me and just allowed me cry. I was exhausted.

There were repeated disappointments and disillusionment. No, meditating in front of the Buddha won't make it go away. Seeing a therapist won't make it all disappear. Saying "don't worry" doesn't make the fear subside. Saying that I've had worst transits does not make the plundering of my heart subside. I was a volcano erupting and others were putting a lid on it, because they didn't know how to do otherwise. But rather than say just that, I received placations. I felt really alone, lonely, afraid, and angry!!! I was in the midst of a turbulent ocean. It was imperative I learn how to swim. Otherwise I would drown. The next years of my life was about swimming with grace while supporting myself in life. It was all a GIFT.

Practical Application for you:

1. When was the last time you felt raw and naked? What was that like?
2. Imagine you are in a boardroom meeting. How many parts of yourself are running your show of life? Are you familiar with them? Take a current situation in your life right now and diagram how many voices are competing for attention and being the primary decision maker?
3. What is your experience of non-ordinary states of consciousness? How was that for you? How did you integrate it?
4. What is the felt body sense of each of these constructed selves?

5. Look at the sky right now. Close the book, go outside and just look at the blue sky or the night sky. Breathe.

CHAPTER 15: SEARCHING THE BASEMENT

As the kundalini pushed its way into detoxifying my bioenergetic system and spewing an excess of unconscious material as part of the unblocking of the physio-psycho-spiritual blocks, I chose to look more deeply into my personal history. Despite and in spite of my resistances, I followed the genesis of my beliefs into the shadowy basements of my past. I invited the dark and the light parts of myself to meet and dialog. I believe that everyone does the best he/she can based on what has been taught by his/her parents, teachers and culture. Part of being a human being is making mistakes. Sometimes though that best has ramifications that leave wounds, later to be hopefully released and forgiven by all involved. These challenges shape our soul journeys. They are also a stage in the journey where we make meaning and extract the wisdom from them that would eventually guide to an easier, more loving and happy life. Unfortunately, many individuals continue to recycle what they've learnt and not break the cycle. It is not an easy task to do this. This is part of why I am writing and sharing this book. It takes a lot of courage and effort to break the cycle. What seems normal is really behavior that is learnt. It is very difficult to to let go of our addiction to a way of being, even when it is painful. The root of our problems is not malice, but ignorance. If we knew better, we wouldn't do the things we do to hurt ourselves and others. This is why deep compassion is necessary for all of us. We all need it.

I am paying homage to my ancestors whose backs I stand on as my foundation and support. May all the healing in this lifetime heal this generation, generations before me and the generations after me.

Being an egg in my grandmother's womb

Since I was an egg formed already in my mother while she was a fetus in her mother's womb, I want to introduce my grandmother ("Lola" is Tagalog for grandmother). At the age of 15, she ran a small store in a village in the Philippines. It was the custom of that culture and time that being simply touched by a man is a ground for marriage. Lola had a Chinese-Filipino suitor whom she was attracted to. There was also another man who had his eyes on her, my grandfather. One day, the latter knowing that my grandmother felt more affection for the other, surprised Lola in the store and embraced her publicly. As a result, my grandmother and grandfather married immediately. By the end of her life, she was to be one of five wives my grandfather had at the same time. My grandfather was rarely present in the family's life and when he was, there were lots of violent quarrels.

My grandmother gave birth to 12 children, pretty much on a yearly basis. Out of the 12 children, five died at birth and one child died when she was one year old. My mother, Amor, was the seventh child. She was born between two stillborns, Clarita and Virginia. My mother remembers her one-year-old sibling, Kristina. My mother recounted, "She had long eyelashes and light skin." She died at the age of one year old. She saw her mother crying and saying, "don't inject anymore". Kristina died of an overdose of medicine in the hospital.

Reflecting on my grandmother's life sends me into sadness and anger. There was this heavy burden that sent her to her grave early in life. As a child, I remember asking my mother why she died and she would reply, "She forgot to breathe." When I asked my mother now why she died, her reply is, "from too much grief." Perhaps, she didn't forget to breathe, but didn't want to breathe anymore. I can imagine the anxiety that pervaded her life, and the anticipation of another child. Will the pregnancy end in yet another stillborn? I wonder how my grandmother felt when she was pregnant with my mother. Not only was her family life insecure, it was also World War II. The Philippines was in the midst of the war with the Japanese killing Filipino civilians without hesitation. My grandmother did not live very far from where the Bataan death march happened. I remember stories of Japanese soldiers with long guns with knives attached at the end. I was told that they'd used these bayonets to stab pregnant women. My grandmother also had teenage daughters and my mother would narrate how they'd place water buffalo manure all over their hair and body as to appear unattractive. These served as deterrents from being raped by the Japanese soldiers. And what about the rationed food and all these children? And the hiding places? I can't even come close to all the fear, despair, confusion that was the environment of my mother's conception and term in her mother's womb. My mother was born in 1944, while the war was still roaring.

My heritage is of mixed races. My mother was from the east, the Philippines, and my father was from the west, Finland.

Less than twenty years later, my mother gave birth to her first son, the first of four children. The circumstance of her life was far from ideal. She was in her second trimester of pregnancy when my father decided he didn't want to be a part of her life. He left the Philippines. My mother was young, unmarried and pregnant in a culture and time where this is a complete taboo. My father was to return two years later and bear three more children with my mother. Their marriage, like my mother's own experience in her family, was filled with quarrels that exacerbated when my father was drunk.

My second brother was born three years later after my first brother. One year later, my parents moved from the Philippines to the United States. I was conceived immediately after the move to Georgia. My mother was unhappy in the south, as she didn't have any "Oriental friends or food". She missed her culture, family and friends. She was in a hostile environment, both within the family as well as the culture. After all, this was the time of the civil rights movement. This phase was characterized with "sama ng loob" meaning bad feelings. My mother recounted making an appointment for the hairdresser over the phone and giving her name "Mrs. Peterson". When she'd arrived there, she wouldn't be accepted in because of her dark skin. When getting in a bus, she would be asked to sit in the back. My mother would say then to the bus driver, "White in the front, Black in the back. I am brown so I go in the middle."

There was also physical abuse from my father as well as emotional abuse. He drank, smoked and yelled very much. It was a hostile time.

I was born in Hawaii whose volcanic temperament I have inherited. I appear calm on the surface, yet closer examination reveals a turbulent movement of heat - that which alchemy is made of. The baby's cry sounded like the voice of an angel and so they gave me the name Kathrina which means "pure." It would take my lifetime to really know what pure or non-being is - that state before qualities of positive or negative are added.

After my delivery, my mother could not walk for two months. The doctors took a biopsy but could not find a cause. When I asked my mother why she couldn't walk, she replied, "because of stress." As I looked through photos of that time, I see also tenderness and joy of having a new baby. I see my father playing with me, my brother watching over me in the crib, my grandmother with me on her lap on the stairs outside and my mother breast feeding me. My mother was so young. I can't imagine how hard it was for her.

A few months after I was born (eight-months-old), my mother took her three children and left my father. We moved to the Philippines. My mother recounted how we lived in an unfinished house, sleeping on the wood placed on bricks. She was pre-occupied as to how she will raise her children as a young, single mother. It was a time of uncertainty. By the time I was eight-months-old, I had traveled across the Pacific Ocean, driven across the continental United States and lived in two continents. My life as I had known it was filled with change and turmoil. I remember not wanting to come out of the womb. I felt the violence and the lack of satisfaction of living. I was a quiet baby, rarely crying. It was as though I didn't want to add more responsibility, more needs. It seemed that my mother had her hands full as it was.

I grew to be a vivacious child, except in photographs where my eyes of defiance clearly blazed. I have a streak of red hair and consequently, do not like being told what to do. Though I love the natural world and basked in its quietude, I also danced with its teeming life that often escaped those in a hurry.

It was final that my father would not be present in my childhood life. Though grief-stricken at the turn of events, Amor endeavored to busy herself in becoming a successful businesswoman involved in different avenues. Along with my three brothers, I lived in a eight-sided salmon-colored house surrounded by a swimming pool, cottages, palm trees and "bird of paradise" gardens. The summers were hot with sweet mangoes and jackfruits, while the rainy seasons were orchestrated with the melody of frogs in the flooded fields adjacent to the bungalow. Since Amor was away most of the time, the siblings were free to roam to the river, play with the water buffaloes, climb the guava trees or kick the can in the middle of the dark night in the balmy province. The innocence of my childhood was overshadowed though with the realities of living in a broken, abusive family.

My mother worked having different businesses and gave the care of the children to live-in caretakers. I am so grateful that my mother found devoted and loving women to act as her replacement in the home in our care. I had a caretaker from the age of eight-months to eight-years old. I called her Manang and there was not a day I was away from here all my formative years. We slept in the same bed and being a girl, I was always by her side. She was very religious and spiritual. She would pray while she washed loads of clothes by hand in the bathroom. So I learnt that praying and working came hand in hand. One did not need to only pray in church. Every night, my bedtime stories were stories from the Old Testament.

You might say there were some eccentricities on my end. I was a child who loved dragonflies and clouds. Papayas ripening on the tree were marvels to me along with the flowers that graced my beautiful and spacious home. I was a natural mystic. I also loved people and also afraid of them. They can and do hurt each other after all.

The spiritual and mundane widened its gap in my understanding. It wasn't until later in life that the abyss would close. The opening of my heart, with all its wounds and scars, would be my portal into this union. So we go back and forth, between the girl me and the woman now I have grown to be.

Not only was I deeply philosophical, I was also very spiritual as a young one already. I prayed to the Sacred Heart of Jesus and Mother Mary every day as a child. There was something about the heart that had thorns around it that echoed. They understood what my heart felt like.

Early on, I knew that heaven and hell are already happening right now and right here. At the age of 10, I knew that God was my friend and I can communicate directly, that I didn't need the intervention of the priest. Whenever I would go to confession up to then, I would confess my thoughts rather than deeds or speech.

My father would come to visit every Christmas for two weeks. He'd bring M & Ms and dolls/toys from America. When he did come, the rules in the house changed. Instead of rice, I would eat potatoes, lima beans, plain boiled vegetable and eat with forks instead of using my hands with the fish and coconut-curried squash. We were forbidden to speak in Tagalog or play loudly in the house. When he was there, the kitchen cupboard would be lined with Nescafe jars and San Miguel beer bottles. I hated the smell of beer and Phillip Morris cigarettes.

Nonetheless, for two weeks each year, I would pretend and bragged to my schoolmates that I had a father in the house. Each year, as the two week limit would approach, my father would disappear one dark night without saying good-bye to his children. He didn't like the children crying when he left. I and my siblings would then wake up and my father would be gone. I'd sit by the door and verandah, looked far away and had to wait another year to see him come back. My siblings and I were not told that my parents were separated - only that my father worked far away.

Although I was very young, I knew much for my age. I knew that life was a paradox. As mentioned earlier, my mother would take me to the different gambling institutions. In the cockfighting pits, I'd speak to the roosters before and after the fights. I felt sorry for them--so regal and beautiful only to end up bloodied over men's lust for power and money. I'd wish I had magic and could turn them loose--everyone even the gamblers. I just wanted everyone to be happy and free.

My mother was also involved with the aborigines in the mountains behind the salmon bungalow so I spent time up with them. There was a gold mining operations there, and I would asked, "Why was the river so dirty?" Since I grew up in an animistic society, I listened to many stories of different realms and beings that cannot be seen, but nonetheless were there. I knew that many beings lived in my house besides my family.

Along with my siblings, I saw many terrible things. Although there was much violence in my early life, my caretakers were very loving, present and available. Manang was a spiritual woman with a committed religious practice. I remember her hugging me all the time. I remember the bedtime stories from the Old Testament. She, my younger brother and I slept together in one bed until I was seven years old. I was very closed to her and loved being near her. She never got angry. She never yelled. She had a calm presence about her. Her presence was predictable and stable. I remember using my whole body to sense where she is as though a magnet or compass. There was not a day that we were separated. Even in her weekend off, I would go with her to her house and attend her church. I felt safe in her presence. I remember that she always prayed, even when doing laundry by hand. I remember not going too far from her physically.

Manang was so devout that she'd be praying even when washing clothes. Consequently, I also had a religious leaning. I went to the Sunday and Saturday masses, Wednesday novenas and visited the church to pray to the Virgin Mary and Sacred heart of Jesus all by myself. I felt safe and accepted there. I began to feel bliss and had feelings of peace. I aspired to become a nun one day. When I was eight-years old, my family moved to the capital city for educational purposes and Manang of course came with us. Not too long after our move, I came home from school one day, and Manang was gone. She didn't even say good-bye. I asked my mother and she said, "Manang left because her religion/church was too far." I never saw her again. I don't remember feeling anything about her departure. All those years I had found solace with Manang.

During an experiential psychology class in a graduate school, I remembered this incident with Manang sensorially. Afterwards, I felt this deep sadness and anger that she left without saying goodbye. I felt betrayed, abandoned. Once again, there was another disappearance. I do not know if she really left for her religion or perhaps she and my mother had a disagreement. Thirty-three years after our parting, I visited the Philippines again. I met Manang in person and I asked her why she left. She said she could no longer take the abuse of my uncles. She had had enough. She didn't say goodbye because she felt she wouldn't have left, and so she left when we weren't around.

Ate was another woman who cared for me and stayed with us in the city when Manang left. I have known her since I was a baby. She was tougher, especially with my brothers. She took me everywhere with her. Her full name is Divino Perfection (pure divine perfection). I wonder now was that her real name or a name I wanted her to have. I certainly needed to see pure divine perfection in my life. She stayed with us until I left the Philippines when I was nearly 12 years old. I never saw her again. She died shortly after.

At the age of eight, my grandfather died and my mother started to become a healer after a prolonged sickness. She underwent a healer's journey and I remember it to be very difficult, alienating and confusing. During this time of illness, Amor was called by a wooden deformed statue residing in a garbage can. Having this vision while in the bus, my mother built a church, healed people, exorcised spirits and many other things. I sat and watched everything. I liked especially the exorcisms as I'd be asked to close the doors and windows, and see firsthand the spirits speaking through someone else. I was fascinated as I sat quietly on the pebbled steps in the huge room.

During this time, Amor also underwent a penance. She was called to carry the cross up the Calvary every Good Friday for seven years just as Jesus had done over 2000 years ago. She'd wear a maroon cotton dress and a yellow cord around the hips. Her head/face was covered with a black cloth and her feet bare. Previous to the Good Friday, there would be days and days of sonorous chanting of the Passion. There would be sticky rice cakes and cold drinks the whole day and night. I liked this time very much. I didn't like the blood that oozed from the blade cuts on men's back though as they flagellated themselves to atone for their sins.

My mother became very popular in town and soon she won the office of vice mayor of the village. Jealousy of her rival forced her to step down as the lives of her children were threatened. So it was--I lived in this big salmon house, orchids on coconut trees, a ghost named Rudolph and fairies and gnomes to keep my company. On one hand, it was really magical with the fireflies, a play-house made of leaves, mountains and fields overgrown with watermelons, etc. It was carefree. Yet at the same time, there lurked the shadows of the exiled feelings of confusion, loneliness and abandonment.

More impressions

Like most Filipinos, my mother valued a good education for her children. She worked very hard to send us to private school. A good education meant a better life. Every parent wants her child to live better off than she did. My mother wanted this for us.

When I was eight, we hired a jeep, packed a sturdy table on top with suitcases full of clothes and a rice sack filled with our kitchen pots and pans wired to the front grill of the colorful vehicle. We all travelled to the capital of the Philippines, Metro Manila.

We lived in a one room apartment on the third floor of a five story building. We and three bunk beds, for my brothers and I, a a boarder and our caretaker slept on the multipurpose wooden table that served as a bed, dining table and homework desk for all of us. We had a one burner kerosene stove and one bathroom with a bucket for taking baths.

I remember staring across the window into another building that have men and women dancing. Something new and unusual for me. Below was bustling students and next to the window were thick electrical wires where birds landed - a reminder of the province I had come from.

My oldest brother was a teenager. One day he was sent to buy food and he instead watched a movie. The next thing I heard was the spanking. The city was more scary for me than exciting. The rivers were black and smelly with pollution. When I blew my nose into my white handkerchief, it was black. The streets were not for children. I missed the open fields and skies of the province. I missed the fireflies, water buffaloes and the carefree, unhurried life we had.

But my mother wanted to send us to the best school. And so we did attend an expensive school across the Malacanang Palace, the presidential white house of the Philippines. Many of the children there were arrogant and spoiled. After one year of this,

155

I begged my mother to return to the province when she told she wanted to leave me in the city. I was relieved to go home to the dark soil and fresh air of my province.

Every month, my grandmother would send us a letter with a $1 for each children. My brothers and I would exchanged the dollar bill at the black market exchanger, the corner store behind the open market, next to the ice seller where we would buy blocks of ice still covered with rice husks for our birthday parties. I remember it melting, dripping cold drops unto our brown feet as we hurried home in the tropical heat.

Anyways, back to the dollar bills. Once exchanged, my brothers and I would take the bus to Olongapo City. We then went to a movie theatre, and bought scoops of Magnolia ice cream. It was our adventure. None of us were even teenagers. The camaraderie and caring of my siblings planted deep seeds in my heart as I grew into an adult. I learnt deep friendship from my brothers and way into my adult life, I am known for the richness of friendship in my life.

While in Manila as an eight-year-old, I went to the slums one day as my caretaker's brother lived there. It was a mountain of garbage and all the makeshift homes made of cardboard and flattened tin sheltered families. It was an eye opener to walk the wooden planks above the open sewage. In the maze of shantytown, we were gleefully welcomed into their home. We only went once and it was the only time Ate shared her life outside of my family with me. It was such a juxtaposition from the wealthy school I went to every day with manicured lawns, security guards and children dropped off by chauffeurs in expensive cars.

My friend Jennifer is the only American friend I have that could appreciate the cuisine of chicken fingers, tripes and blood. As a little girl, life and food were raw. We killed chickens that we had raised for food. I had visited homes where the kitchen was filled with hanging intestines with pork meat - sausages to be sold soon after. I also sat on a big tables with everyone wrapping lumpias for gatherings. I grew up being taught how to determine how fresh a fish was by looking at its gills. I never liked cleaning the insides of heads at all, and since I wasn't very good at it, I was relegated to washing pots and pans caked with charcoal instead. I didn't mind it at all.

Waxing the tiled floors with candles and then scrubbing them with the "bunot" - half of a coconut husk each of us children would swing our hips and legs too - filled with laughter and learning how to dance while cleaning and fulfilling our chores. The coconut was considered a very valuable tree in the Philippines. The broom we used outside is made of the ribs of the coconut leaf gathered together and made into a broom. The sound of the swishing of the broom still brings sweet memories to me in the early mornings. There was a different kind of rhythm then than the gas powered leaf blowers of today.

The decade I lived in the Philippines was a decade of martial law placed by the then President Ferdinand Marcos. I remember one year when the armed forces took over one of our houses and lived there. I don't remember much then except I was supposed to be quiet. I do remember going to a field trip to my first museum visit in Manila. One of the museums was dedicated to Imelda Marcos, the first Lady, and all the fashionable expressions she was infamous for. I was also very impressed by another museum about the diversity of Philippine culture. It was the first time I had a view outside of the provincial paradigm I was raised. I was eight-years old.

Once the year, the traveling circus would visit my village. The dusty vacant lot sandwiched between the basketball court and the local market would come to life. There would be lots of games with darts that fly in the air and balloons and beings that were half women/half snake. There was a makeshift movie theatre that had two by fours on the dirt to sit on. The black and white films were old and would flicker the whole way through, yet it didn't hinder us from eagerly paying our few centavos to be part of the festival.

Several times a year, we would load the wooden cart with sheets and curtains and we would jump into this caravan on the way to the river. The cart was pulled by a water buffalo. It would be the big laundry day and we would spend the whole day in the river, bringing picnic of rice and other delectables. The children swam in the swimming holes while the women washed the heavy loads of laundry. I had very fond memories of those trips in the heat of summer.

When I was eleven-years old, there was a lot of talk about how it was to be a woman and what menses meant. By this time, many of my classmates were starting to grow breasts and were having crushes with the boys in class. I don't remember much from these classes except I wasn't supposed to harvest eggplants and other vegetables in the garden when I have my period! The sex education part was to come much later in the American school, except I was the only one in the whole seventh grade class who wasn't allowed to be part of sex education because my mother thought it was inappropriate. So I studied and read independently about drugs in the library instead. It wasn't until my freshman year in the university that I saw a beautiful film with sperms swimming for the egg, then conception, gestation and the beauty of birth. I even made a one on one appointment with my university clinic to give me a sex education class. I wondered why I wasn't shown this earlier.

Very early on, I fell in love with adult comic books. The booklets contained many serial stories with pictures and dialogs. The genres included romance, science fiction, drama, comedy, action, etc. They were like television soap operas except they were illustrated in a comic rather than enacted on film. Often, the week's story would end at a climactic moment to be continued in the next week's edition. They were addictive.

Reading comics was my escape from a turbulent family life. It was also an initiation for me into the world of the adult. Or should I say, my way of trying to understand the pain of life through the eyes of a child. Comic books taught me about sex, well sort of. I knew that when a man consumed a woman, the comic picture showed fire consuming oil. Or in its gentler form, a bee entering a flower.

In the village I grew up, there were comic stands that rented comic books on the spot. There I'd spend hours, my bottom balancing on a narrow bench not too far from the stall that sold fried sweetened bananas and yams. My Catholic school forbid reading such "vulgar" pieces of literature and students caught got a beating for it. I lived in a different village than the school I attended because my mother and the local priest did not get along. Therefore, I was never caught by the nuns and continued my exposure to ideas varied in nature. It was very funny. By the time I was addicted, my hair was cut short as a boy's and some of the wildness of my brothers and cousins definitely exhibited in me.

To subsidize my comic fix, I sold all the bottles and jars I could find in the kitchen to the bottle seller. A middle aged man with dark leathered skin, the bottle seller would pass by my house pushing an old wooden cart filled with empty bottles. In the Philippines, one brought his own recycled bottle to the market to use for fluid products. We used empty gin bottles as containers for cooking oil. Since the bottle seller paid the highest price for gin bottles, I would empty the gin bottles of cooking oil into a cup and sell the bottles for 25 centavos. I'd sneaked into the kitchen when everyone took his afternoon siesta as I was supposed to be doing too.

Mischief laced my resourcefulness. Sadness also laid behind those deep, dark eyes penetrating souls passing their way. The empty bottles of my mother reflected the lost longings of each member of my family. I fled my home to seek solace in the different worlds of the comic books. Somehow being lost in the stories of others (even fiction) meant not feeling my own confusion, anger and betrayal. Long before I learn to write cursive, I already have deadened myself to the spectrum of feelings inside. However, it was the introduction to death that reminded me of the full feeling life dwelling within myself.

The first time I saw a dead body, I was six-year-old. Someone went amok in my village and chopped up two people. Because the nature of the death was bizarre, the funeral, rather than being held in the home as tradition has it, was instead held in the church. It was a way of protecting against evil. It was the way shame was dealt with. The whole village gossiped while their hair raised in fear and shock.

The imposing church stood between my school and my home. That day, its ringing bells did not breed comfort nor solace. Nor was its huge open wooden doors an invitation to the pious to kiss the exposed foot of the kneeling black Nazarene. No holy water could make us forget. The church became instead a shell that

159

protected the weak from the unknown. It sanctified our deepest terror. That death can take anyone at anytime anyway it wants to.

One balmy afternoon as my classmates and I headed home, everyone sprinted pass the church and quickly made the sign of the cross as to not catch anything evil or peeked at ghosts. I lagged behind, pretending to run, and when only the dust kicked off by fleeing heels kept me company, I snuck into the back door of the church. I just wanted to know what everyone was avoiding.

It was quiet and empty, except for two simple caskets with flower arrangements that you find only in funerals. Dropping my heavy school bag by the aged pews, I inched closer to the smell of formaldehyde, not knowing what to expect. Barely perched over the caskets, my eyes met these lifeless, old mannequins. The caked on foundation did not hide the blood that had drained from their faces. They were cold and hard, unlike the warm suppleness of my hands. Both their hands were folded on their bellies, in an act of repose. The sewn up pieces of flesh fascinated me. I've only seen torn blouses sewn with needle and thread up to that time. They were dressed in their Sunday best and they looked lonely, alone in a culture that revolved around family and community. The late afternoon sun streamed into the colored stained glass windows. There was stillness and without knowing it then, death came knocking on my door to be a permanent guest in my life.

It was then that I realized I could die at any time. At the age of six, I began to sleep with my hands folded on my belly as a preparation for death. I wanted to give God a sign that I was ready.

One main road went through our village. It was the same road I'd sprint towards when the bottle seller screamed his presence. It was the same road I and the others would run to when a funeral's marching band played the music that called everyone to pay respect to the one whose feet now point to the heavens. I was to see more funerals than weddings as a child.

I mostly remember my grandfather by the muted sound of his voice behind the bedroom door. He spent the last years of his life in quarantine. He had tuberculosis and had taken the upstairs room overlooking the vast fields, the mountains and Mt. Pinatubo. That used to be my bedroom, until it became my grandfather's. Once a week, I would leave jaggery sweets and sticky rice cakes in front of his door. When he thought I was gone and was downstairs, he'd open the door and retrieved the sweets. He didn't know that I hid behind the wall, just on the first step of the wooden stairs. I watched his eager, wrinkled hands and I'd imagined the tattoo of his white wife on his forearm. My grandfather had five wives and one was an American. During his youth, he was quite a vital, amorous soldier. There was no birth control then and I ended up with lots of uncles and aunts. As a child, I didn't understand because he was so old and not exactly attractive to a young child.

It was the same stairs I sat on as I looked into the casket he now laid in the living room. Only his face and hands were exposed from his Sunday best clothes. His perfectly ironed clothes were a contrast to his wrinkled skin. I had forgotten how he had looked. I wondered where he had gone for I knew then he wasn't the corpse that lain below. By then, I've learned to keep my thoughts to myself. Questions were not welcomed in my family. This was very hard for me as I am an extremely curious person.

The black banner across the balcony expressed to the village that this house was in mourning. The house was bustling with activity. Funerals were like festivals. There was gambling: playing cards and Chinese majhong (Chinese cards). Money was raised this way to help the family with the funeral expenses. Women gathered cooking mostly pork. Men exchanged tales over palm wine. Children circled around an upside down charcoaled wok. It was a game of truth and dare, and somehow, we all ended up having the charcoal on our faces like war masks ready for battle. It had something to do with warding off evil spirits. Just the same way that we'd all have to be washed in vinegar water and jumped over the dead body as well as a fire to purify us and make us spirit proof. Since he was a soldier in WWII, there was a flag and gunshots to honor his death.

Soon after we'd sent Lolo away to the white washed cemetery, our living room again was graced with another casket. A young woman dressed in a lemon chiffon beaded gown, her velvety black hair against her light skin, unmoving in her silence. She was friend of my mother's. As she alighted from the bus, she was run over by a drunk driver - hit and run. She didn't have a family, so we offered the funeral. The yellow gown was my mother's. I remember how beautiful she was in it while she sang in one of the local gatherings in the village. From this tragedy, the cautiousness with crossing this particular road began with ferocity.

My interludes at the comic stand couched these losses. They filled the lack of communication with the adults in my life. One way I held the changing life cycles was to imitate the way comic strips portrayed the world. I began to see my life events as a series of boxes with serial static pictures and people speaking blurbs over their heads. It was simply a series of moments that get connected together and you have a story. The lack of continuity and the jumpiness of a feeling/emotion tended to mirror my days. Yet, at the same time, these boxes contained experiences I did not understand. And of course, the "to be continued" at the end of a series echoed "life goes on no matter what happens."

Again, I smelt a certain floral scent, a sign that death was near. Soon afterwards, my father's father died. I've only seen him in pictures. He was from Denmark and entered the United States through Ellis Island early last century. It wasn't until years later that I was to learn about the character of my grandfather, and how he affected the lives of my grandmother, father, and consequently, myself. I remember seeing a very handsome picture of my grandfather in uniform and a sword. He was a soldier in WWI.

The Scandinavian land he was born in and his death in New Jersey were so far away from the tropical island I grew up in. The contrasts were enormous. One of the exciting highlights of my village life was running to the radio to listen to our favorite soap opera. It was quite tricky as we had to fiddle with the internal wires of the radio so we wouldn't lose the reception while the story blasted amidst static. I, along with my cousins and brothers, were mesmerized by the talking box.

Even though I've encountered several deaths already, I didn't know death's impact until I watched my aunt pleading and begging every person in the house to bring back her son. It was her wailing that led me to her trail. I stood by the iron wrought glass door, and saw her body half on the earth, the other half searching the spirit world for my cousin. Death and life awakened in me as never before and I just wanted to hold her tightly next to my heart.

I wanted to make all the pain go away and knew that I couldn't. I was nine years old.

I met the news of my teenage cousin's death with disbelief. How can anyone joke about this? How can the umbrella that shielded me from the torrential rains be also the same weapon that stabbed his eyes and murdered him? The fragility of life was so apparent. I realized then that which connects us to each other was so tenuous. As I sided to one corner, I overheard a conversation, "Parents shouldn't have to bury their children."

My cousin Jimbot was handsome with a lithe body, even as a corpse. I thought I saw a tear come down his cheek when I peered into the casket. He was born of mixed race, just like I. He was the only child and the reason for my aunt to live after her husband left her. After the funeral, my asthmatic aunt flew into more frequent rages and frantically poured herself into gardening the dark earth of our garden. When I heard her curses early in the morning, I knew to stay out of her way. I don't remember ever mentioning Jimbot's name again after his death.

Life went on with our games and chores and school. We chased fireflies, beetles and spiders. We found ourselves gorging on plump mangoes on tree branches, diving into rivers while women washed clothes by the riverbanks. Life was simple. Sorrows and pleasures were scattered throughout. The typhoons came and we went through candles faster than candies. There were lots of festivals and processions that punctuated the seasons. The stories of people's lives embroidered the days as vignettes passed from the mailman on a bicycle to the vegetable seller balancing a basket on her head to the uninvited guest hungry for lunch at our home. Everyone knew everyone. There were no secrets.

The texture of fabric

I was at a Japanese fabric store recently where they sold remnants of colorful fabric for a $1.50. As I sat on the floor fingering the different textures of fabrics, I began to remember memories as a nine-year-old going to the local tailor and seamstress asking for remnants of fabric. I would gather these fabric pieces and walk home with a big smile on my face. My mother had a sewing machine that faced the big window. When my mother sewed, I would be asked to thread the needle since my eyes were sharper than hers. I learnt how to sew by watching my mother. I got pretty good at hemming skirts because when I did them incorrectly, I would have to un-hem them and then hem again! My mother was very tough with me then. It wasn't a tender, warm love at all. It was as though having lost her own mother to death at a really young age made her heart towards her own daughter guarded. I've often wondered if tenderness with me came too close to the tender love she shared with her own mother as a young child. As both she and I matured, there has been more room to allow a wider repertoire of feelings towards each other. As I've grown older with the experiences of life, I've understood her more. I've realized that "mother-daughter" relationship do change with time. I see that I've had so many more resources just by virtue of being of another generation and exposed to a cultural timeframe that looks at the human potential movement to include individual psychology. I don't take this for granted. I have now deep appreciation for my mother. I can't fathom the sacrifices required to be a single mother raising four young children.

This memoir is like collecting all the fabric remnants of a lifetime and sewing them together to make a tapestry. Telling the story of my young life is to make more sense of how far I've come to live a life that says "no" to abuse. So with these fabric remnants, I would sew simple and beautiful clothes for my doll! I was pretty creative. I even made a desk from a cabinet door and hammered three legs unto it! I had a pet chicken that slept with me in my bedroom and then flew outside early in the morning. My mother had built me a toy house based on the traditional Filipino house outside in the garden. I spent my days there playing either alone or with my family members. Children are so creative in making the best out of the life they have been given.

One day, my oldest brother had to be sent to the United States to join my father. He was fifteen years old. Less than a year later, Pekka my brother had ran away from our father and Amor felt urgently to search for her lost son. At the age of 12, my siblings and I moved to California, not merely to reunite with our father but really to search for our lost brother somewhere in the south of the US.

All of sudden, I had a mother and a father in the house and it was strange. They were authoritative. Life was harder, also poorer. I assumed the role of family caretaker as I began cooking all the meals and between my siblings and I, did the housework. Both my parents worked, sometimes they lived under the same roof and sometimes not. There were periods of time when my mother left my father, and my siblings and I lived with my father.

Birthing a new me in a perinatal workshop

The perinatal workshop has had a profound affect on me. It's opened up pre-verbal experience in a different way than cathartic work. Issues of trust permeated my process work. I am not surprised as trust has been such a delicate dance for me throughout my life. Questions posed in the experiential exercises reverberate in the three decades and a half I've been here. Do I trust her/him to do the work? Do I trust her/him to take care of herself? Can I feel safe and just enjoy the experience of living?

The first exercise of being a baby opened up my process of relating. As a baby in the exercise, I was quiet and restful. I wanted to check out and sense whether "my mother" will respect me as a baby or impose her needs upon me. As I sensed that she was giving me a lot space and attentive to my needs, I began "to wake up" and looked her directly in the eyes. I saw myself playing with her hands and smiling and feeling safe and satisfied. I felt that I could explore and I wanted to relate to her. I was no longer just observing from the sidelines, but I wanted to be in relation to her. After the exercise, my partner mentioned that she might not stay in the class because of personal reasons. I felt saddened and angry. After all, I entered into this relationship because I thought she was going to be there the whole time. I felt betrayed. I felt she should have said it at the beginning. Perhaps I wouldn't have opened up to the degree that I did. Frankly, I wasn't sure if she was going to show up the next day. I just held my silence and was determined to rein in my exploratory process to the surface.

When we did the second exercise of being touched with my eyes closed, I was adamant that I also be touched on my hands and feet. It was clear that I didn't want any surprises. I was also taking care of myself. I wasn't interested in diving into the pool of the unconscious. This process of stating what I felt comfortable with at the onset of the exercise was important. I could easily have opted to not participate. I did not want just to flee or just bear it either. I made a choice of what I needed. My partner in the exercise actually felt more at ease with this arrangement and when it was her turn, she asked for similar parameters.

I've struggled over the issue of getting what I want. For a great part of my life, getting what I want was an accident. It wasn't a conscious process. It felt almost like by chance that I get fulfilled or satisfied. I learned early not to ask for what I want because I didn't get it anyways. Somehow, as a child, I gave up trusting that others could really give me what I want. As protection, my sense of wanting was blurry. The wanting was there, but I wasn't connected with it.

As I've matured, I have a better sense of myself, my wants and not wants. I remember though for a long time, not even knowing what I want. A few years ago, a friend of mine had to repeatedly ask me what I wanted. I remember feeling really confused. I had gotten to a point in my life where I could finally say what I didn't want and that took so much courage. And now I had to also learn to say what I want! It was such a revolutionary and revolutionary struggle. The exercise we did the second day of the workshop was a yardstick to show how far I've come in being able to ask for what I needed and wanted. My partner showed up for the next day, to my relief. I was able to drop down to a deeper place. Being touched on my feet for a few minutes brought me to a kinesthetic memory of one of my caretakers and how that was when I was a child. I was surprised that such a memory came.

I am so thankful for the workshop in dispelling a "myth" I carried about birthing. The films of birthing into the sea and the tubs were powerful and awe inspiring. I was touched. Birthing wasn't just despair and turmoil and burdensome. I felt in my life that I wasn't wanted. I felt as though I was just on the way. I tried so much to be invisible and not need so much. I was so quiet. I felt at times that I shouldn't have come. The class showed me that babies need to be wanted and need to want as part of their development. This is part of a healthy life. Birthing is giving life. I felt my womb opening. My womb in the sense of the womb that held me in my prenatal phase as well as my womb now that opens to carrying a baby if I choose to do so. It wasn't just about fear and constriction. It was also about expansion and joy. My birth was also life. I can honor the sanctity and the miracle of birthing. There was something prayerful in birthing.

2013 on a family visit

Walking on the dry earth again reminds me of those long solitary times I had in the desert as a teenager. The breeze gently blows the creosote bushes while the Joshua trees still pray even though they are scorched unto the ground. I stop to take in the view, the rocky formations of hills. The Bear Valley range and the San Bernardino mountains act as embraces to this huge desert plateau. The lone jackrabbit runs and then pauses to look at me, then runs again. I am reminded of the walks I took on this very place when I was fourteen years old, a ninth grader in junior high, walking to the high school. I had joined track and field even though I was in a different school. I used to walk many miles to go to training and run the hurdles. I reminisce to that time and appreciative of the qualities of dedication and commitment I already exhibited as a young person.

Running was essential for my sense of control. There was something about getting ready on the sprinting block, my shoes screwed with spikes, while my adrenaline pumped away, my eyes focused, the energy ready to burst forth in running. Something about jumping over obstacle after obstacle and not falling down! I felt that I was flying in the wind, and nobody could catch me. I waited for the gun to blast and off we went to the finish line. As an adult now and working as a professional of trauma resolution, I see how significant my early athletic endeavors were for the regulation of my nervous system. It was a way my fight/flight response could cycle through from a freeze response. It was really the only time I could physically run away from a tumultuous family life.

Over the years, every time I entered the high desert elevation on Cajon Pass and soon after seeing certain landmarks, I know that I am almost home. Except now, my home is no longer here. My family still lives here, having moved to other locations and created their lives. The town has changed enormously. Where there was open desert, now you see whole subdivisions and big box stores. It is a car town. Hardly anyone walks. Yesterday when I walked, I saw two others walking: a teenager who is skipping school and a woman bundled up with a small dog.

My parents bought a home in the Mojave desert in 1981. As a teenager, I loved walking in the wide desert. The wind would blow and our two dogs would run wildly amongst the creosote bushes. Sometimes, I would just sit under a bush and be silent. There were so many tiny flowers close to the sand. They were like little orchids the size of my thumbnail. There were parts of the desert that were fresh...the sand was undisturbed. There was the moonrise above the desert hills. There were the magnificent dynamic colors at dusk that reminded me again and again the changeability of life, and if you are patient to listen and look, you see the nuances and beauty underlying creation. Those solitary walks saved me. They gave me peace, solace, something bigger than our petty dramas. They gave me strength and taught me that I am part of something grander, and that there is oneness to creation.

When my oldest brother was found from being lost, there was just so much problem. He was physically found, but the lostness only became more apparent. It glared at all of us, for we really were all lost. Pekka took drugs, was kicked out of school, entered juvenile hall, jails, etc. Even Pekka's artwork (he was a gifted artist) spoke of the pain. He took me aside one day when we were teenagers, handed me a comic strip he had designed, and requested that I write the story of his life one day. Once, I visited the county jail to meet Pekka and I was horrified to see this building. I didn't know what to expect. There was no preparation for it. The concrete prison walls and all the screams and steel cups clamoring with Pekka's quiet, eyes down broke my heart and shook my soul. I didn't know what to say. It was awkward.

I loved Pekka, but I was frightened of him. I was also ashamed of him at that time. I was also ashamed of myself. I had so much shame inside me. It wasn't until the kundalini rising that I was to face this internalized shame. I wanted to be as different from him as possible. Little did I know at the time that we were so alike in that we were both responding to the deep pain in our family and life itself. So I excelled in school, avoided even the dust of drugs. I took the opposite pole and became the "angel" "perfect child" in hopes that I could forget all that was going on in my family. I never spoke of my family and forbid friends from visiting my home. In order to have some semblance of an understanding, I wrote in depth articles for the newspaper on issues of abuse, dysfunctional families, alcoholism, etc. I became an over achiever. I was very involved with school activities as well as a way of not spending so much time at home. Though on the outside I looked like any other normal American teenager, I wasn't. My life with my family was uncontrollable, unpredictable, lonely, scary and messy.

Practical Application for you:

1. What are the rites of mourning that you have in your family? In your culture?
2. What are the wounds of passion in your family history?
3. I invite you to take a piece of paper and with your left hand begin to express with crayons or/and paint the colors of your mysteries.
4. When you are angry or hurt, what are the ways you express yourself?
5. With both your arms, give yourself a hug. Squeeze your upper arms gently and firmly. Say to yourself, "I love you, (your name)." I encourage you to call a really close ally/friend and share what you feel is right for you.

CHAPTER 16: THE WORLD IN LABOUR
SPIRITUAL EMERGENCY CONTINUED

The spiritual emergency felt like a tremendous volcanic eruption of my unconscious. I had 24-7 access to both personal and collective ancestral patterns. Repressed and suppressed memories flooded my consciousness. Looking back now, it was no surprise given my early family history. It was also a time of embracing both the light and dark. Spiritual awakening for me included a broken heart. I chose to work through all the muck and find the jewels in it. As I did, it made complete sense why the journey had such magnitude. It was exhilarating, mysterious, scary and painful. The letters between Bonga and I continued. I felt that he was the only one who could really understand first hand what I was experiencing.

Below are excerpts from letters exchanged back and forth between Bonga (B) and myself (K).

B: October 31, 1999

Waves of fatigue and exhaustion, the story of my life seems more and more vague and blurred. I often have this image of you in the bathroom with pillows and the utter loneliness of this devastation tightens my heart. I hold you in my heart, you are the world in labour, a kind of new prototype going through the pains of birth...

I hope life will bring you to quieter waters and that many blessings are flowing towards you. I am in awe when I think of your courage and flexibility. You are surely an old and great soul. Take good care, sweet child of the universe.

K. November 1, 1999
Why am I so terrified of being together?
Why am I so terrified of being held?
Why am I so terrified of being loved?
Why am I so terrified of being demanding?
Why am I so terrified of being needy?
Why am I so terrified of wanting affection?
Why am I so terrified of wanting to be held?

Why am I so terrified of wanting and needing support?
Why am I so terrified of being abandoned and hurt?

It is important for me that when we meet that it is really as friends. I need a friend who can be there for me. I don't want this meeting to be a meeting to work on a relationship as lovers. I am not in any space to confuse the two because I'm already full with all these things going on....If I had a friend that is going through what I'm going through, I'd dig in the garden with her and encourage her and sing with her and rock with her and walk in the moonlight in the evening when she can't sleep or bury her...you know...I'd hug her so she doesn't have to hug pillows and I'd put my body on her so se doesn't have to fly when she doesn't want to and I wouldn't tell her she's crazy or possessed or need to go to church or maybe even psychotic and I wouldn't have all the readymade answers to really appease my own worries instead of just being being with not knowing. I'd tell her she's awfully courageous and she's wonderful just the way she is and she doesn't have to perform any way to be loved. Even when she's confused, I still love her and even when she's in a rage, I still love her and even when she's terrified, I still love her. That she is okay just the way she is. And even is she starts to panic because the kerosene stove won't work and the fire is everywhere, that it's okay we'll just have something else to eat.   And I'd join her under the sleeping bag and help protect her and we'd weave golden webs and colorful feathers and we'd laugh at all the craziness and all that stuff and cry together and be wild together and sing row, row your boat together...and do you qualify for the job of bodyguard/friend/accomplice?

B: November 11, 1999
    I hear you and I full well understand your fears and terrors. It is a big jump for you, and for me as well and I do understand that you need a friend and not a lover in this case. The last letter was very touching indeed and if you ask me if I qualify for the job, I'll show you my SB letters on my chest, not Santikaro Bhikkhu, but Super Bonga. If you feel that it would be easier for you that I come to the States, that is possible too, you know. All is open, and

as I told you earlier, it is up to you to choose what is best for you. Your story is as beautiful as it is difficult and in as much you tell me that deep down you know it is all right, I feel that this knowledge is shaky. I can hold you in my arms and walk with you by moonlight and build sand castles and listen to your stories and laugh and cry and wonder at this big mystery. I do feel very concerned for you and I know that any one else in the world would already have collapsed or fallen apart or freaked out. But you are so strong, and above all, stubborn.

Should we meet soon, I also would be glad to be a friend, a soul brother, a companion and although I do not claim to be the perfect match, I trust that my heart will be able to contain your process. Take very good care of your self and do not think that you are alone. The forces that have brought you in this condition are also the ones that will guide you.

B: November 30, 1999

I will take rest for the next week and check the email to know your dates of arrival. I will check places around Maenam beach to start with. I feel held by the holy mother while everything I know as me is falling apart.

K: December 1, 1999

Dearest Jisan,

I hope the panics have subsided and that you are receiving as much support and love. Please be gentle.

I want you to be very honest with me please. I am not really all right. I just said that because I didn't want you to worry, but by saying that I was denying what was really going on inside me. I don't want to deny my needs or my feelings. I am on my reserves and I can't take care of anybody. I'm using all my energy just to be together. How will it be when we're together? Is it wise for me to join you when you yourself are in a crisis? When I'm in a crisis? Will there be other support?

Please write as honestly. Call me. I am scared to go to Thailand and will have no support system. My survival is at stake here. And so is yours. Please let's really reflect on this.

B: dec 2, 1999

I hear you very much and I do feel that it would be foolish for us to meet on an island and freak out together. I have not been able to have a decent night of sleep for the last week and last night's panic ended in a kind of death experience and an explosion of energy so strong that I left my body and wandered in different realms of reality. Somehow I survived and I feel so exhausted and also at the edge of insanity....What is it that binds us? I feel so touched by what you going through and very frustrated not to have the opportunity to be with you. I am very much at the end of my possibilities and need real support....as soon as my mind dives within, I am confronted with an immense chaos and feel so much at the edge of annihilation. I am totally lost and do not know what to do anymore.

I perfectly understand that you are not in a position to help me and hold me and feel so grateful that the honesty that we share is still at work in these crazy moments..Please, keep record of all that you are going through, to help yourself and others too. I know that we are on our way to freedom. This is certain. What we do not know is how long it will take for us to come to terms with this stuff.

I love you immensely and after this new crisis, I must congratulate you for being so brave and courageous in your path. I truly admire your courage and endurance. It is truly wonderful how you manage this.

B:

Let us take it one step at a time. It is so rapid, the changes we go through. I am very glad that we keep on supporting each other and I trust that there is more waiting. Do be kind and gentle to yourself and do not expose yourself too much. Let us keep in touch, you are really a central piece of my mandala.

K:

...hang in there. Don't forget the strength that is within yourself. Please don't beat yourself deeper and deeper

B: January 10, 2000

...To say that I am desperate is weak. I feel devastated. Our relationship was the cement that kept my fragmented self together and now I am falling into pieces.

Universe so dear,

Please help Bongaji right now. I can't take care of him. Please open his eyes to the options that are present. Please hold him in your arms. I trust that your mysterious ways know what is meant to be. I shall accept whatever will happen. I send my prayers to Bonga. May you heal my friend.

Another letter:

Please let Bonga learn to love himself and find his own power. Let him take responsibility of taking care of him.

Another letter:
Dear universe,

Please keep Bonga safe and let him go to England where Bob, Nicki and Kate can help him. Embrace my cacahuete (peanut) close to your heart.

Practical Application for you:

1. Do you remember a time in your life when prayer did not look like anything you thought it is?
2. When was the last time you exchanged letters by snail mail? What did they smell like? What was the texture of the paper? What images were on the stamps?
3. Have you had a break-down or supported a loved one through his/her break-down? What arises for you? In your emotions? What are you sensing in your body?
4. If you were to name this rite of passage, what would you call it?

CHAPTER 17: ANOINTING THE DEAD

Just like I wanted to show my brother in the spirit world how it was to live life to the fullest, I felt this same pull to show Bonga that one can go through the deepest despair and come through it in one piece, alive!!!

When Bonga died, I was pissed!!! It took a while to fully show others this rage I had because I had to feel it more fully, know its nuances, know the passion that lay behind it. It was a storm that took me...the deep grief that propelled me to run wildly for miles, my long hair flying in the air, throwing myself into the cold Pacific ocean and cursing the skies and God. It took the roaring waves that kept tumbling over me to drown the loudness and fierceness of my despair and anger. The bigger the wave that swept me, the more ferocity from my belly came out, until all I could do was wail. It was like the ocean was washing away everything inside myself. The Great Mother could hold it all. She was anointing my entrails and reminding me that the depth and intensity of grief was equal to the depth and intensity of love I felt.

I learnt that he died through an email. I felt that a bat had hit me on the back of my head. The shock was astounding. I walked home from the bus stop and I looked at the full moon that spring, and I knew he was watching me. That evening, I began to make a list of things to be done before I could fall apart. That was my pattern: very good in emergencies!!

I called ATT the next day to get an overseas calling plan to Switzerland, England and Canada. I knew that there would be a series of phone calls to be made so I could ascertain what had happened. I got the bare facts: cold, numb, details of what happened that day, but no emotions. They were like puzzle pieces being placed together to make a coherent whole. But it wasn't coherent. It didn't make sense. How could it? We were all reeling from the fact that Bonga had just taken his own life!!

His family planned a funeral to be held in two days in Lausanne. I was in California. But Bonga didn't want a funeral. He wanted to be cremated. But funerals are not for the dead. They are for the living, to help them with saying goodbye. I didn't see his dead body in the coffin. My experience from the past was that it was already hard to accept someone dying, and even harder still if you don't see the dead body. It took me a while to accept that he really died. Even a year later, I was still waiting for the blue aerogrammes to arrive from him in the mail. That perhaps a blue letter arriving in my mailbox would wake me up from this dream called grief.

No more letters came. Instead I read and reread the ones I had received the last year before he died. Where there any signs? Of course there were. He told me when I left a year ago for San Francisco, "If you knew I only had a year left to live, would you stay?" It was a bit macabre. Yet, wasn't our spiritual enquiry about this very question of living life to the fullest especially if you had only one year or one day left to live. We said goodbye in a bus station in Tiruvanamallai, India and I wept like I have never before in my life. I felt that I was saying goodbye.

The first part of that year, he seemed fine, apart from missing me, and realizing my place in his life and there was the deep longing for this love. He sent many blue colored letters reminding me that we shared more than a bank account. He yearned for the opportunity to show me his love and care. Then I had my spiritual emergency that spring of 1999, and I broke into a million pieces. I was trying to keep it together with grad school, work and all the altered dimensions accessible to my consciousness. It was mind-boggling and crazy making, and yet deep within, it was all in order. I was in a process of transformation. This is what I had been training for all my life.

Bonga volunteered to come to California. I was scared. I was in such shambles. I knew I could not take care of no one else but me at the moment. I told him this. I was also very scared to be dependent and be taken care of. It brought to the fore my frailty and a shattered sense of identity. I was picking up the remnants, yet there was no way to put them back together. They were not meant to be glued back, for I have shed the old skin, a new one was forming. I was raw, naked, exposed in the big city.

Yet I also wanted him, anyone, someone, to take the reins for me and let me rest. The inner horses were so wild, and the city wasn't a place for me. I was lost. The waves of the unconscious were tossing me turbulently, and I was in the midst of a simultaneous shamanic journey and a kundalini rising that didn't stop. The life force of Mother Shakti showed its powerful and tumultuous expression within my physical body and psyche. My kite was flying into unknown territory, and I needed someone stable, secure and trustworthy to hold the thread steadily until I could find my way home.

And there I was in my apartment in San Francisco, having made a spare key and bought extra clothes for Bonga just in case…just in case he came…I wanted him to come because I really wanted him to meet me. Haven't I been waiting for this for so long?

As my journey got more out of control, Lyle, a mutual friend, invited me to temporarily live in Canada and offered to take the reins of the horses. I met Lyle right before my father died. Bonga, Lyle and I met in Bodh Gaya in India. After meeting, I soon left to help care for my father before his death. Bonga and Lyle lit candles for my father at the Mahabodhi temple (where Buddha attained his enlightenment). I would faxed letters updating Bonga of my father's condition as he was in a coma.

When I went into a spiritual emergency, Bonga was very worried and so he asked Lyle to check-in on me when Lyle was on a visit to the bay area from Canada. It was a short yet meaningful meeting. Before he left, he said that if I ever needed anything to let him know.

I so wanted to surrender and let someone else stronger than I take the reins of the horses that were out of control. I also felt it unwise to do it with Lyle, since he didn't really know me well. I didn't want the cauldron of deep vulnerability and need from me to incite conditions of romance. You know the damsel in distress and the knight in the shining armor mythology! I also had a hard time surrendering my deeply rooted hyper-independence!!

Simultaneously, Bonga coaxed me to return to Thailand where he would take care of me. We'd rent a cottage by the sea, he said, and we'd play by the sand building structures like Carl Jung did when he went through his spiritual emergency. This time in Jung's life is what inspired Jungian work and sand play therapy. It was his initiation into bringing these gifts to the world. Bonga recognized the transformative power of this time. There would be no pressure to even be romantic. After all, we had already broken up. He'd bought the pots and pans. The cottage was waiting by the sea. I had a plane ticket ready. Lyle bought the ticket straight to the islands as a way to show his support. I'd taken a leave of absence from school and given my notice for my apartment. I was jumping into the net of support for the first time in my life in my deepest vulnerability and incapacity.

Then, the phone rang that day. Bonga had not slept in 10 days in this island waiting for me. He saw spirits and they wanted him to jump in the river in Thailand. He was losing his mind. He needed help. I made a decision not to go to Thailand. Instead, I called Lyle at one in the morning and I asked to take his offer of help. I asked Lyle to take care of Bonga in Canada. I was so unwell at the time and I knew I couldn't do it.

And so…the journey unfolded beyond my imagination. We managed to get Bonga to meet Lyle in Canada while I stayed in San Francisco. It was deeply moving in so many ways. There was this profound love between us and all these bizarre scenarios of cosmic play were trying us. I prayed and prayed. Then I learnt I didn't know how to pray anymore. The only invocation was: I surrender to whatever the universe feels is the best for our highest good. The abyss within my soul kept widening and burrowing into the bowels of the earth. I felt horrible.

While in Canada, Bonga called and told me all the different ways he wanted to end his life. I reminded him over and over again that this period in his life was calling for the death of the old, not the literal death of the body through suicide. It was a death-rebirth that has been told of countless eons through mythology and religion. Movies such as Star Wars and the Matrix allude to this fundamental journey of the soul. He would get it, really understood it, but then the riptide would take over. The depression was so deep and thick. There was so much clearing out of his system in this purification, and I wondered how to help him with the backlog in his system. Taking a breath got harder and harder. The beating of his heart became more laborious. He didn't want to go on anymore.

What are the different ways to convince someone why to stay longer here on earth if he didn't want to anymore? He was a mountaineer. Did planning pilgrimages to Santiago de Campostela help? No. Did planning a six month walk along the Pacific Crest trail help? No. The only wish he had was for us to get together again, to make a try again. He felt I could make him want to live. He was convinced that I was his north star and now he felt so lost. I reminded him this power only resided in him, and can never be handed to another person, not me, not anyone. I didn't want to be emotionally blackmailed into believing that I was responsible for his death or life. It was some of the hardest conversations I ever had with anyone. I was finding my own north star internally in my falling apart universe. In the midst of so much sorrow and anger and despair, we spoke and asked forgiveness of each other for all the wrongdoings and pain we had caused each other. We were letting go of each other.

I hated the telephone. I hated the phone ringing. The pit of my stomach felt like its knotted cords. I wanted to throw the damn phone away. Break it into a million pieces. Yet, it was the lifeline. A lifeline where I felt hopeless and helpless to make any difference to the man I loved. Many times, I felt my bondage rather than my freedom. My journey was to find my liberation in the midst of so much pain and confusion.

Bonga entered a psychiatric ward for one month. He was the one that volunteered to go in. We were all relieved. At least, he couldn't harm himself here. At least he could get professional help that none of us could give. At least, there would be many people working there 24-7. At least, he could be angry with me and get support there. At least, he could let out all the pain in his life from really early on and get holding. At least, there would be help…to extend his life.

He called me when he left the hospital. His spring had broken and his vivacity and vitality had disappeared. The medications took it out of him, squeezed and buried his spunk. He really did not want to live anymore. He couldn't see continuing to live his life forward this way. He felt he'd lost his dignity. He'd asked me if I understood. I said, "Yes I understand, but I don't agree. It can change. This too shall pass." He was finding a way to make peace with his decision. We went through many conversations of completion. We asked forgiveness of each other as well as shared our gratitude for the life we'd shared. I was exhausted of hearing the different ways he wanted to end it. It's been so hard the years of pain and turmoil with the tumultuous kundalini rising for him. He felt his spring broke, He lived a life whereby he didn't know if he'd make it the next day. He saw his body as an old man in his thirties. He was so scared. I wished it could have gone away. I'd hold him and rock him. It would go away, but then it would come back. I would run away. I was fed up. But I never stopped loving him. I thought maybe he'd stand up on his own if I wasn't there watching. I didn't know that it would break him. I didn't want to break him. I wanted to help him be strong from inside himself. I wanted him to be strong without me. It was so painful to fully hear that he really was going and we were saying our goodbyes.

He said he would see me in the next life. Shortly afterwards, I received the email that he had died. Even though we talked so much about dying, I was so devastated when he died. My magic friend chose to leave this life, and I had no say in it. The years that followed was a constant returning to choosing to accept his decision. It has been a journey of my own healing into my joie de vivre.

The night I received the news of his death, I wrote in my journal:

I feel much sadness for my dear brother. I love him so much. He's given me so much of himself...the magic, the vitality, the wildness. We are both of the same tree. I look at the full moon, it is his face I see...I feel so much gratitude for him. I trust the mystery unfolds as it needs to. I wish him well in what is to come. I hope he keeps me posted. It's such a shock for me. I let the feelings flowed...the frustration, the anger, the guilt, the sadness, the grief, the gratitude, the magic, the passing of one mystery into mystery. Why the fuck did it have to happen? God, I have to call his parents and they don't speak English and my French is so bad. Bonga, please help me. I know you're here. Come to my dreams tonight and tell me how you are doing.

That evening I dreamt a huge ship got stuck in a small cul de sac. Then a big white bird flew from the ship into the sky.

The next day it hit me as I listened to the voicemail and heard Bonga's voice in the machine that I would never get a call from him again. It was as though a thunderbolt stroked me. I took the ferry with a white gardenia, and just like in the dream, I went to the ship's bow and released the white gardenia symbolic of the white bird in the dream. I directed the energy towards the ocean so he won't be in this small cul de sac. I told him that I need him to stay with me now but I know that he may have other plans too later. I said that the door is always open for that release/freedom of going. I understood that from the depth of my soul. But, nonetheless, I began bawling and I just screamed, "NO, no, no! Why did you have to die?" I did another release at a later date of encouraging the gardenia into the big ocean at Tennessee Beach. The gardenia coming back to me and I kept throwing it back in the ocean, "You can make it. You can make it. You can do it." until the waves took it into the sea.

Since I wasn't at his funeral, I made my own ritualistic burial. I sewed a Bonga doll. He used to make Kasha dolls. Now I was making a Bonga doll. I sewed all the anatomical parts correctly. I sewed clothes for him. I made a sarong tied just the way he tied his. It even had a small patch on it. I sewed a khadi shirt, loose and free and an Indian type bag. In the bag, I put rupees for the galactic beggars (he was very generous to beggars), a condom so he's safe when exploring sexually, a picture of Ramana Maharishi, my message of well wishes in a note and a flute because he is Krishna! I even gave him a mala (rosary) in his hand. I made a burial with all the things he loved in this life, and might be good to have with him in the next. He was very generous. I included bubbles, paint, calligraphy pens, wishes of dharma and happiness, some thread, a feather, some seeds, my hair, a mirror, a peaceful scene with dhammic inscription from Sister Mechtildes, some trail mix and water, a rock, condom. Before I buried him, I bathe the Bonga doll in a salt water mixture very tenderly, caressing each of his parts very gently. I chanted Buddhist chants and mantras and also "Suzanne" by Leonard Cohen, except I substituted "Kasha takes you down to the river." It was very healing to do this burial alone in the forest. I stayed for a very long time until the mist came once again. I went up the ridge and saw the hillside blooming and I was reminded of life. As I walked down, a snake met me and we just stared into each other's eyes. We knew.

Journal entry: March 23, 2000

Was it a senseless act? I do not know. Could it have been avoided? I do not know. That was part of the pain. There were so many questions and no way to answer them. How could a person who stuck his hands in the toilets in Asia to save ants from drowning kill himself? I had a hard time reconciling all these paradoxes. I could see how he did it out pain, but at the same time, could I see that he did it out of love? Can I hold all of it in my heart? I knew he was pushing through with his insights, breaking out of his shell but I also saw the fragile ego. There is dawning an understanding of the soul's dimension of nothing being a mistake.

Surrendering to the mystery got harder and harder. I was boggled. It was the biggest spiritual lesson I had to contend with. It challenged me on all levels. I wanted everything to be neat and all in a box tied up. This wasn't going to be that. So I spent a lot of time looking at the stars so my mind's questions could just disappear and my being could be silenced. Up to that point, I tried to hold his pain and I couldn't so I tried to hold him in my peace. I could no longer live some else's life. Even though it was excruciating, there seemed to be a glimmer of hope that he would come out of it and we would look back and laugh. I wanted so much for him to reclaim his power. I wanted him to be alive….and now he was dead.

I never cried so much as I cried those years. I cried with friends. They reminded me of the bigger picture, and those that knew him, relayed Bonga's love, affection and gratitude for what I've given him in his life. Our long term friend Ed reminded me that the last thing Bonga wanted was to hurt me or make me sad - that his death was part of his journey. I cried more when I was alone. I never knew a person could cry so much. I flowed like a river. Friends and family reminded me that I am here to stay on earth for a reason. They wanted me to stick around. Several offered a 24 hour hotline for me. I told them just checked in and asked if I'm eating 3 meals a day, sleeping and drinking. My friend Lucinda said in shock, "Now I know how Job's friends felt." My friend Marty brought food, and diligently showed up every Friday.

My friend Jonathan tied a green string on my wrist so others could hold me and I won't fly away. When Michael offered his phone number, he added that we don't even have to talk. We could just be in silence on the phone. When I retorted that it will take a really long time, he added that he's got 8-10 years!! Eve took me out to remind me of balance. Many people really reached out at the beginning, "We care for you." Victor, another classmate, chimed in the elevator one day, "Little butterfly, keep out of the rain. If it starts raining, call me and I'll bring an umbrella." My eyes were very tender. He added, "Those that are most sensitive get hurt the most. Butterflies are beautiful!"

It was all very touching. The world kept telling me that they care and that I am loved. There was a huge part of me that couldn't take it in. I was so used to being the one who gave care, not receive care. This was a time to learn to receive when I was feeling the most needy. Somehow, I just wanted to crawl in my bed and hug my hot water bottle against my heart. And it was really hard to come out with so much rawness and vulnerability. I learnt to let go with those friends who did not feel threatened with the intensity of my feelings, and held in with those that could only give their limit. Claire, my therapist, urged me, "It is a privilege to grieve with somebody. Not only are they giving you a gift, but you are also giving them a gift."

I'd feel Bonga's spirit healing my heart. I learnt that life and death are not too far apart. I learnt to trust the Great Mystery and rest in her arms. I knew that it was all really about love, and not to wait until someone dies before we say it. That was the message that came through again and again.

I entered seclusion for the most part. Phone calls and letters came in offering solace, reminding me that when a big star explodes, it affects everyone in its vicinity. Even my dreams portrayed me grieving. There was no break. I asked my therapist, "How long will pain be here?" She replied, "As long as it need to be." It scared me to feel so much pain. It scared me to love someone so much. It scared me that I might join him because I had a hard time letting him go. It scared me that I may fly away. I knew I was crossing a lot of boundaries and we were traveling in my dreams. It scared me that I just wanted fragmenting. Did he not wish that I would die first before him because he felt it would be too unbearable for the person left behind and he said that he didn't want me to bear the loneliness of his death? Now it was reversed, and his spirit was telling me I must go on with my life.

Journal entry:

I almost lost it. It is the farthest I have been into fragmentation. I called Lucinda and I said it was bad. I said I'm no longer on the edge. I am falling. It took my witness to walk me through inch by inch to get me a banana (food in my stomach), a shower and a smudge. All my meditation training kept me going. It was simply moment to moment awareness to keep my foot in this world. I was shaking the whole way, my voice even cracked. I promised myself then that I am going to be all right. I am going to take care of me!!! Bob from England called. I said, "Bob, it is bad. I want you to name words of objects in the room so I can repeat them and bring and keep my awareness to this reality. One by one, he said "shoes, clock, phone, window, bed, desk..." One by one, I repeated them to bridge the multiple dimensions that were seducing me to leave one permanently. I was in the midst of this when Lucinda came and took the phone away. She held me on her lap in the sun, stroking my hair. I knew I was going to be all right, for that moment.

Dream:

Someone went to my drawer and took my wallet. He gave it back to me and I saw that my cash was still inside but my identification and bank cards were taken away.

After 10 years as a strict vegetarian, I walked to the Burger King and ordered a double whopper!!! I now needed to be a meat eater to ground myself through this journey.

Lola, the oak tree, kept carrying my weight as I hung out on her branches those many months. While up on the tree, bobcats and coyotes would visit and sit underneath while I was up there. The shamanic journey continued with all the initiations. There were many spiritual operations that occurred while Lola held me on her branches. It was a remarkable time.

The body died, but the soul and the intimacy stays...and continues to grow

It took me 10 years to remember Bonga primarily, not through his death, but through his vital, joyful, funny self!!

You see, when someone dies, it is important to keep on talking about them with the social network of family and friends that were part of his life. I didn't have that very much. I had moved to Marin County to live a fresh life. I needed to grieve, but I didn't have our common circle here. There were a few new friends who, out of their love for me, offered so much patience and generosity for my bereaving heart. I read them our love letters to introduce Bonga, who he was, his personality...his strengths before the depression and the suicide. I wanted them to know the Bonga I knew before, not only the one who was caught in deep despair and pain. I wanted to be fair and give a fuller picture. You see, I wasn't just grieving for his death. I was grieving for the Bonga who was full of life, of magic, of love.

I was angry at some of my new and old "friends" who felt and told me that Bonga killed himself to be revengeful at me. I was angry at them for saying that I should be "relieved" now. I was confused when my spiritual friends said I "shouldn't cry because I was hurting him in the afterlife." That crying wasn't spiritual. I was deeply hurt when some of our closest friends blamed me for his death. I know that I wasn't responsible for his life. I was so upset that when someone told me I had to start dating quickly and that he'd "checked out". And it all hurt. I felt betrayed on so many levels. I withdrew into silence for many years.

I didn't enter a Buddhist monastery for a long time. I didn't want to read any of the dharma books that we shared together. Yet, paradoxically, the wisdom in them kept guiding me to return to something so fundamental in my meditation training: feel the body in the body, feel the breath in the breath, the feelings in the feelings, the mind in the mind, the dharma in the dharma. These tenets of the Satipatthana Sutra saved my sanity and my life. I understood Kisa Gotami and the Buddha's teachings to her.

Once a week, I took the ferry into the city to work and see my therapist. I would put make up on and beautiful, professional clothes. On the outside, I looked so well put together, but those feral eyes betrayed any semblance of normalcy. I was spending more and more time in the spirit world and I began to realize that I had to stay connected with this plane with people that were alive. When I'd go to the city, I'd boil a dozen eggs and make sandwiches and I'd hand it out to the homeless. It was my way of staying connected. There were days the boiled eggs I cooked to give away were still warm when received. The joy I saw in their eyes were bridges to me to this world. I dedicated the merit to Bonga that he may be in a better life on the other side.

One afternoon, I waited for the ferry and a homeless man named Christopher sat next to me. I shared the bread and cheese I had with him, and he sang me songs. I felt his pain, sadness, anger ad lostness. He thanked me for giving him love. Love really is a meeting.

Claire, my therapist, was very important to me at that time. Having a person that is steadfast and solid in her/his love for you while you are going through a rough time is tremendously important. I had just met Claire two weeks before Bonga became suicidal. She was the one person that was constant. She gently coaxed my letting go in graceful ways, "Bonga is a part of you, but he is not the whole of you. There is also you. Don't forget that."

Journal entry: April 4, 2000

I feel that I am a mother who lost her child. If only I could sing a lullaby that would wake him up from the grave. I feel like a child who lost her most beloved sibling. Lost my magic friend. Lost my Krishna. Lost my fellow meditator. Lost my co-pilgrim. Lost a dream. Who will collect garbage with me or sleep under ancient huge bells and listen to thunderstorms and cradle each other in our special hammock? Who is going to go with the cows and answer my calls from down the hill and bring them in when the snow falls? Who's going to make chapattis with me and grate the beet and carrots and catch pear blossoms and watch the birds just glide in the canyon?

I am angry that he took it all away. He didn't give me a choice. He made the choice that shook my soul and everything I believed in. He took away with him his promises, our plans, our hopes. He took away a big part of me. I feel powerless, helpless, frustrated, sad, angry, regretful. He took his life and he took part of me with him. Damn you, why did you take away my heart?

My beloved
Where have you gone?
In the chamber of my heart
Waits a warm cup of chai

The spiritual emergency I was in continued. I thought the spiritual emergency was the lowest in my life. I thought it was the bottom. Well, the bottom kept opening and I kept falling. I learnt how to master falling many different ways. Before then in my life, I had succeeded so much. I was gifted with intelligence, beauty, ease in whatever I touched. I didn't realized how unfamiliar I was with the full expression and feeling of failure. In the midst of deep, utter failure, I had to face my terror of failing. Well, the syllabus in this chapter was definitely Failure and Falling 101. I don't know what kept me going in those dark years. Something so much deeper held me: a love so beyond what goes between two. It was Oneness. I experienced Oneness in all forms, and it was deeply humbling. In the midst of separation there was unity. Somehow, I felt so held by the whole universe, and in this holding I could just surrender to all the feelings that my heart and guts felt. It was the universe expressing itself. The absolute and the manifest were playing as one. I never knew I could wail and scratch the earth with such intensity of a feeling life. I learnt what true intimacy of self meant. In the midst of the deepest grief, I also made a promise that I would never stop loving.

Forgiveness Path

It took me three years after he died of doing forgiveness practices every single day, each morning and each evening, before I could truly mean the forgiveness prayer for him, for Lyle, and for myself. It took that many times, going through all manners of emotional somersaults before I could I say it with an open heart, feeling the tenderness of the raw wound without anger. I went through the black hole of grief, and found stillness in the end. It's like a fulgurite. The lightning bolt stroke the center of my being, and the aftermath required a finding my self after such a perturbation. Another formation arose as a result.

Journal entry: April 20, 2000

"When all else comes and goes, what remains? What is it that is left unchanged/untouched? I need to connect with that because that is my center/my ground. It will help me tremendously when everything is getting destroyed in my life. Who is in the mirror when the mask is taken out?"

I kept remembering there is more to this than the struggle.

Even after Bonga left his body, his spirit stayed with me for a year. In the morning, he would chimed in that he wanted cinnamon with my oatmeal and that he wanted to wear the red skirt when I chose to dress myself. He didn't have good boundaries when he was alive. He had worse ones after he died. In one way, it was charming and endearing that we had this year of transition. It was also helpful for me somehow. He and I had spent so much time away from each other, not seeing each other physically, that the energetic/psychic connection was very strong and ingrained in our relating. The only difference somehow was that he didn't have a physical body now.

You see when he died, my spirit went looking for him in the other world. There was a place that was like a big cafeteria and I would go from person to person there, checking their faces to see if it was he. There was a frantic eagerness on my part because I didn't want him to go. I didn't want my magic friend to die. I traveled astrally to look for him. I entered buses meant for the dead and I would be asked to leave because it wasn't my time yet. I was reminded that it wasn't good for my physical body to travel to the other worlds. So Bonga's spirit came to me here, in the beginning, to console. The level of attachment between us was so strong.

This, however, also created difficulty for me in accepting his death. It also meant letting go of him differently when his spirit was called away. There were times that I stood outside the big gate that separated the world of the living and the world of the dead, and I wasn't allowed in. I would bang on that gate, sobbing and demanding, "Let me in." And Bonga would be on the other side, but he was no longer allowed to play with me this way.

I was lonely, and I traveled that path so I could arrive on the other side. The process required that I accept that our relationship was going to be in another form. It was extremely painful but necessary to make that metamorphosis.

In the process of letting go, I had to learn to look at life not just horizontally, at the level of personality, but also include the vertical relationship with the divine. When I went vertically, above and below, I found my core, my strength. There was a sense of boundlessness, and all the emotions did not matter. I found the strength, stability and safety in me. I also realized that it was important to own and feel fully these feelings. It was the calibrating of controlled exposure to the pain that was the challenge because the lid of my instinctual and affective bodies just blew opened. I was giving myself permission to have boundaries, even within myself. It became years of mastering how permeable do I want to be at a given time. Healing included all of it.

As time went by, I asked my friends to bring me laughter. The death, the kundalini and the health issues around the reproductive organs were a bit much to take on all at once!!! I must say though that the visits to the gynecologist were very healing. I wasn't surprised that my uterus and ovaries enlarged, flared up and got infected. I was grieving so of course my womb would be grieving too. To have someone asked me before going inside me and encouraging me to say, "Stop, or no, or slow down" gave me a choice that felt was missing in my life. The circumstances in my life were changing so radically. The only place I could exert some control was my attitude.

Journal entry: April 29, 2000

Lucinda was very specific telling me of the differences between Bonga and I. She wanted to be clear to me that I know that I am a separate individual from him. That we took different ways and I will not make the same choices he made. She reminded me that I made the choices that were necessary for my survival. That I did the best I could and I am not responsible for his killing himself. She reiterated that I am taking very good care of myself, not like Bonga who expected me to take care of him. She also reminded me that it's ok for me to be angry. In fact, Marty chimed in that Bonga would be very proud of me to be angry, to not hold my feelings in. If I cleared myself out, it would be clearing him out too.

Bonga pushed me so much. He was desperate. I knew he needed help and there were others who were offering him help but he didn't want them. He wanted me but he knew that I was in a crisis myself. He couldn't see anymore. This played with my wanting to protect him and wanting to hide the dark sides because I felt if I spoke of them, then I'd be betraying him. At first, I just wanted to remember the good and beautiful. But there were also pain, cruelty, confusion, fear. I learnt not to keep hiding the truth at my expense. I wanted to believe that he could hold me. As much as he wanted to be my container, the truth was he couldn't. This disappointed me greatly. It hit a chord so deep in my center, that echoed way before I even met him. At the end, I also accepted that I couldn't hold him. I accepted that the biggest "no" I said in my life had to play out this way. There was utter disillusionment. It would take a while to unwind this knot more fully. Many friends and mentors for years supported me in this unwinding.

I asked my friend Nicky, "Will my heart hurt so much in my life?" He said it depends how much I allow myself to feel now. Most people don't allow themselves to grieve. I grieved like a sick dog. I did not understand except I loved. We loved each other so deeply even in the midst of our confused selves. My life just kept falling apart...home, jobs, school, death, friends, sanity...I just kept planting flowers and staring into the sea. I also bought a car for $700 so I can walk dogs except I lost my eye-hand coordination and had to park my car for one year without driving it. I took odd jobs to make the rent. The universe was funny. One weekend, I glued hundreds of matchbox cars to cards and I made exactly the amount for my rent!!

Dream: March 16, 2000

I peered between my legs and there was a huge crystal formation like in a cave – from my vagina to the ankles. There was a word written on it. It said "effervescence". It was a safe place to be.

Ritual in Suan Mokkh: 1995

I had very long hair all the way down my waist. I had Bonga shaved my head and I took my hair and buried it in the forest monastery. I made a vow then that I wasn't going to have physical children this lifetime, though I would be a spiritual mother to many.

At thirty-one years old in San Francisco, I revisited this vow and had an opportunity to make a new ritual if I so wanted. I chose to leave it as it. Spirit wanted to show me many other facets of life. The birthing that awaited me was my own spiritual birthing.

I couldn't have survived through this period if it wasn't for my spiritual practices. The nature of mind held the space where everything, including the different faces of grief, to dance.

I've written a few of those tenets that been most useful for me as an anchor. May they be of benefit to you as well.

According to Buddhism, there are different kinds of sufferings. Again, dukkha means disastisfaction:

1. dukkha dukkha: gross level – pain, grief, ambiguity, insecurity, getting what we don't want; aging, death
2. viparinama dukkha: more subtle and more difficult to see – sensual pleasure, rapture; will end eventually
3. sankhara dukkah: existential suffering; sheer existence dukkha

Meditation allows us to develop mindfulness and wisdom in order to see what the causes of suffering are and then the way out of that suffering into a form of release, and coolness. Mindfulness and wisdom together are like the bread ends in a sandwich. When you see harm, you naturally let go. This is wisdom. It is like touching a hot stove. You know and you don't burn deliberately.

Know when:
1. mindfulness is present
2. mindfulness is not present
3. why it is present
4. why it is developing

"The present moment is the mother of the future. Take care of the mother and the mother will take care of the child."   Maha Ghosanda

When we taste wisdom, we want more of it. We then want to share it with others. Let us look at different ways to comprehend a situation in daily life.

There are four Kinds of Sampajanna (Clear Comprehension):
1. Sattaka Sampajanna: concerned with suitability. What would be most suitable thing to do right now?
2. Sappaya Sampajanna: concerned with beneficiality. What would most beneficial to apply right now? What is likely to work best?
3. Gocara Sampajanna: understanding that there are just mental and physical processes, that there is nobody there.
4. asammoha Sampajanna: understanding anicca (impermanence), dukkha (suffering), and anatta (non-self)

An example in life is to observe what do we do when relating to another person. Is it possible to relate to another without wanting them to fill our needs, gross or subtle? Is it possible for another to relate to me without wanting to fill my or his needs?

How am I generous to others, to myself? How do I cling to my ideas? Do I make sure that I have the last word in a conversation to make a point – to elaborate myself as something special, spiritual, etc? How do I use my skills to manipulate others?

In this investigation of self, we get to see what we take for granted and how that affects our happiness. Five spiritual faculties that play with each other anytime we are cultivating a maturation into true understanding:

1. faith – Do I have confidence in what I am doing?
2. effort – How much energy are you using? Do I have the right motivation?
3. mindfulness – observe mind states without changing it
4. concentration – one pointedness
5. wisdom

True stillness has right effort, right mindfulness and right concentration. There is lightness that is solid. Vipassana comes from right view, right attitude and right thinking with continuity of awareness give the mind stability.

When concentration is high, but wisdom not keeping up, investigate: Am I clearly aware of what is going on in my mind? What does mind know about object and mind? Look into the balance of relaxation and interest, rather than just effort and relaxation. When we are interested in something, there is an inherent effort that is natural and uncontrived. Remember that awareness is a mental activity that is already part of our daily life. We simply are bringing more consciousness to sharpening the quality of awareness. It's like using an ax to chop wood. We want it to both heavy (weighty) and sharp. Both qualities are needed to chop wood more efficiently.

The four abodes of the gods (Brahman Viharas) are very important teachings in Buddhism and in my training. These qualities are essential to cultivate in the path of transformation and in living one's life. These practices include: One sends love to another. One sends compassion to another when he is suffering. One feels sympathetic joy for another for his good fortune. One meets life with equanimity.

1. metta – loving kindness; equal – someone in similar situation
2. karuna – compassion; when someone is suffering more than us
3. mudita – symphatethetic joy; when someone is more successful than us
4. upekkha – equanimity; we are faced with situation we can't do anything about

Simply put: physical and mental suffering with aversion leads to unwholesome state of mind. Understanding dukkha and setting and letting go of grabbing to it as me or mine lead to wholesome mental state.

Practical Application for you:

1. Has mental illness been part of your life? Have you loved someone who struggled with a mental illness?
2. How open are/were you in speaking to your community about it? Was it helpful? Did you feel received by them?
3. Is it easier for you to be happy for someone or have compassion for them? Why?
4. Which room in your house is forgiveness a guest or a resident? If you were to draw a path to forgiveness, what would it look like?
5. I invite you to make yourself a cup of tea right now, and sense the warmth of the mug in your hand.

Part III: Light and Dark Dancing

CHAPTER 18: A NEW LIFE IN MARIN - HELPING OTHERS HEAL

"The miracle of life waiting in the heart of a seed cannot be proved at once." - Kabir

I moved to Marin in the spring of 1999 into a bright yellow bedroom...yellow walls, yellow duvet, and yellow flowers in bloom outside my window. I called my room Ananda for bliss, and made the intention that joy be one of the pillars of my life. I embarked on a training that would cultivate this seed. I desperately needed that kind of joy.

That first week, so much coagulated blood came out of my vagina as though I was giving birth. After restricting my breath in the city and the spiritual emergency in order to hold myself together. There was so much rawness and fragility, I felt I had to cement my girth. My pelvic cavity held so much in, and now I was letting it go. I took it as a sign that I really needed to breathe deeply. I was picking myself up with dignity from a series of humiliating blows to my sense of self.

I continued deep psychological work: depth psychotherapy for more than 10 years, EMDR, SE. I also received Rosen Method sessions for two years. I studied Diamond Logos for another five years to deepen further my understanding of self. I continued with Feldenkrais and Anat Baniel Method as a practitioner. I studied NeuroVascular Integration and also Core Individuation. I spent a tremendous amount of time in nature. There were very special trees that took me under their limbs, and loved me so devotionally.

For more than a decade, I completely allowed myself to feel the range of emotions around betrayal, abandonment, humiliation, and the link to my behaviors and patterns of hyper-independence. I sank into places of hatred, terror, jealousy, powerlessness. I made friends with shame and dread. I faced the constriction of my prison walls and felt the immobility, the tightness and the dishonesty with one's self. At first the screams were silent, then I found my voice. I physically shook so much the shock out of my system. The second half entailed deliberate, conscious focus on joy, generosity, positive worth, gratitude, gentle loving kindness. I had to learn and live from a place where crisis wasn't the center of my life. Neither do I have to refer everything in my life back to it. It wasn't a linear process at all. Before I could truly understand, I had to feel all of these, and sense my belly deeply. I was owning my full self. In the process, I began to separate self and other, love and dysfunctional coping mechanisms. I also saw deeply that the people that have hurt me the most are my greatest teachers. I took a vow again to grow old gracefully, wisely and lovingly.

Before Bonga died, he wrote me this in reference to my kundalini:

"You must understand that all your life has brought you to this point and now there is no going back to the old. You are sitting on a volcano. You are blessed and no matter how dark and painful this phase of your life may be, believe me that each moment is worth the price...surely it will lead towards more joy, more space, more love. Above all, the forces of the universe are going to work for you and I pray that you might relax in the midst of it all... God's grace is overflowing...you have fought the battle, oh you beautiful and daring Don Quixote. Now it is time to leave the driver's seat and to enjoy the ride...You are in touch with raw, naked life and it is such a lovely blessing."

Dream: march 13, 2000

I was in a dark forest and I was very "primordial" in my being. I was a dark goddess and I took a deer and cut her belly up. All these organs spilled out with blood. I jumped right in and curled inside the entrails.

During the years of the spiritual emergency, I had to learn to really cherish myself. I was in a psychology graduate school that was focused on experiential classes on the deconstruction of self. Doing more deconstruction wasn't really healthy for someone who was already in the deep throes of deconstruction due to spiritual emergency. When everyone in my classes was asked to open, I had to close. Voluntarily not tearing myself apart was my opening to my self. It was a journey of learning how to protect myself. It took me many years to learn titration. What I needed was a safe container instead of more deconstruction. I saw how tearing down can be a form of self-abuse as well. It can be a way to prove beliefs around being "damaged good, second best, unworthy, unlovable". It can be a way to maintain the split. I examined my tendency for intensity and reflected on my life. Research points that abused children's brains are geared to look for traumatic stimuli, not neutral or positive ones. Negative self view cycles to prove itself in destructive ways. I also knew that synapses are not permanent. They can be healed and that new neurological patterns be created. It was clear to me that I wanted the cycle of abuse to stop with me.

I entered the phase of my life where I was giving myself permission to have boundaries. I had to go through a long apprenticeship into healthy boundary setting that challenged all my beliefs and identities. And I accepted the terrain into feeling the incredibly wide range of feelings I was capable of. I began to feel myself in ways that were foreign to me, and I asked myself, "How come I have never experienced this quality of movement of ease before?" And now, I do.

Often modern science looks at medical conditions, whether physical or mental illness, as a set of symptoms to be fixed rather than going to what causes the aliveness of the body-mind to expand or contract. Looking at causes and conditions just don't go deep enough to the roots of what it means to be a human being and what happens when there is a compromise to its vitality and health. People are seen as parts rather than wholes, disjointed rather than connected. The body becomes a battlefield rather than a love field that needs attending. Solutions become patches that temporarily alleviate a discomfort, but underneath the initial emergency is really a call for something new that will elevate the whole system to a higher level of functioning. Often this means a shift in how one is living. When there is a break in the system, it usually means that something in the lifestyle or/and coping skills need to change. This invitation is a positive one. How many are willing to accept the call?

The body-mind system is like a circuit board of energies. It's not very different than the circuit board of a car or your computer. When the connectivity between two points is obstructed, the points don't light up and therefore the function of that pathway is hampered. Neurological wirings that get created from learning are pathways that work for certain situations early in life, but then get corroded and unusable, even dangerous, the older we get. How do you repair these pathways of learning? You learn new ways to add to your possibilities of living. Learning means taking risks to put yourself in an unknowing place to discover different ways of unknowing to arrive at a known. Sensing the body is the best way to do this and you can start at any age.

What do you do when there is an influx of energy coming into your body-mind system? Do you open up and bring curiosity to explore and feel yourself? This may happen in a sexual excitation perhaps or a delightful meal. What do you do to tolerate pleasure? Do you saturate into this experience and bring a sense of wonder and joy inviting more of this? How do you use breath to widen yourself or inhibit yourself into fully sensing your aliveness.

What about if the energy influx brings up painful sensations such as overwhelm into your experience of life? What do you do then to experience pain? What do you do when anxiety arises for you? How do you manage the tiny tremors that ripple through your nervous system? Or even that nagging feeling of being out of sort? Does your tailbone tuck in or your hip pull back? Do you notice a pulling of your vagus nerve in your solar plexus or does your chest collapse? Or do you catch it more as a numbness or a blurring of your vision? It could feel like a fragmentation or a sense of a part of you just died.

For most people, the questions I have just asked are not obvious because of a lack of awareness directed to the experience of being a human being at this level of aliveness. Most people are not home in their bodies. I invite you to take this moment just to notice what is happening with you as you read these sentences and track your responses between pleasant and unpleasant. The best place to learn is yourself, your experience of aliveness in your body. "Dead" places are actually very rich in sensations and stories. Some questions to ask yourself, "Does this dead have a color? Is it heavy or cold?" When we start to bring this kind of curiosity then our "dead" parts come back to life to teach us about ourselves.   This is the beginning of a long love story of being a human being.

Practical Application for you:

1. How have you inherited the cycle of abuse in your life? How is it playing out in your life now?
2. Make a graph of your life. Make an x and y line. Write below the x line all the unpleasant events of your life. Write above the x line all the pleasant elated moments of your life. Make the x line with chronological age numbers in your life. Now connect the dots of events chronologically with a line. What do you see? What have you discovered just now?
3. In what way is the story of your identity continuing itself?
4. What are the ways you cherish yourself?
5. Look around the room with your eyes and head. Make sure the torso is also moving. Look above and below, to the sides, behind and in front. Allow your eyes to be soft. Say, "My name is _____, and I am _____ years old. I am sitting right now in the town of _____. I am safe." Breathe.

CHAPTER 19: BUDDHA AND THE SNAKE

"When you were young you said, "I am a student", next "I am a married man", and now "I am a sannyasi (renunciate)." It is useless to change the attribute when the subject remains intact. What you have to renounce is the "I". The crux of the problem is to tackle the possessor, as the things he possesses are ad-ons. So long as the true nature of individuality is not understood, the problem is not even faced." By Ramana Maharishi

Daw Setra spoke to me before I even met her in person. I felt called to go far away to Burma when I read a paragraph in a newspaper with an address just outside of Mandalay. I've had many interesting messages all my life that it seemed very much in tune to follow this strong calling back East.

She didn't speak English. I didn't speak Burmese. It was my first time entering Burma, called Myanmar. I arrived in Yangoon and felt at home immediately with the Burmese people. The evenings were dark except the kerosene lanterns on the street. Much of the city was gray except the gold pagodas that shone so brightly all around. I took an old bus that broke down four times to Mandalay. What was a ten hour trip lasted 21 hours. But who's counting time?

I only had an address and did not know where I was going. I simply showed it to the taxi driver and I found myself in the monastery. I was in my 30s and Daw Setra was in her 80s. She had been a nun for 52 years, and had not touched money for 40 years. She was a tough business woman when she was younger, and was known for her courage in standing up to notorious thieves back then. She became a nun under Ledi Sayadaw.

We loved each other from the first moment we laid eyes. When she laughed, her missing teeth stood out. She embraced me so tightly as though she wanted me to stay forever in Burma already on our first meeting. She asked me to ordain and remain there to practice. I took ten precepts and wore the brown robes. I was given a Burmese name of Daw Pinna Cari based on my birthday. It means Miss knowledge seeker/owner.

Daw Setra was so kind and generous with me. We meditated together in her hut, along with Tanzen and three other women with her. They would direct so much loving kindness at me and their meditation practice was impeccable. Their deep love for me kept me going there. It was very difficult at times. She was the first person who really got me in the kundalini purification phase and was able to guide me step by step.

The monastery when originally built was isolated, but as the years passed and Mandalay grew, the monastery has become nestled into the outskirts of Mandalay. It wasn't quiet like my simple home in Sausalito. The mosquitoes were smaller in Burma than in Thailand. Nonetheless, my body was like a pincushion for these mosquitoes. I was given a hut to live on my own. There were bars on the window, and the city blared outside the high walls just outside my hut. The practice was concentration on the breath and then mindfulness of the sensations (vedana).

I ate my two meals with the other Burmese. I was the only foreigner. We had breakfast at 5:30 in the morning and lunch at 10:30. There was no dinner. Everyone watched me eat. Burmese meals of fish and meat were difficult for me to eat, so I tended to go for the vegetables. Even then, I became ill. I said nothing, and ate what I could for the time I was there. This did not escape the attention of my hosts. Soon, Tanzen would go and buy vegetable dishes without spices for me to eat. I was so grateful.

Journal writings:
"This time of silence is like a purging. All these pictures, memories, all coming and going. The mind pulls all its tricks. I see all the belief systems and how they rule me and how much energy is placed their way. I see how psychology is so much a preoccupation of how to make more pleasing belief systems, more workable systems, but it doesn't really address the bubble like quality it has. I see all the stories I tell myself. At first, I kick and scream and find all the reasons why I should leave or why this isn't for me any more. These are just thought formations. From years of meditating, I knew that this was just the monkey mind.

Last night, the "mariachi" band played practically into the wee hours of the morning. They were playing just next to my hut.

The men and women serenaded each other karaoke style with loud microphones. I figured it was a special occasion – a wedding or a funeral. When I went to breakfast, the women were laughing at the situation. I was told that next time, I should just close my windows and meditate! This was to be a recurring event every single night. There was a silent reprieve, brief, then the dogs began to bark.

I was certain at that point that this place has many conditions for realizing dukkha (dissatisfaction) and anicca (impermanence). Again and again, I was shown how it was up to me to grab or not to grab the sense object and whether I was going to attach to the pleasant or unpleasant and be driven wild. Who is grabbing the noise, the sights, the odors, the taste? All my senses in the monastery were assaulted. The feeling of unpleasantness was definitely my meditation object. My body was sore. I just kept observing discomfort and my choices whether to grab it or not. I watched the play and no one was directing it. It was simply phenomena parading one after the other. This was anatta – non self. Who is watching? The mouth and throat were simply dry.

Daw Setra took a bowl of sugar next to her, showed it to me, and with expressive eyes and a beaming smile said, "dhamma" while pointing to it. She then took a newspaper and wrote in Burmese letters sugar on it, then took her big tongue and swiped it on the newspaper letters. She made a big face of grimace, "no dhamma." This is how she conveyed teachings to me. Otherwise, it would be through a very loose translation of English by Tanzen. Truly though, it was her kindness and care that were teaching me beyond any words could convey.

The goal was nibbana – enlightenment. I got tired of hearing of dukkha, anicca, anatta. I wanted to go home. I just wanted to practice easily and give myself lots of loving kindness. I've been so hard on myself for so many years. There was so much austerity."

A later journal entry 9/26/2002

"Vipasanna instructions were given this afternoon in the hall and U Min Swe was there to translate for me. We were all standing doing the body sweep when I began to feel sick. I trembled and perspired profusely. I got very hot as though a high fever had descended upon me. I kept on doing the practice. I then got this huge abdominal cramp so badly I had to bend over lying on the floor. I kept practicing the body sweep. I tried not to think or to stop. There were so many sensations. I was just so sick. I felt I was dying. U Min Swe kept reminding me nonstop of the practice "creation, destruction" over and over again "impermanence", "suffering". I was getting sicker. The thought of checking out came quickly. I kept practicing. He was fanning me and encouraging me, "don't hope, don't disappoint", "don't apprehend", "the pain will go away". I didn't even know he knew I was in so much pain. His encouragements helped me very much. I kept practicing, and bringing attention to the objects of meditation. He sent loving kindness and it alleviated the fear. I felt the entire hall of Burmese meditators sending metta (loving kindness) to me. I kept practicing. The fright went away. I could witness the creation and destruction on so many levels. The pain in my abdomen subsided after a while. There was a coolness and lightness. A huge weight had been taken away. There was an opening. I felt different. I don't know what exactly it all meant. I just knew that something lifted.

"Daw Setra told me that I will be a dhamma teacher. She said that I have parami (cultivated perfections of certain virtues) so just keep on meditating on the creation and destruction of everything. She doesn't understand English, but I can understand her dhamma teachings. They all tried so hard for me. I would meditate extra in the hut with them. I could see that they sincerely wanted me to come to a deeper realization and be free of ignorance and suffering. They send their loving kindness, presence and awareness my way. They've become like family to me. When I vomit, they come and remind me to see creation and destruction.

"Purification is happening. There is a lot of phlegm leaving my body. The phlegm had a bad smell. It smelled putrid, death like. There were times it was punctuated with the sweetest tasting saliva. It was delicious. There were lots of shaking and movements. Sometimes my tongue felt ice cold. Sometimes it was so relaxed and laid flat way down my mouth. I can really feel where the phlegm comes from in the body. My body knows how to make it go up. I can even help it by guiding it with the hand where there is difficulty. Sometimes, its gets stuck. It's very similar to when my father was dying and his body was expelling all the bodily fluids. Am I dying?

Daw Setra and Tanzen practiced intensively with me. 'Leave the akusala (bad deeds) here.' These wretchings I am told is like a sweeping/cleaning of my body. She said, "don't swallow it again. It must come up and out." I carry a spittle wherever I went in the monastery. Daw Setra says to ignore what others are thinking as I am wretching. This is dhamma. I sense distinctly when the right side of my channels was being worked on and cleared by the wretchings, and then the left. There were different yoga positions that spontaneously arose to press the phlegm out of certain spots. My awareness is so keen that I can follow the point of beginning, the traveling and getting spit out. Then the body sits up straight and opens by itself. The flow of energy unobstructed -lightness, effortless and naturalness resulted. Could the yoga asanas have developed out of the yogis going through this? And the reason they are done is precisely because of clearing the way?

She says she wants to give me what she knows – like an heir. She says that my dhamma is wide/big and I have parami (the culmination or perfection of certain virtues). My other teachers have said similar observations. She encouraged me to be a dhamma teacher and open a center.

The wretchings subsided, and now the sneezing has taken over. I can feel the head fluids moving about. I am peeing more, sweating more. There are lots of strong odors. There are lots of sensations. My bums are being attacked by pins and feel like a worm is crawling under the skin. I am more convinced that transformation is physical. At least my body doesn't ache as much as the earlier nights.

Last night, my face did movements spontaneously – very gentle and subtle ones. I can feel the pumping of phlegm and air from pockets within. Fluids are coming out of all the holes of my body. Muscles and other areas I didn't know are moving in isolation of others. It was fascinating to observe all the contortions. It is like there is a preparation of my physical structure to function more optimally. The movements, involuntary stacking of the spine, the twitches in the face allow for proper, deep, and unobstructive breathing. There is this intelligence that does its own thing. I feel the channel next to the right of the spine. Tension is releasing in areas I didn't know. In the brain too, there is a rearranging happening! I realized that having my left foot half lotus does help one side so I switched to the right lotus and sure enough, the left side began cleaning and so much phlegm came out. I am in awe at the intelligence of this organism.

I was dying. My face melted away. Who I am and who I thought I am melted away. There was such stillness, spaciousness and joy. There's a reason I came here and this is it.

"I feel the energy shoot up again. My whole body jumping in one complete circle. I feel the energy shooting up my spine to my head. I see the yoga postures arise to clear up areas that are blocked. Where there is a block, there is a stronger shake. It is almost as to shake off and clear the pathway. And sure enough, phlegm or air or fart is expelled from that part of the body. Daw Setra knows about these "sweeping" of the body. I've begun to guide the energy upwards instead of it going everywhere in shakes. There is a way the spine straightens, and the shoulders fan out as though a cobra's head. The head aligns a certain way. I can feel the big pathway and the many minor ones like nerves all over. When the energy goes there, and hits a block, the body feels open, light, like a fire burning and at the same time, a deep coolness. There is a disintegration of the face, the body...a melting.

I saw big fireflies while the crickets sang in the muggy evenings. The nuns chanted and I also heard the busyness of the lives of people outside the high wall. I presumed petty concerns as well as family joys. I like the cloistered life. There is something "cooling". It is like the heart is not constantly on fire. The simplicity in living allows for the interior to unfold.

Daw Setra parted these words to me. She wanted me to return and stay for good. Don't go away for too long. Come back and become a nun. " You need a teacher to guide you when the energies go all over. When the pot is boiling, don't take it away from the heat and cool down. If you know that water washes dirty hands and if you don't use it, don't blame the water. You don't need a degree from a university to know dhamma. Here, you've got a certificate from Mahaboudi with honors." And a last teaching to take with me, she said, "Your teacher is your body."

Daw Setra reminded me to practice very slowly in the US when I returned because I have no teacher here. She said that I am (yogi) like a patient, and she is a nurse. She can give me dhamma medicine as needed. She said, "Don't practice too hard in America because you will die soon otherwise." She narrated that her own teacher asked her to stop meditating for two years when the same things started happening to her. She said that I have very strong parami and I try very hard. She wanted me to return to Burma before she dies so she can hand me over the dhamma.

Before I left Yangoon, I had a personal interview with Sayadaw U Pandita. He said that I must know myself thoroughly before I could be of true help to anyone when he found out I did a lot of counseling and teaching work with children. I took to heart his admonition to be attentive to intentions. I miss Daw Setra's kindness and warmth. Panditarama seemed sterile compared to where I was staying in Mandalay. I still see Daw Setra laughing!!

Practical Application for you:

1. Sit quietly. Now start with your feet and sense what it feels like to touch the ground. What is the sensation of your legs. Is it prickly? Warm? Cold? Can you feel the fabric of the pants or skirt touching the skin? What does your belly feel like? Is it spacious? Tight/tense? Go to your heart. Does it feel present and alive? Does it feel numb/vacant? Continue your awareness of sensations into your head and face.
2. Now continue your sensing to the back side of your body. What do you sense? What is prominent? What is absent?
3. What virtues in your life are you cultivating? Which ones do you want to cultivate more of?
4. Put your right hand on your belly. Sense the belly rising and falling as the breath comes in and out.
5. Open your eyes and thank yourself for giving yourself this time to sense yourself.

CHAPTER 20: THE DESCENT AFTER THE ASCENT

True love and prayer are learned in the hour when love becomes impossible and the heart has turned to stone.
   -Thomas Merton

   I want to take this time to bow down to the universe and offer my gratitude for all that she has bestowed upon this humble seed. I venerate her for the space of which contains these fleeting clouds of forms. With open hands, I thank you.

   I was having dinner with a friend recently and he asked me as to how I managed during my spiritual emergency. It was really grace that kept me going in all those wild times. At first, I increased the volume of my compensatory ways of striving to hide the fact that I was falling apart. Somehow, I thought if I looked put together outside, then I must be together inside. Except it didn't really work. I went to graduate school and worked to support myself while my psyche spewed like Mt. Pinatubo and I could no longer contained the unconscious material unleashed into access. I was afraid and was too scared to let anybody know that I was terrified. And that I needed help - really needed help. I was drowning and pretending I wasn't drowning. At first I felt that if I admitted my lost of control to myself, I would be annihilated. I could do it for a year pretending to be superwoman. Then I couldn't anymore. I was lost. When I lost my ability to read the Roman alphabet for a while, I knew that I had to stop. Then I surrendered to that. It took years to just be with the new state. I didn't have to do anything with it because it was just about being. I still had to function in the world and be cognizant of its rules like money to provide shelter and food. I focused on the freedom, not on the limitation. I had different eyes to look from. There was a deep trust inside me. I felt grace.

   On a material level, I had money only to pay one month to the next. I found odd jobs that didn't require me to be fully present in all my capacities. At first I ran psycho-spiritual workshops as an assistant, but then my capacities for that diminished so I stuffed envelopes, glued match box toy cars into paper cardboards, watered plants in a nursery before it opened. I ate very simply and foraged for fruits in the forest. I interfaced with the world only as necessary. Almost all the energy I had was devoted to spacious activities that demanded nothing from me. Sometimes all I could do was be with my shadow, without moving. It was a liminal time. I performed many rituals to commemorate the internal cycles. I had a plain poster on my bedroom door to remind me to eat three times a day, take calming teas, walk, breathe and pray. I ate meat and root vegetables when I needed more grounding. I had cards I had cut and wrote sentences of affirmation of what I can do, like "I do laundry." My outer performance level was low. I had to remind myself of the love, care and the sacredness of what I was able to do and be. There were few friends that came to fulfill my person to person contact. I saw a loving therapist once a week. She kept reminding me to trust the wisdom within. I was in silence most of the time. I painted hundreds of paintings and I wrote poetry. I listened with my whole being. I stayed with the present moment. I walked. I prayed a lot.

I spent a lot of time listening to the waves of the ocean. The elemental world was very prominent then and resonated to the primal internal landscape I was going through. The elemental world also helped as my ally and teacher.

Non-ordinary states of consciousness continued. The turtle appeared, crawled and kissed my toes. She spoke these words and said, "Dear child, you are one with us. Do not forget our kinship. All that comes to you will also pass. Just remember, the waves of the ocean, they come and go. They will remind you and hold your hand in this time of transformation. You are in touch with raw, naked life. These are the seasons of the universe. It's all going so fast, but be still, child. You are taken care of."

In the middle of a warm autumn day, I sprawled on the beach, caressing the sand. When the worlds of my heart take me to different spheres, it is the natural world that keeps me here. She listens to my toils. She allows me to express deep what is my soul. With empty hands, intuitively, the sand guided my hands and Turtle appeared to remind of these bountiful gifts. The storms had come in succession and uprooted many sea kelp beds. Along the shore, these thick stems of the sea lay as beacons to this lost child.

The storms had unrooted me in my life. I desperately needed an anchor. "Turtle suggested, "Hold them in your hands for they will you to the earth. The tides will come, but you will be safe. Rest assure, you are my child." When the mother sea otters have to fetch food for their young, they tie their children down with the sea kelp in order that they will not be swept away. I didn't know this fact when I gathered the kelp. It was reassuring that nature was guiding me in these storms that were breaking the foundations of my inner house.

I laid down beside turtle and began to caress her back in a circular motion. I began to cry, and this voice uttered, "You are safe now. I will take care of you and not let you be forgotten. You are not alone. I shall not abandon you. I love you and I promise I'll be there with you." In that moment, my world shifted as I caressing the pregnant belly of my very own mother, and I was inside her. I mean this in both a metaphorical and literal sense. Tears, sobs racked my body as I just held the pregnant belly. I caressed the grains of sand as though they are my children and I am their child. I was caressing the grain of sand who is me at the same time. I was holding her and this very act was a simultaneous holding of myself. Myself included all.

The ocean called. "Come wash yourself in my waters. Let me bathe that which pains you away." Guided by her words, I performed this ritual unknown to me before hand. Songs and prayers come out of my lips. Gestures with my hands to meet the embrace that she was holding me tight. This call had not happened only once but many times. Once I woke up in the morning and I couldn't get up. My back had given out. The ocean called to "come and wash your pain away." A friend and I went to the sea and I was well afterwards. Another time, a vision appeared and I took a bus going to an unknown place. I got out in the middle of nowhere and began walking up the steps in the fog. The oak trees and eucalyptus forest began to carry my weight and the exhaustion disappeared. The chaparrals were smiling and sending me their nectar. The flowers bloomed- how could it be in the midst of autumn? I kept following the rabbit in the mist. A few paces to the right and there she appeared in sight. A huge boulder with white and green stones – a cleft in her middle especially to cradle her child.

I laid my tired body unto her lap, closed my lids and let her take care of my plight. The mist embraced me and the bird with the spotted tail came so close to my heart, "Yes, you have arrived." I fell asleep and when I next opened my eyes, the horizon vast and clear replaced the mist. I recognized that I was on a journey where boundaries did not exist.

I felt the cells and atoms of my body. I felt the cells and atoms of other living beings. An entry into my journal illustrated some of these experiences:

The images kept coming. Many snakes, cells, ribosomes – fluorescent in color. Some are bright yellow green, magenta; others are orange. Everywhere it is bright. Inside my head, in my brain, there is so much activity. My head wants to explode. It is like all these tiny snakes want to go out. My body is too small. Sometimes, I see the image of a volcano ready to explode. There are many dark men who are naked. They have white marks all over their bodies. I want to pull my hair out. I want to bang my head against the wall. Break it open so it can go out. I shake, shake, shake. So much energy…

Another entry reads:

I just placed a halt to everything. I can't afford to go on like this. I'm going to break down. The other night, she was so strong, and she wasn't alone. Not only one white cobra, but my head was full of many little ones. I was like Medusa. There was so much energy in my skull and they were all moving. I was being whipped on my spine as I did the child pose. So many different languages. So many stories. I feel wired and electrocuted .

Being so raw and sensitive, I heard and felt the cries of the world. I didn't stop at my skin. Sleeping or waking states didn't differ from each other. When in a bus, I could feel the people's suffering so deeply. When I laid in my bed, images of massacre after massacre of people and animals from different times and places came one after the other. The constellations of suffering opened its doors to me. Time away from the city helped me. Just sitting under a cedar pine or holding a boulder or dancing with ocean waves or just caressing the warm sand along the shore made huge difference between sanity and insanity. There is a rhythm and simplicity in nature that asks for nothing. Nature revealed to me that we were never apart. I feel like I'm in the heart of a caring mother. And I am also that mother as well as that child and the space that holds both mother and child.

I've also come to accept the wildness in nature. I am wild. For a long time, I tried to ignore my inner wildness and wilderness. It didn't fit in the properness young ladies were supposed to be. The wildness of the thunderstorms met my inner thunderstorms. The raging ocean waves dwarfed my rage. As Slow Buffalo had stated a thousand years ago, "Remember...the ones you are going to depend upon. Up in the heavens, the Mysterious One, that is your grandfather. In between the earth and the heavens, that is your father. This earth is your grandmother. The dirt is your grandmother. It is just like a sucking baby on a mother...Always remember, your grandmother is underneath your feet always. You are always on her, and your father is above."

It was the natural world that I sought solace in the times of deepest despair in my life. I always had a special connection with the elements of nature. It made sense that now it would also be true. For me nature is not a place, but a relationship. It is a play – the sun playing with the waves or the sun playing with the sand or a play of my toes with the waves. It is passion. It is communication. To be able to recognize, appreciate and venerate this interrelatedness of life is my way of living in a sacred manner. It is not an idea or an ideal. When I transgress this basic law, I hurt others and hurt myself. A Crow elder had said, "You know, I think if people stay somewhere long enough – even white people – the spirits will begin to speak to them. It's the power of the spirits coming up from the land. The spirits and the old powers aren't lost. They just need people to be around long enough and the spirits will begin to influence them."

I do believe this. If only we can open our outer and inner senses, then the spirits of the land will speak to us. We don't even realize that we are eating the very ground that is holding us. "Home" has become foreign to so many, yet the yearning remains. I remember Thich Nhat Hahn describing Americans as being uprooted – like hungry ghosts. There is a lack of respect and care exhibited in the way people live. I notice that everyone wants to be happy and whole. Most of us just don't know the way to do it. Breath is spirit and it is the way of connection. We yearn for connection and yet it is the very thing that gives us life.

Shakti is not only tumultuous. It is also soft and nurturing. The years that followed became the training ground for me to create a life that supported the transformation I was in. I erred on the side of moderation as my subtle body did best under these conditions. I entered a renovation and restoration phase that purified, fortified and repaired my subtle body system. It was to last for years. There were many levels of initiations and the corresponding unloading and shifting of my physio-psycho-spiritual body.

Below are helpful areas to explore if you or anyone you love is
undergoing a spiritual emergence.

Issues that can come up in the session

For the client:

1. Who am I? How come I feel everything?
2. Am I being punished? What did I do wrong?
3. I know I suffer from delusions, but sometimes I also feel God's
   presence. How do I tell which is which?
4. Who dies? What dies?
5. Why me?
6. Is it okay for me to be angry at God? Which God?
7. How do you make the sensitivity not be so painful?
8. Is this going to last all my life?
9. Who is to say that I am healthy or sick?
10. Is the counselor listening to me? Am I being judged? Can I
    trust her? Does she think I'm crazy too?

For the counselor:

1. View of counselor: Does she/he think of religion as a crutch/
   defense or something else?
2. Is he mad? Is this spiritual?
3. What spiritual resources can I offer him? From his spiritual
   tradition? From my spiritual tradition? Can I offer myself?
4. Is it okay for me to be angry with God?
5. How does one distinguish between a mystic and a madman?
6. How can I acknowledge the authenticity of his experience and
   offer a needed help with disturbed personality structure?
7. How can I validate him? Can I make him feel not alone in
   this? What ways to do this?
8. Can he trust me?
9. Do I know deeply that there is really no problem?

My own transformation necessitated visiting the raging fires to the cooling waters of life. Whatever shadow lurked, I dove into it to keep finding who I have become - now! I've found that understanding the stages of grief are essential. Part of my healing was to provide service as a grief facilitator supporting children dying with cancer and children in bereavement because someone they love is dying. I also offered Attitudinal Healing "Power to Choose" and resiliency curriculum to a local school following the same group of children for two years. Being alone and being connected were incredible partners in my recovery.

Below is a wheel of grief adapted from different sources (Dr. William Lamers)

Death can be death of a person or the death of our identity. Remember that we live in a society that pushes death aside, and as a consequence, most don't want to talk about death. It really comes out of a lack of understanding, a fear of the unknown and an ignorance. If you or anybody you know are grieving, find someone that is willing just to listen to you. There are free groups around that specifically support grieving. Take time to cry. Eat well and exercise regularly. Postpone major decisions for the time being. If needed, get professional help.

1. Shock: numbness, bluntness, not quite sure how i feel, denial, confusion.
2. Protest: anger, yearning, crying, irritability, self-criticism, guilt, bitterness, "if only", loss of appetite, nausea, disturbed sleep, bargaining, bitterness, feeling of emptiness or of having been cheated, desire to run away and become very busy, overwhelmed by intensity of feelings
3. Disorientation: depression, apathy, withdrawal, decreased socialization, loneliness, exile, loss of interest.
4. Re-organization: finding new meaning in life and death, acceptance of loss, change in patterns of behavior, new or renewed socialization.

Not everyone experiences grief the same way. Everyone has a different timetable. Understanding the various stages helps you cope and knowing that others also go through this process helps give you hope. And remember that it will take however long it will take.

PART IV: CHRONIC PAIN AS ENQUIRY INTO TRANSFORMATION

CHAPTER 21: LIMITATIONS ARE INVITATIONS TO GREATER FREEDOM

We all have some kind of limitation. One of my gifts is I see wholeness, not just brokenness. I can look at anything and see possibilities. I see this not just in my work, but when I see a fallow land, a chair, a canvas, food items and relationships.

I look at a plant and know it will grow bigger, bear fruits and flowers. I appreciate it in all its stages of wholeness. I don't hurry up the stages because it is not developmentally not there. I don't get impatient with the plant. When we are invested in the plant giving us something now, then we get frustrated with the plant. When this happens, it is a great opportunity to see how we are being confronted with our wanting and what all that means: fear, anxiety, desire…and the grief of not having it the way we want it. We are all plants and we are not exactly the same plant either.

Why do we turn our backs on the preciousness? Love is true a meeting and it is who we are and it is also rare and precious. Why do we squander it?

In my rush to get it settled, am I rushing this little fragile plant in growing? It (grief) is a little plant too. The break up is a little plant too. I remember the process of my breasts growing from small to big. Endings are beginnings too.

Here in the Tetons mountains, all the wildflowers are re-minding me that "right conditions" for growing are not about a judgmental right and wrong. Mountain wildflowers grow in the toughest conditions and so they are strong and also fragile. Like I.

Hold on to the beauty that you see. No one can take that away even if they disagree. It is your experience. Don't give it up. It is your specialness. Your preciousness. You are adorable, sexy and sweet! Believe in yourself!

MCS & CFS: A journey into who am I?

I was healthy again, in a new relationship, teaching school, and taking another advanced professional training. The journey into physical wellness came crashing when I began to experience

Multiple Chemical Sensitivities and chronic fatigue. It began with a root canal, tooth #30. Within 24 hours of a root canal and placing a $1600 crown, I began to have sensation in a root that was supposed to be dead. Next step was a double root canal on the same root because chemicals had leaked into my system from a crack. Then more swelling and an extraction under anesthesia followed– all within a few days. Lots of injections and my physical health crashed. The level of toxicity in my system from all these procedures started a condition of Multiple Chemical Sensitivity or Environmental Illness. I stopped working, even pumping gas for a few minutes made me very sick. Going inside a mattress or furniture store made me nauseated and my breathing tubes closed in. I became disoriented. Breathing in paint or scented laundry soap made me ill. My eyes and top of lips would twitch. I knew that my neurological system was not okay. (talk more of symptoms)

I was in a professional training program and my level of sensitivity was such that I couldn't bare being in the same room with so many people, or smelling the new carpet glues. My physical structure and psyche was overly stimulated and overloaded. I had to do the first part of the training using DVDs and doing them alone in my home. That was how much I wanted to do the training. Even when I was at home, I had to stop and paused many times because my system got overwhelmed so easily. I had to titrate the reorganization happening in my entire structure. No one taught me this. I was on a new frontier doing it alone. When I spoke with the trainer, she said she was training the 99 students out of a hundred. I was the 1 student that needed a different way of teaching, and she wasn't teaching to me. I had to figure out a way I could teach myself if I wanted to stay. I wanted it so badly. I was tenacious and finished the training.

I learnt a great deal about failure that year. I learnt a great deal on how to fall down, and pick myself up again and again. I learnt about fear and still learning about courage and strength. I could only do two segments of the training off site and I had to join the class, but still it was so hard. I couldn't bare to be touched just by anyone. I showed up for everything in the training, but I was in a special room in the back all by myself, and when I needed to do the practical component with another person, one of the assistants would come to me to practice. I don't know what kept me going. It certainly felt like I was touching a live wire again and again. Something inside myself knew I had to figure it out somehow. I had to wire myself neurologically in a different way!!

The traumas of my life were activated as my sympathetic system went into overdrive. The PTSD was full blown in its expression. I had a map to hold it, yet still, it was really difficult to be going through it. I shook more, I vomited more, I became very anxious. I couldn't walk very far without fearing that I could come back. My world became smaller.

I was living in a beautiful home with a garden and a hot tub (without chlorine). The walls were lined with precious artwork, golden Buddhist thangkas (paintings), and the home was spacious -a wonderful place to land and heal, so unlike the Mission home I had in San Francisco. I tried to keep counting my blessings, as my life fell apart yet again. I surrounded myself with beauty, in form, in sound, in taste, in textures.

I did an intensive treatment with Dr. Raam and Sophia in alchemical medicine. He was trained as a siddhi doctor and gave me 12 intensive treatments in a period of 90 days. I flew to Los Angeles. Every hole of my body was cleansed with different kinds of oils and herbs in order to balance the elements of air, fire, earth, ether, water. Each treatment lasted 4 hours. For eight months, I took many pills that were made of herbs, minerals and magic! I would place drops in my eyes, my nose, my ears, my vagina. Purification continued. I was devout to this routine. I watched very carefully what I ate, what color I wore, what scents were around me, etc. Everything that came into my senses was medicine. I began to get healthier and stronger. He encouraged me to hold myself as a little bird in the palm of my hand. I became even more judicious who was around me and how much time and energy I was giving away. I was so exhausted and my life force necessitated being discerning.

I had to look at my life patterns with renewed focus. What didn't serve me had to be released. I had to see clearly what got in the way, and these were long held identities of being loving and how the convoluted ways I knew how to receive and get love. I saw how tortuous some of these detours were. It was another level of saying "No". It was a journey of authenticity. It was a path of love. He said, "Why are you still carrying all this garbage around? Let it go." The garbage was all the trauma and beliefs around what happened in my life. I had to keep facing me in the mirror. It required courage, commitment, discipline and forbearance. I faced the swings of my life: all the waiting for love, waiting for my parents, waiting to be healthy, waiting for enlightenment, waiting for me. In this waiting game, the pattern was overextension and then collapse. These swings were tiresome. I was tired of this particular movement. I am creating a new neurological story and living confidently in it.

My partner did not support me with these treatments. He thought I had Multiple Sclerosis. My mother thought I had Parkinson. Some people thought I had seizure disorder of some kind. Both my mother and partner felt I should have gone to a neurologist and go the route of MRIs and Cat scans. I was determined to stay away from hospitals at that point since I had MCS, and I knew that my whole system was so reactive to chemicals. Years later, when I injured my lower back, had convulsions again and severe headaches that didn't go away, I went the medical route and had at least 7 MRIs and 3 cat scans and EEG and many other neurological tests. They wanted to see if I had a brain tumor. Thankfully, none of that came up, but the physical symptoms kept unfolding and I had to find other ways of finding peace and wellness through so much physical discomfort! I came to terms of healing even if there was no cure.

My then partner was seeing many children in his profession that had seizures, and other neurological illnesses. He was really scared, but did not know how to tell me. He was scared that he was going to be stuck with a woman who was sick. He was in the prime of his vitality. He wanted to get married and have a family. He wanted a woman that wasn't sick. The relationship was at stake. It was lonely to be going through this illness without much support from those closest to me. Friends loved me and I shared what I could of the despair and helplessness I felt as I lost control of my most basic functions. I was scared, as panic would seized me when I was alone in the house and I had to work at calming my nervous system down. My extrasensory experiences kept widening and opening. I began to see and hear more things of non-ordinary consciousness. I knew that this was part of the unfolding of the kundalini process. Of course, I had wished that it would have been easier, more graceful, yet the fire in my belly kept burning. The rushes of energy from the bottom of my spine kept churning and shooting up my crown. I continued to have spontaneous kriyas (movements) and breathing patterns that were unusual. Speaking in tongues continued as well as the visions. I had to keep surrendering to the illumination. My partner did not understand. I couldn't tell him what was happening completely as he was only in his familiar model of looking at what was going on. I look back at it now, and I can see he was really scared. He was at his edge of knowledge, and I was experiencing a life that was outside of those boundaries. I continued to see Claire, my therapist, for support.

My brother drove me sometimes from Orange County to LA to see Dr. Raam, and he tried to understand, though I don't think he really did. His love for me kept me connected. Chronic illnesses really reveal what a relationship can hold or not. It wasn't long after until my partner and I were separated. I was determined to try Dr. Raam and I am so glad I did. It took a leap of faith. I borrowed money from my credit card so I could pay for these treatments.

I wrote extensively in my journals. They became my solace. At least I could express myself in them. At this point, I couldn't paint with acrylics or do ceramics as the paint fumes made me sick. I did a few watercolors, yet the feeling life inside myself was of the nature of deep primal and instinctual intensity. The brushes felt too refined for my sense of urgency of expressing myself. I wrote. Voraciously. I was my own laboratory.

I wrote down my strengths and weaknesses as honestly as I could. I saw patterns of wanting an authority outside of myself to tell me what was best for me. The illnesses taught me to find my inner teachers. I had to accept that I too mattered and am precious. My needs also mattered when there is a negotiation between two individuals. I saw how I repeatedly gave my power away bargaining for love and approval. It was painful to see all these self-imposed limitations. I had to face my own self-hatred. These same portals opened me to trusting my own authority. I began to touch essence in different ways, not just the blocks.

Who's Got your Back?

I had gotten my life back from the MCS. I had paid all my medical bills. I was the assistant director at a local adult school overseeing programs and classes designed for adults with disabilities. On the weekend, I worked one on one with an adult with disabilities. Little did I know that I would end up living with a disability myself. I was used to being in charge then all of a sudden I wasn't. Again. Just when I thought that life was getting easier, flowing gently after the train of crises that spanned years, events halted my activities and dreams as my back unexpectedly gave out on me.

It is in the season of persimmons that I finally succumbed to the urge to put pen to paper and write my story. It was nine months previous that my back first grabbed and I had spent the whole year healing. That's enough time to have a baby!

I was excited, happy to start my spring vegetable garden. My neighbor Don had a piece of land lain fallow and I overlooked into it from my balcony. I had envisioned lots of greens and colorful flowers. We agreed for me to start a garden and we were picking up soil amendments and other garden implements. He did all the lifting, except for a pound light trellis. I twisted slightly, lifted a few inches and ....my back grabbed. I didn't know what hit me. Pearls of clammy sweat dripping down my forehead, almost fainting spells, I half laid on the soil amendments on the truck bed, except every centimeter of movement pained like hell. After an hour of this in a Home Depot parking lot, the only reason I wouldn't agree to an ambulance being called was Don saying, "They'll still have to move you." Like a crab, I crawled sideways towards the left bracing the car (that was the only direction I could move with pain) and Don carefully and slowly drove me home, avoiding bumps, potholes. As he approached my driveway, I saw the long flight of stairs. I lived on the second floor. "God help me climb those stairs", I muttered under my breath.

Back then, little did I know that the injury would take me into an odyssey. I thought I'd spend a day or two in bed. My negotiations with time went to a couple weeks, to months and the prospect of years.

Needless to say, I lost my jobs as I spent my time healing myself. I spent thousands of dollars on all kinds of healing modalities: allopathic doctors, acupunture, Feldenkrais, cranial-sacral work, siddhi medicine, medical intuitive, homeopathic, osteopathic, psychotherapy, diamond logos work, meditation, shamanic healing, Russian neurotransmitters, etc.

I did it - perfectionism - even and especially on my own personal healing. I was starting a business to help people with pain. Such irony. I've tried so hard to heal. Somehow in my circuits there was still the belief that I must have done something wrong to be ill, therefore must do something right to be well, and if I am not well, then I'm not doing enough. Equals I'm not good enough. With renewed focus, I began another level of the dismantling process.

My siddhi doctor said that I can't maintain my health and that's why I am still in pain. The thoughts in my mind inflame me, and thus the pain. Pain is inflammation and for it to go away, you take away the inflammation. My mind was in flames so I tried to look out for flames and put them down before they transform into body pain. Well, I'm still in pain. He says, this is the human condition. Buddha had to go through this himself. He gave me 48 hours to look at my mind and see its causes and conditions. I was so pissed, and whether he meant it or not, I took it that it was my fault that I was in pain. I am causing pain to myself. Am I a masochist? Why would I want to do that? Is my identity so closely related to suffering that I have to perpetuate it? If not externally, then generate it internally.

Buddha's first noble truth is there is suffering. Did I not understand this too well and that's why I spent the decade of my twenties sitting in monasteries and ashrams in Asia that I may find the second noble truth: there is an end to suffering? Craving to be born is what links the two together. That's why we watch the mind and when seeing occurs, birth is death.

The bags of frozen corn, half-compressed and sticky, laid on my aching back and butt. I've learned that ice is great for calming tormenting nerves. If left to their own, the prickly nervy sensations would throb down my left leg until I'd be scratching walls. These bags of corn have been my best friend that year. I've done all my somersaults, exhausted my healing agendas and I've come to this: I've poured the honey and now it's up to the honey to take its time in dripping me all over. I used to fan the honey or put a heater so it will melt faster. Does healing mean the pain will go away? I hoped.

I had to accept that healing and the physical pain going away were two different things. I didn't know when the pain will go. I accepted that I had no control over it. I did have a choice to mentally suffer or not about it. I chose to look at how I can lead a happier life regardless of what conditions were in my life.

Garden of Delight

lost in the overgrown woods of my heart
forced to stop
surrendering to the dew bathing my hair
listening to the leaves succumbing to the earth
finding beauty even, especially in their last flight

with my back stopped
to prowl in the night
to dance wildly in ecstasy
to climb mountains eternal
to inch across the block
to crawl to relieve my needs

in my garden
tending the young saplings
watching the shadows marking time

kissing evaporating dreams
hopes dragging butterfly's wings

the darkness of the night
when pain abounds
my solace is a spiral tunnel
a fractal this kernel can hide

as identities stripped one by one
who am I
when only the stars illuminate the evening

Who am I
when only the child screams
breaking door, windows
angry at the world
ashamed, scared of my needs
opening Pandora's box
breaking camel's back

whales of the universe
please sing me your song
in my garden
I dig up the seeds of tenderness
hidden long ago
only to find husks of rage
begging for forgiveness

if I spoke as softly as the breeze
I wonder if my longing will tiptoe
out of its cave

if I caress its snarling cheeks
if I let my tears water the seed
if sunshine is to touch my heart
will tenderness remember
it can sprout?

under the sage covers and golden canopy
I learn to utter
Please help
I am safe

Journal entry:
"How can I still have so much gratitude and optimism when inside I want to die? This life has been long and filled with hard trials, and I am tired, ready to surrender my will. Have I failed swimming in a dry lake, make believing even this has run dry? I've always looked at the bright side and I also want to give up now. To dive in the ocean of my inner world and not come up. To swim like the seaweed descending to my pearl, having light illuminate my journey. Which part of me wants to die?

"Today I experienced space while I was completely in my body! It's not just a spacious mind, but the reality is space and materiality is in space and space holds materiality. There was a seeing and experiencing the body cellularly – space has dimensions, tangibility and my experience is that the objects were coming to me, and I not to them. That it was the natural order of life. And believe it or not, my doorway was through my feeling of wanting to die!

"My arms started to get blotches of red and white and went very cold, like a corpse. It was strange for me to look at my arms as though they belong to someone else. I grounded lovingly in the white and red essences. I felt this pillar of pain in the middle of my torso. I kept letting the white permeate everywhere that wasn't this hole – surrounding it, keeping my awareness wide. I started to have different movements, and the contractions changed. I felt like a baby was being born, but coming out the other way – through my mouth! I felt like an amphibian coming out of my skin.

"My body structures are being redefined essentially. I see the grids longitudinally in and around me. I am running these essences through my muscles rather than my central nervous system. The effects are profound: more integrative, gentler, slower. It's just what I need right now."

Do you know how it is to live with pain? It's taken me a year to drive 20 minutes, walk one mile meanderingly without pain. I didn't know if the pain would ever go away. That year, I had to train myself differently in how to do the daily activities of living. It was like being an elderly in a thirty some body.

I've come a long ways. In the beginning, I crawled to the bathroom, crawled to the kitchen. It was hard to prepare food. Opening jars and slicing vegetables were very painful. I've asked friends to shop, to do my laundry, to drive me to all the appointments, asking my community if anyone would give me free sessions, assist me in dressing. I felt like a child. There was a time my eight-year-old niece came to visit and as we prepared to go to the ice cream store, she bent over and tied my shoe laces for me. It wasn't too long ago that I remembered teaching her how to tie her shoe laces!

Asking for help was very difficult for me. I was so used to doing everything myself. Wasn't I supposed to be superwoman? I felt that by asking help, I'm even more vulnerable. Will people say no? Will I think myself less than? I felt vulnerable and tender while the world seemed harsh and dense right now. I just wanted to hide under the soft covers. Then there is the notion that I didn't want to overload anyone. If I overloaded another, then I wouldn't be liked and the only the social contacts I had would also vanished. This pattern of belief was a double bind for anyone, but especially for me because I really needed people's help. I once was told by Bonga, "What would it take for you to stop? A broken back?" This dynamic and identity reorganization was part of my spiritual emergence. My sense of self was so tied in to being hyper independent. My "preciousness" was my wound, and because it was so tied in with my survival mechanism from the get go, life had to unlock my knuckles one by one as I wrestled with letting go of what I thought were some of my most valuable possessions. I am afraid that when grace appears, it doesn't always look so graceful. I was a hard nut to crack in some ways, and it took hard lessons for me to get it, repeatedly!

How do I receive the different ways friends give? They don't always look like how I want or think help looks like, yet they are offering help the way they can. How do I integrate the help of pushing beyond to give/be present and then pulling back afterwards? I'm seeing both the generosity and the holding back. In what ways do I do these? How do I not take it personally when I continue to work through my fear of abandonment? I am lonely, alone, wish just to be embraced, know that another body is near and I'm not doing this by myself.

There was a frustrating balancing beam between putting a facade of everything is okay and then the gritting teeth of when I just wanted to break all the windows! I felt somehow that asking someone to take the time out of their busy schedule to bring my groceries and then vomiting all the rage of being confined by a back injury and my whole world turning upside down and inside out would be too much. That I would be too much. And I wouldn't be loved. Worse than the rage would be my tears of helplessness that I kept at bay. If I wasn't producing, giving, providing, pretending to be strong, then who am I? Who would want me? If I cried, would I stop crying? Remember that I cried so much when I grieved for Bonga. I was afraid the grief wouldn't end and I would fall apart - again.

When I could finally stand up, I was so proud of my achievement. It meant I could use the stove and make hot chocolate. One day as soon as I poured the hot water into the glass, a crack formed and all I could do was watch the glass open into two while the chocolate spilled unto the floor. I knew I didn't have the speed, agility nor strength at that moment to make any kind of difference. I watched, waited and prayed that it didn't spill too far so the clean up will be easier. Kind of like life.

When I was injured earlier that year 2007, I made an oath to walk the eight hundred kilometer pilgrimage to Santiago de Compostela in Spain when I felt healthy again. Even though the best I could do was take a few steps in my apartment, I felt that I've begun that pilgrimage and there are so many thorns on the route. It is a physical challenge. An emotional one. A financial decline. A spiritual bankruptcy. My illness became a solitary confinement, and I had to face deep beliefs around experiencing life!

The year before this time, I was planning on buying a piece of land and building my home on it. My state disability ended and I had applied for federal disability. Eighty percent of applicants are denied and must appeal. The interview was rigorous, the questions aimed at diminishing one. My carapace was thin. After a two and a half hour interview, I could barely cross the street. It was my first conscious thought of my fear of being crippled. I came home and cried. I couldn't move the next day. I decided that I wasn't going to go through with that type of powerlessness.

I was losing who I thought I was. I was being forced to let go of who I wasn't. Who am I when I can't perform the way I think I can? What are the possibilities and abilities I've come to discover with all these limitations? Can I have tolerance wide as the sea for my self? For all what I perceive to be my failings? For my fear of failure? I was always the best, the number one, the 100 percent, the superstar and now...it takes so much to keep my gaze straight. Have I been beaten? The proud insulted, humiliated. I am angry, sad, lost, desperate, seeking solace. I felt exposed and vulnerable. I've worked so hard to be seen, but never expected that God would undress me to my naked bones!

I listened to a tape of Tulku Urgyen Rinpoche (a well respected Tibetan Buddhist teacher) a few days after the injury. I am grateful for his teachings on impermanence, this precious human rebirth, blessings. I'm seeing that life goes on without me and that my responsibilities don't really need attending to immediately. I saw that my roles were dispensable. That I am more than my roles. The key is: who am I? I've made a choice to take these days, this year as a chance to reconnect me to myself. There are so many stories I tell - even to explain away why I've hurt my back. I used to believe that there are reasons for everything that happened. Now, I see that it's not about seeking for reasons, but rather finding meaning. Somehow, reasons sound almost fixed, handed down, like a blind person grasping for some object to hold, but meaning is created, allowed to be born. It takes time.

I was just stopping. It felt right to stop. This was extremely hard to understand for me. I used to think I was a very quick student. Now, I realize it takes time to learn really important lessons well. For months, all I could do was walk down my tiny Sycamore street. I would extend my walk house by house. You see, I rehabilitated myself with the way Moshe Feldenkrais did when he injured himself. He would increase the weight he lifted only by a 10 penny weight increase each time. This way the nervous system doesn't feel threatened and retreats and contracts into trauma to protect itself (its job). This difference, although seemingly insignificant, actually amplified the brain's learning tremendously, and made successful rehabilitation. Anyways, I would walk down this street and a big part of the first months was that I would push myself to make it to the big red stop sign at the end. Even though I couldn't do much, I made that stop sign my goal no matter what, gritting teeth, pouring sweat, excruciating spasms. Until one day, I got it. The stop sign wasn't a goal for me to physically reach in my walk, but to actually read and understand, "STOP!" I had to learn to stop before I had pain. I had to stop and listen to what the present moment was asking of me, not how I want it to be (future) or how I did it this way yesterday (past). My operating systems of my early life were now up for upgrading. It was taking samsara and mixing it with compassion. Hurray!!

I'm honing in with my coccyx. Help me find home. Somehow I'm lost, seduced by something lesser than what I have come here for. I sit here in my darkened living space, the rain a comforting pitter patter. This reminds me of the endless days meditating in the tropics. Sitting helping keep the walls erect. Was it the external wall of my abode or was it the internal walls of rigidity, of ideas, of beliefs, of identities? I used to sit lotus style for hours at a time, unmoving. Now, I can barely sit for 20 minutes without discomfort. Do I hear my voice judging me? You're doomed! Yuck to all these darknesses that feed my fear, that keep me tucked under a thumb unable to breathe, to move, to be me. Away with all of you! These became great opportunities to reflect: How do I sabotage myself from feeling peace? Hatred took my hands and led me to those places I could not bear to tolerate feeling. With practice and time, I began to rest in the emptiness of shame. Rather than merely identifying with the ego, the shift in awareness brought deep curiosity to simply what it is to be a human being. Within the confines of withholding, hatred and love became one. The path of directly familiarizing myself with my own hatred brought me to my own power and peace.

What beliefs did I protect under this guise of will and strength? The world is not safe. People are not safe. Not trustworthy. Only help because they want something back. To be weak, vulnerable is to be prey, to be eaten alive. Do I really believe these to be true? No. There is basic kindness, basic goodness. I have been helped so many times in my life, here, there in all my travels around the world, the monasteries accepting me and giving me soap and toothbrush. The nomads who sheltered me when I was lost in the Himalayas. The individuals who handed me as a precious doll from one to the other that I may make it safely to my destination in the then communist Poland. The strangers who've wiped away my tears when I've fallen into pieces and all I could do was be a child with phlegm dripping down my nose. All the pilgrims offering food to us along the Dhamma Yetra (Pilgrimage for Truth) in Cambodia. Friends and neighbors who continually come to offer support. No. The world has elements of safety and also elements of non safety. I touched these parts of myself that are hard like steel, uncompassionate, sadistic, pointing a finger at me, "you deserve all this pain." NO. I do not deserve pain. I have a right to a life with joy and peace and contentment. I do not need to ruminate suffering again and again. The world is benevolent. I live in beauty and love. I am safe.

When did this realization first dawn on me in this life? It was when my ninety-year-old grandmother died when I was 18. I realized that I could die too right then and I have not lived my life as of yet. I bought a plane ticket and backpacked across Europe for 10 weeks. I barely had money, but my soul yearned to be free. An unplanned journey was the closest I knew to freedom at the time. I was always a searcher, both religious and spiritual in nature. As a child, I went to church alone, prayed to God as my friend, spoke to the plants in the garden. As a teenager, I took long walks in the desert, taking in the changing colors of rocks and my life. I knew that I had to go then. It didn't matter that it was Europe. I just had to go. It had to be then because tomorrow I may not want to anymore. I didn't want my dreams to depart without me.

I traveled extensively around the world. I created adventures most people only dreamt of. The external voyage soon lost its appeal. They became pictures in my mind that lacked the substance I was seeking in my heart. I needed another kind of travel. An internal journey where the Everest and the Death Valleys were those of my internal landscape. I saw through the collecting of experiences, exotic or not, as an extension of keeping my image. There was truth that I was collecting good party tales that made people drool. But what did they have to do with me?

I dreamt and counted the clouds and birds in the sky. I started dancing again. At the beginning, I ended up spending a lot of time on the floor, lying down or sitting against the wall, making tiny movements that express what the music evokes in me. I didn't dance like I used to, but nobody dances the same twice ever either. The first time I went, I met a woman who came for the first time in 17 years. She had fibromyalgia amongst other things. Her car is specially built so her gas and brake pedals are hand operated. We spoke and congratulated each other by dancing. You see, I haven't given up on life. That's why I walked that hill so I could see the river otter feeding and the hawk on the branch over the ducks. I want to be positive and visualize a positive well being. I don't want to focus on the pain, but on my wellness. I am given a gift now. I am taking the opportunity to know its preciousness.

I definitely felt some humiliation at times, yet I knew it was not personal at all. This was not a time to add self pity. I was grateful for whatever came my way. It was continual teachings on appearance-emptiness. What creates suffering is how I'm looking at it, not so much the object. I chose to not dwell on one channel. Since it is all movies, I switched channels.

The roles are reversed. I've spent so many times being on the other side. The giver. I've been volunteering since I was a child. My mother believes in generosity very strongly, so I have quite a strong ethics in this regard. As a little girl, I was called Princess of charity, as a pre-teen, I was a candy striper, as a teen walked for march of dimes, volunteered as a teacher in the slums of Nairobi as a college student, worked with Mother Teresa when I was 21, worked as a grief counselor for children in bereavement, and many others. I'm making the point that I've taken comfort in being in the role of "giver", and consequently, receiving has been difficult as I haven't had much practice at it (at least consciously). Funny, I thought it was enough to see that giving is receiving.

Years ago, when I was in a monastery in Thailand, I taught meditation retreats to about 100 participants every month. There was one particular retreat, whereby so many students were getting Dengue fever and I took care of them too in addition to all my responsibilities. To make a long story short, I was exhausted at the end of 10 days. I had my laundry in my arms ready to wash them by hand when one of the people there asked me to give it to her. I had the most difficult resistance to this request. She said, "Giving is a virtue. Receiving is a harder one." I know this to be true for me.

The day has been filled with rain. The berry tree across my living room window is filled with finches, hungry for its ripe blue fruits. As I meditated earlier today, I realized that part of the anxiety I've been feeling these days remind me of the last time I spent two weeks away from a lover. I left and never returned. How is it that in the midst of my inadequacies, I am finding my truest strength and power. I feel strong, vital, full of possibilities. I ask myself how would I like to live my life now with all these challenges and changes? I am on a crossroads in my life. Frankly, I do not know what tomorrow holds. There's a big part of me who just wants to pack my suitcases and be the adventurer I am. To connect to the excitement of safaris, taking dhows, sleeping on beaches and train stations, doing archeological surveys, etc. Except this time, I can barely lift a few pounds without pain in my back. How do I be an adventurer without moving physically? How do I explore and stay with the different terrains and cultures that pervade my thoughts and feelings? How do I explore the unknown with all the fear I've learn of the known?

For now and the foreseeable future, I stay close to my sanctuary, whose walls I've painted with dye, whose every knob I've changed with something hand-crafted. Yes, this very abode that flooded the second night I moved in. I know it is my baptismal place. It is where I made love and opened my womanhood. It is where the gardenia blossomed and exuded its fragrance, reminding me that I am not just a pretty, plastic flower. It is where I have countless dates with myself enquiring into the nature of when did I forget who I am. When did I leave that behind and made a decision about the nature of the world? That same sigh that drove me into the solitude of meditation and now calls me to lay my fears and remember who I am.

Today, I don't have back pain. It took a while to rehabilitate but I am now ready (in 2015) to walk the 500 miles Camino across Spain to Santiago. Back then in 2007, three months after injury, these were my concerns:

What are the things I'm frustrated about?
1. Not being able to walk too far.
2. Not being able to dance.
3. Not being able to have sex.
4. Not being able to bend without pain.
5. Not being able to lift a little thing without dizziness.
6. Not being able to carry my groceries.
7. Having to stop myself from enacting many thoughts from intention to action.
8. Not being able to stand long enough to do a really complex meal for friends.
9. That I got tired so easily.
10. The idea that I shouldn't feel frustrated.

What are the things I am loving doing?
1. Watching the dragonflies, deer, egrets, cats, birds by my window.
2. Enjoying the flowers and vegetables in the garden.
3. Walking my half block.
4. Being artistic – painting, imagining, weaving
5. Being able to order online - it gives me a sense of control.
6. Cooking for myself.

7. Giving my belly a massage.
8. Foot massages.
9. Having time.
10. Connecting with friends.
11. Spending time alone.

4/18/07

I am ashamed of my needs. I am ashamed of needing. I am ashamed of being helpless. I am ashamed and scared to be needy. There is a resonance of waiting, abandonment, uncertainty and the lack of support in my lower back. Ouch!

I made friends with shame. Shame's foundation is hiding. It persists when we continue to hide. In the exposure and acceptance of shame, I was able to see life as a description rather than than a conscription. I began to invoke a different response pattern. Compassion blossomed.

A dream on March 20, 2007

I was being tested for something. My pulse went up from 150 to 190 in just a few minutes and I had to ask the tester to stop. I was upset. Why did I have to ask her first. It's her job to keep me safe. I realized that it was a myth. It was my job to keep me safe!!

Practical Application for you:
Helpful Tips for back injury:

1. Get a good pair of running shoes with insole especially made for your body. It really made a huge difference for me that year of recovery.
2. Imagine all the actions you want to do and still can't physically. If you want to again climb mountains, imagine it. Imagine dancing. Imagining movement is very powerful as the brain doesn't know the difference. It starts to built neural connections that will help you make the transition to moving physically.
3. Sleep is essential as it is the time the body really recuperates. If you are in pain, make sure you look into herbs/teas that keep your system calm before going to bed. There are electronic de-

vices on the market that help balance brain waves to help with this. Invest in it if sleep is an issue for you.

4. Get into a Feldenkrais or Anat Baniel Method class to learn new ways of moving that will support you.

5. Keep going to activities you love, except modify it to your physical needs. If you can't sit for long periods of time but love to go to a play, get a seat all the way in the back where you can sit and stand as often as you like.

6. Break down activities into segments. When I wanted to drive to San Francisco, I made a plan to drive and make three stops along the way so I can walk in between for short periods of time. This plan gave me the confidence and joy that I could do it with as little pain as possible. This was part of my rehabilitation.

7. Learn how to say "yes and can we modify it this way" with family and friends. Remember that it is not about the activity, but the connection and spending time together. Don't be afraid to ask for what you need. Most people out of pain do not know how much certain activities take for you. Explain and include them. You'd be surprised at all the creative options that may arise. This is how intimacy develops as well.

8. Alternate high impact activities with low impact activities. Be realistic what those are for you. Remember they continue to change as your health shifts daily.

9. Make sure you are engaged in pleasurable activities too. Joy is an important part of recovery and healing. Sometimes chronic pain and depression loops unto each other.

10. Take walks. Two or three shorter walks that are manageable are better than one really long one where you are in pain.

11. Look into taking a diet low in anti-inflammatory food. Wheat and sugar are inflammatory.

CHAPTER 22: MIGRAINES - THE HEART ATTACK OF THE SOUL

Just as I was recovering the use of my back to a greater extent of health and decreased pain level, another health challenge knocked on my door. Here was another opportunity for transformation at a deeper level. Of course, it had occurred to me that it was fascinating that I was having both ends of the spine flare up in my system. Could this be kundalini related?

The migraines and light sensitivity that lasted for eight months everyday were true teachers of love for me. In a way, it was my good fortune. This neurological illness allowed me to understand deeper truths. Paradoxically, the migraines healed me. In the darkness of those eight months, I asked these questions, "Who's gonna be my friend in the dark? What does a friend look like in the dark?" As I bowed down to the Mystery, I found darkness to be my friend. I clung to divine guidance in the midst of all the changes. I kept dropping to that place where pure love resides for it is love that withstands the tests. It was a repeated choice to keep turning to the knowledge of love in my life.

By keeping a multi-modal headache diary, I was forced to look at my unhealthy patterns of giving myself away at a minute level. The question became: Am I choosing a headache by doing this or by being with this person? With the courage to ask it so bluntly, I began to see clearly that I was choosing a headache. I saw that attempting to take care of other people's disappointments was impossible. I can care for another, but they are responsible for their feelings. I saw my tendencies to put myself through boot camp and marathons and how I lacked the lubrication of kindness to my self at those moments.

"I had just finished a week of retreat on the bardos (intermediate states between two lives). The next day I was in the emergency room. The left side of my body was numb, like novocaine. My left arm and left leg felt as though they were in buckets of ice cold water or dry ice. The weight was heavier on my left side. I was alone and I did not know if it was a stroke I was feeling. How was I going to leave that room in what condition? I didn't know if I would die right then. I took deep breaths and let the air out through my mouth repeatedly. Tears silently glided down my cheeks. I was scared. I searched for the face of God. I wanted a personal God. My Buddhist practice did not provide me with one. Somehow at that moment reminding myself of clear light was not enough. I called Ammaji, and she came, kissing the left side of my face, stroking/caressing the left side of my body. I remember the instructions from the bardo teachings, "You can't get hurt. You're dead already." Repeating this to myself over and over again brought deep peace and acceptance.

I thought: was I ready to die? No, not in the way I thought I would. I saw how unprepared I was and how preoccupied I was with conditions. Who did I want to be there with me, to help support my transition to the next phase? And would they come? Would they drop everything and come just like that, to help usher me? And if it was a stroke, would someone be there patiently calling me their love, knowing that it would be my anchor between the worlds? I thought of who was on my emergency contact. I wasn't sure. I hoped it wasn't my mother as it would kill her to hear that something had happened to me right then. I laid down on the bed bringing awareness to different parts of my body – calling them not to sleep or to go deep into forgetting. Somehow, there was no room to be afraid because I had to remind myself all that. I felt the loneliness. I thought of my sangha (community) and wondered was it in name only? I thought of my family and their love and wondered would I want their panic, fear, anger, confusion alongside mine at this time? I took deep breaths to calm myself and remind myself to be in the present.

I was wheeled into the CAT scan room for my head scan after they've pasted all the medical gadgets on my body just in case I have a stroke/heart attack so it will all be ready for medication. I shook vehemently and was asked if I was okay. Was I scared? I answered truthfully, "I don't know." I called Ammaji to hold me gently but tightly so I knew that I wasn't alone. The doctors and nurses kept asking me to lift my arms, my legs, to smile to see what was changing. I hear the noises of other patients, bells and intercoms and flashing lights. I remind myself of the bardo instructions not to be distracted. Stay in clear light awareness.

Thankfully I didn't have a stroke. I had hemiplegic migraine – a migraine with stroke like symptoms. That was the medical diagnosis.

The headaches came full force and stayed for eight months. That first night I was very scared and Peggy held me. "You are perfect as you are." She repeats. "You don't have to do anything. You are God." And I asked, "even my fear." Yes, your fear is God. "Even my anger." Yes, anger is God. "You don't have to be good." You don't have to try because you are God. I felt safe. The next day, light blinded me. I covered all my windows with extra blankets. I couldn't stand light, even the cell phone or stove digital light. I got irritable, anxious. I shook, got dizzy, felt this hang over. There was a pressure pressing my head from the outside and at the same time a pressure from inside pressing out. Groggy, stomachache, my thinking also dramatically slowed down. I had a hard time answering questions, following directions, being asked to reply to where is what? Conversations that included time and space felt like snags in the sweater of my consciousness. I felt confused by these gaps and changes. I've always relied on my quick thinking and ability to articulate and navigate my world. Even when my body ached, I knew I could rely on the prowess of my mind. It terrified me that I was thinking slowly and had to ask for the first time in my life another person to say it again slowly.

I thought when the back injury happened, it couldn't possibly be worse, and here I was realizing, of course, it could be worse. I realized that I really don't know what dying means - whether it's the final dissolution of the body or the many deaths we have throughout life. I peeked at my arrogance that had masqueraded, hiding a naiveness fed by ignorance and insecurity. Here I was reminding myself to be kinder and saddened by how much I pushed myself, the judgment and shame and skyscraper high expectations of myself. I asked the questions: what am I committed to? What am I praying for? I had to let go of assuming that I have to think through this. In the midst of feeling abandoned, I found I am never ever abandoned.

Dear Me,

247

You are loved no matter what. Mommy said that tonight. I too am saying it to you. Clare says God never leaves you, even when you think you've been abandoned. You are always loved!

Is death like birth? Birth into something new. I want to go home before I die. Catharsis after all means clearing out the dead. Then I am letting the dead out. I am blessing the weed seeds and then throwing them out. I want to die while alive.

As I get older, preparing to be lighter, what will I take with me as I depart from this world? One reason I saw why I am here in this body is to experience my body. I definitely have experienced pain. If pain and pleasure reside in the same coin, I must find the key or the precise turn that I get the experience of pleasure proportionately. Universe, guardians, angels, gods and goddesses – help me please!"

Journal entry:
"I got a massage last night. It was the first time I had a non-medical, non-therapeutic bodywork. I realized that my relationship to my body is being in pain. No wonder I don't want to inhabit it or the earth. The woman was large, loving, motherly. She gave and I received. I said what I wanted, what I didn't like, deeper, softer, here, there and I did not feel guilty, ashamed, apologetic or looking at hurting her feelings or not. I wasn't taking care of her! I felt so much pleasure in my body. To feel my body without pain or fear of pain! To feel my body not as an arena of self-discovery, growth, exploration, insight, psychological, spiritual, medical. It was touch that was not PTSD. I told the masseuse, "Touch me this way that touch will call my spirit back to my body. I realized that I have been in pain for so long that I forgot pleasure. That I can feel good, that it's ok to want to feel good, to long and get it. Now I know it.

It was different than a lover touching me. I didn't have to reciprocate or to show pleasure or have expectations. That pleasure wasn't just orgasm. I felt a coming home to myself."

I was coming home to love as a body, in the body. The sensitivity to light was my way home to love. It forced me to look at my life force and how I want to use it!! I started to see where I was wasting it and giving it away needlessly. I placed side by side my migraine thresh holds and triggers. I saw how I was setting myself up: to fail in my intention as well as be sick. This was recipe to be unhappy. Simply because it was a pattern.

I wanted to be good and helpful. Consequently, I had all these ideas of what compassion looked like. I had to keep hitting the wall of my limitations and self-judgements around love means being a martyr and not having needs. Life presented many situations where people I cared for needed help, and I had to choose to not help them because I just couldn't at the time due to my illnesses. I had to learn to take care of me before I could take care of another. The issue of sacrifice and savior were core beliefs. I had to wrestle with my demons. I had to find strength in my separation, and not just the merging.

When the head medical doctor who was the specialist of chronic pain "declared" that I was going to be in pain the rest of my life and will have to take pain meds, I said, "You are wrong. This will be not the case with me. I am here to find out the cause of all these and I will change it."

I chose to succeed in my wellness and health. A big part of this was to look at my choices, and the compulsive ways I was habituated in executing my goals. Think of life force as stuff. How much clutter do you want in your energetic body or your living room? I had daily diaries with maps and graphs tracking how I used my body that day, what I ate, what level of intensity was present, what emotional landscape and what were the environmental factors. Were they low, medium or high impact? I tracked what I did to respond to myself. Did I alter the course of uneasiness or stayed with it? Did it work, how? It was comprehensive. It was honest. I couldn't hide, nor could I lie. I wanted desperately to stop the migraines. It was intense self-research. I had a tiny thermometer I held between my fingers to measure my body temperature throughout the day and corresponded them to the factors of stress valleys and peaks on a daily basis. I did my self graphs for 8 months straight. At the end of each week, I did a synthesis of what I learnt that week of my patterns, good and bad. I used those to build on my intention for wellness the next week and so forth!!

I recognized where I learn tolerance for the intolerable – from my mother. Her insistence of my being patient, forgiving, of embracing differences, of what I grew up believing what love is supposed to be were all turned upside down in my investigations. I knew love was everywhere but the form and intentions surrounding the forms were questionable. When I hear stories of my mother's stories in relationships, both past and present, I wonder how different and similar I am. As I allow more room to feel my wonder and delight as well as my fears, disgust and anger, it gets clearer to me what my shadows are as opposed to someone else's disowning theirs and blaming. I began to see that decisions are made not in a vacuum, for myself or others.   Sometimes, in our self-absorption, we forget to inform those around us of what really is going on. It's a patterned habit of relating, but also one of lack of skill or capacity to sense it or/and communicate. I learnt to look at how to provide the needs arising internally and how to meet those self-needs, rather than doing a long detour of creating an agenda and strategy to get someone to provide those needs and love my way.

I am practicing in my daily life keeping only those things that I love and this makes me happy. By getting rid of those I don't want in my life anymore, I am recognizing sometimes practicality feeds the toleration does not necessarily serve optimally. I've created this as a practice in pleasure and wanting. In this process, I get to see the "what if?" come up. I find it to be another opportunity to be with ambiguity and numbness in myself.

"Tonight I started a God jar. It is a jar that used to belong to my grandmother and had sugar in it for decades. I am praying that all the sweetness will coat all the prayers and situations that I am having a hard time swallowing."

What gives you pleasure? What do you want to give you pleasure?

1. my Adam's apple being caressed by eyelashes
2. exchanging gazes with the black feral cat in the morning
3. the blackness of the evening
4. the smell of lemon
5. orchids
6. watching a funny movie
7. picking fruits from trees

8. cream
9. seeing others happy
10. a real dialog

This was part of changing the garden of my head. By planting different flowers there, I wanted the fruits of migraines to shift. As joy penetrated, underlying layers of deep disappointments came to the surface.

Hello Loneliness,

What shape are you that permeates my skin, oozes through my saliva and I run and run quickly as to not feel you and still seep you do. It's like I'm running away from my heart. How can that be so?

Activities are good diversions. Lonely – who are you? Is it the same as not feeling accepted? Is it being rejected?

Lonely is when I prepare dinner and I wish someone was there to share it with me. Lonely is when I put back my dreams of togetherness in my little suitcase. Lonely is when I curl in my couch and stare at the sky. Lonely is when the phone rings but I don't want to share the annihilation I feel. Lonely is when I lose transparency and righteousness because it's easier the loneliness. Lonely is when my lover can't appreciate the preciousness that I am. Lonely is when I can't even cry when I know I'm the edge of tears.

Lonely is when I want to share the beauty around with a companion person and it is only I at the moment in all beauty. Lonely is when I jump to what it could be and not here now as it is. Lonely is the gap, the abyss. Lonely is missing my companion. Lonely is having a hard time accepting that to myself.

Journal Entry:
"I did a very important enquiry today around mistrust and uncertainty with people I care who disappeared. I felt the sadness and my heart opened like a flower and the sensation was that of misty fall. I felt the brain stem holding tightly and the vagus nerve pulled up, like an energetic shunt to support myself. As I stayed

with this tension, there was a flow that unwounded. I saturated in this release and there was joy.

I did so much research to try to understand why I was having these headaches. One person had similar symptoms when the sharpnel from a gun came towards his eyes. Another woman had her husband leave suddenly taking all the money in the bank with him. She became legally blind from that incident. I thought about it and its relationship to death and survival. Animals when they are injured go to a dark place until they are okay. The eyes receive so much information, even before the body flinches.

The cranial nerves, especially the optic nerves are next to the amygdala and limbic brain. No wonder flight/fight response and migraine lighting each other up in my system. I also see the pattern of the element of air imbalance in all the illnesses these last years. Ocular disturbance is a metal/air imbalance. I am taking this as an opportunity to re-pattern my ways of looking and seeing!

Watching my body when I am in joy, I notice that it is like magic and all boundaries disappear. I get light and spacious, airy. It is now time to bring earth energy with joy together. It is interesting to note that when I am happy, I forget I have a body. Joy while in staying in my body is my answer and my medicine!!

Solidifying my identity with the illness, whether for or in repulsion of it, is my bondage. Here, I am given an opportunity to see through so clearly, again and again, who I am and who I am not. Use it!!! See where my bondage lies. There too in the same place lies my freedom. This path is liberation. Illness is a play of consciousness. How can I turn this illness into delight?"

My neighbor moved the rocking chair underneath the fig tree so I can read in one of my favorite spots. Friends and family send me gifts of clothes to cheer me up. I was being met in so many ways, and the beliefs around not being loved just couldn't hold up!!

"Date with Magnum tomorrow (MRI for brain scan). I was surprised that I was nervous and scared to do it. The whole procedure itself is so foreign, even though I've done it plenty of times by now. It's not so enjoyable. Even when I imagine the sounds of hammering to be the songs of the Gods and that I am receiving their blessings...and what if they find tumors that's making all these head symptoms?"

Thankfully, I had no tumors. I continued on my search for wellness and relief. I cried and felt the passageway in my head opened up. Have I been burying my sadness in my head? I have been hiding behind anger because the loss was so deep. This migraine cluster is me grieving!

Do I trust myself? Do I feel safe enough in myself that I can take risks, be tender, be vulnerable, ask for the exact help I need and want- knowing I will not explode, not disappear, will not let go of myself even if the answer is no or not favorable to my desires?

Today in enquiry was the closest I've come to wanting to no longer be in a human incarnation. I felt my exhaustion and I just wanted to stay inside the black crystal, frozen and waiting to be re-energized in a much later date. The being in the cave of the black crystals cajoled me to come out, "Don't you want to feel the grass on your feet or the wind on your hair as you run down the hill or to make and be in love?" I felt my tiredness of earth human living. I felt so battered here. I felt that at that moment I could will myself to stop breathing." I decided to stay.

Relationship to addiction:

Although my parents wanted the best for me, it didn't always happen that way. They didn't know that for themselves. How could they know that for me? Right now, I am taking responsibility for myself. I take responsibility in being clear with my needs and wants. Whenever it feels funny inside, I am to trust that intuition. I will ask questions. This is not a time to lie to myself. Denial was such a big part of my life. My boundaries have been tested and violated so much. The pushing is so familiar.

Of course, I so want to be loyal to the people I love and I want to do it without compromising my integrity and sense of self. I don't want to give away my sense of safety and self-worth. Clarify and clarify some more. Notice when I am lying to myself. Notice when I am minimizing something. These are red flags. Notice when I am compromising and what part of me I am compromising.

Am I for or against myself? Notice the ways I run away from my feelings of dying inside and how they get translated to colluding in an unhealthy pattern of behavior. This is an epiphany for me. This is a relational whole – a fit in a puzzle learned as a family. Parents were in an addictive behavior because it was the best way they knew how to cope with pain. The best way then I knew how to cope with pain was to make it seem better with them in the expense of myself. This was typical behavior for a child. My parents had a tendency to engage in out of control behavior to avoid feeling their pain. My sense of safety and familiarity is to collude with them not feeling the pain or my pain with this out of control behavior. To fix things and make it okay – that's what I've learnt to do. Now I am choosing to shift my way of being with pain, in my self and others.

As I take my stand as an adult and see her an adult, I began to have conversations with her in this way too. Instead of just listening and checking out from a distance from my feelings being triggered, I allowed myself to feel and to listen to her questions as to how she feels.

One recent Mother's Day weekend, my mother and I were driving through the desert en route to the hot springs. She sang many Tagalog songs of a child longing for her mother. I could hear and understand viscerally the effects of my grandmother's early death on the child that was to become my mother. There is something about songs that bypass the cognition and pull the strings of the heart directly. The immediacy of emotion is palpable. Right then and there, I really got it that my mother missed out a lot from her mother dying young.

The generation of women my mother belongs to is different than my generation. The availability of choices are not the same at all. I was having a conversation with a college friend around mothers. Our understandings and judgments of them for wanting to be taken care of by a man may not be so different with the same longings we have about being protected by men. We all want the same thing – to be loved and the ways we want that expressed in our lives. That maybe it is not about compromises, but negotiations.

I have been looking at the systems we are operating from. I've allowed myself to feel my pain real time, meaning not after 10 years, but as it is evoked in the current moment in a current situation with a current person. I've allowed myself to take sides of right and wrong without losing love for either side. I've allowed myself to thaw and be impacted. I allowed myself to ask questions – and open to receive the answers I did not want to hear. I saw clearly that I didn't want to hear many things. It takes a lot of courage to hear. I allowed myself to feel feelings I did not want to feel.

I just allowed myself to be. I was afraid that asking questions of my mother on those issues that bear so much pain that it would break her and she wouldn't be able to handle it. Or/and then I would have to take care of her and my own feelings would overwhelm me. My own discomfort with other's feelings evoked by me was uncomfortable. As I've noticed that I can be with this discomfort of myself and others without having to change or fix it (not 100 percent but pretty good) – this is my grace. I'm learning not to step in too soon, that it's okay for uncomfortable feelings to land on both parties and that is part of relationships. I won't die, neither will the other.

Practical Application for you:

Which pattern do you have? Do you recognize yourself in one or more of these?

Bear the pain and /or leave or die
or
Fight, get beaten the crap and die
or
Numb out and pretend the world is peachy rosy
or
Keep taking ownership of my feelings but giving no/not acting on consequences of not being met
(addressing/talking about the issues but still accommodating him)
or
Leaving – failing ideal of love

Failing loyalty to my ideal of love

Superego steps in and cycle of self-punishment

Unless Witness steps in and sees with clarity and true love

CHAPTER 23: COMING HOME TO LOVE

I have been blessed to have loved and been loved. Let me preface this chapter by saying that love is always perfect. The delivery of it gets mixed in with so much hurt and wounding, however. We all do our best based on what we know, and our capacity at any given moment. Sometimes, though, it is really hard to distinguish love from the scars of love. It especially gets difficult to discern when one's own attachment and relational history is not conscious. What is love? Really let this in, and see what answers arise for you right now. Is it your story or did someone else hand you that story?

I saw a clear picture of this when I attended one of Leonard Cohen's concert. The whole venue was full, and then Leonard came out, singing one song after the other. He sang with his soul. At times, his knees were locked in as to not have to let go of whatever angst it was in his belly. We can all relate to this. Sometimes, the pain of love is such that we hold ourselves so tightly, yet our longings and tenderness resound. I was dismayed at how each song was about dysfunctional relationships and filled with co-dependency. The whole audience was mesmerized. He was singing their, our experiences. He was singing the cultural experience. I felt sad, then I began sending lots of angels, and I said, "It doesn't have to be this way." What are the songs of your love?

"If there is a habit or quality in your mate that rouses unlovely traits in your disposition, you should realize the purpose of this circumstance: to bring to the surface those poisons hidden within you so that you may eliminate them and thus purify your nature."
-Paramahamsa Yogananda

Relationships have always been a spiritual path to me, as I have used the dynamics to investigate the foundational relational templates I have come to create as a child. It's been a path of creating new pathways of relating that are healthier, happier and truly more caring of self and the other. Warm lubrication is the quality of love that feels nourishing. It's a gift that keeps on giving. To partake of this in union with another is such a blessing, an offering of the deepest magnitude. Lovership and relationship become containers within a larger container of spirituality. The men in my life all became my teachers. I took love as my guide, and as wisdom grew, I began to see the ways I overrode some deeper intuitions and wisdom. There are ways that I didn't want to see, and I decided to overlook them initially, until they revealed themselves again in retrospect. As I age, I am accepting more and more that love and discernment come together. With maturity, I've gotten to accept a level of ambiguity in the expression of the form loves takes. The essence, without a doubt, is unquestionable, yet the form shifts. Life has thrown me so many curved balls that I've had to look beyond the forms to truly keep opening my heart.

It wasn't just personal history though. It's too simplistic to think that way and this is where I find psychology to be too narrow. There are cultural norms, historical influences, and of course, the gender and biological expectations that shaped my relationships, or anybody's for that matter. Then of course, there is a trajectory that is more than one lifetime. There is the soul's journey that traverses a mere one hundred years in a physical body. What we do now as behavior is not only an effect of one point from the past. I don't see the logic of thinking we can pick point A in space to cause point B in space. Space is made up of many points. Who are we to pick one point over the other and pretend that this is the whole truth and nothing but the truth. I am simply pointing (pun) to a much bigger trajectory that is beyond the linearity of our cognitive renditions around concocting a familiar and digestible explanation that may not really be it, yet makes us feel comfortable, for the moment. Think quantum physics rather than just Newtonian physics.

As I matured as a young woman, I certainly showed up differently in each relationship, having had learnt and ripened from the relationship earlier. Who I was as a twenty-year-old was certainly different than a forty year old! In my younger years, I definitely put up with a lot in the name of tolerance and pushing my edges, overriding my gut feelings. I also played out what I knew up to that point from my earliest relationship with my parents. As I grew older, there was a cultivation of qualities that served me and the other better. I knew myself better, and didn't need to use detours to get my needs met. I simply asked for them directly! Or got them another way. I also gave of myself very differently, more authentically to how I was expanding into a bigger sense of self that wasn't just ruled by the egoic and superego structures that were shaped by psychodynamics.

I looked at my relationship with my father to shed light on my structures. My father never talked to me about men and the importance of loving. I wish he did. I wish he taught me how to use the tools in the garage. I don't remember ever playing with my father. He didn't help me with homework. He was absent the first 12 years of my life. He died when I was twenty-nine years old so I didn't get to see him aged in wisdom, and have the opportunity to have a changing relationship, adult to adult. I missed out on this. I didn't know my father very much. We were in each other's lives for six years when I was a teenager.

He encouraged me to travel so I could know the world firsthand, and not just rely on books for knowledge. He gave me my first radio where I can listen to stations in different languages. I enjoyed the lunches we had at truck stops that served cherry pies. He laughed when I got my first traffic ticket and reminded me it won't be my last. He loved watering the garden and we often looked at the desert together. He wanted to make my mother happy at times, but didn't succeed. He was very proud of my intelligence. He was the first person in my family to ask me about what meditation was. He loved meeting the few friends I brought home. I was with him the last month of his life and held him as he took his last breath in this life. I am grateful that I was with him. I am glad that I got to see my father's essence before he passed away.

There is a poem by Hafiz I like very much:

Every time a man upon the path
does not keep his word
some angels grumble
and have to remove
a few of the bets

259

they had placed upon his heart to win

In my experience, when I meet someone, I see his/her essence. I might forget it soon after, but nonetheless, there is that acknowledgment. Next I see certain patterns of the personality. Humans are habitual creatures after all. What are some foundational determining factors off the bat? Defense patterns, passion of course, and what level of stuckness each one of us is in. As I've gotten older, relationships have gotten shorter. I see this as a blessing, really. At first, I used to joke with Spirit and lamented, "How come the honeymoons are getting shorter and shorter?" Then even the honeymoons disappeared as the reality check of compatibility became more accessible and the courage to act on them became more available even in the getting to know friendship phase!!

I learnt to listen to the man in front of me on a first date and believed him. I let go of the belief that I was going to change him or he was going to change me. I listened to what he said, what he didn't say, what energetic demeanor he had with me in the interaction. Did he listen to me? Did he ask me questions? Was the questioning truly curious, or was it a cross-examination? Was sexual chemistry leading it, and the rest was in the toilet? What was my belly telling me? I listened to my intuition more. Was there congruence? I had plenty of opportunities in relationship being an attractive and pleasant woman so I had lots of practice with these enquiries real time with different kinds of men from different cultures, generations, socio-economic backgrounds, etc. When the object of desire and probable pleasure is seemingly attainable, one gets to check the level of honesty, virtue and fidelity of those involve. I learnt a lot about how men worked, how I worked internally. Could I live with this? Could I live without it? How did each accept a yes or a no in a given situation? If you observe, you get lots of information. Now you have more of a choice whether you want to do it or not. All the above is also true for the other person determining how they receive me and whether they want to move forward with me/us.

I once had a relationship where the man suggested we do a flow chart of each other's lives side by side with multi-colored pens for each category. I was hesitant at first. I wanted the getting to know phase to be organic, natural, flowing, not forced or business like. Then I thought, what the heck. We pay more attention to job interviews than romantic relationship interviews. I agreed to the flowchart. It was new, refreshing, and I saw that it was his way of gathering information about me and our compatibility potential!! He didn't want to waste much time. That is what happens when you get older.

One caution though. Remember that not everyone is truthful in showing himself up. Truth is one of those malleable words. It is one thing to show up with your best, but it is another to deliberately lie and mislead a potential partner. This happened to me, and it wasn't until years later that I learnt of the basic lies that were the foundation of that relationship. It was simply disillusioning and disappointing. That really hurt!! When I asked that person why he lied to me in the most basic important values I specifically asked for, he replied that I wouldn't have gone out with him in the first place if he told the truth. So he lied, and the whole relationship was founded on those lies. It took me a long time to catch on, and when I did, I left the relationship. It deeply opened an enquiry for me on whatever unconscious lies I was telling myself. The pain was so profound that it encouraged me to look at shadows of my past more pointedly, and update it real time in my life.

I developed more and more courage to be able to just see, without judging. As I grew older, I became more discerning. The veils of my egoic structures began to melt and I could be with the transparency of what is the truth. I knew what I wanted and I wasn't going to pretend that someone was going to give me something that really only one's self (me) can give the self. I became braver with loneliness. I also knew that I am not an island, and wanted a companionship that was compatible, nourishing and elevating for both involved. I was interested in a partnership on all levels.

Of course, there were also reactionary decisions that were not carefully thought out, but isn't that the nature of learning? Knowing what to do (successful learning) requires a series of not knowing how to do it in order to arrive at that place of knowing. Then it starts all over again. Knowledge is to be on the edge of our knowing. I saw that if I stayed only within the parameter of knowing, stagnation results. Life is dynamic. I invite dynamic stability in my life knowing that change is inherent in existence. Intensity is part of that. To feel one's aliveness means to feel lots of movement. It's like living in the same valley and never leaving it to see that there is more than what is in the valley. It is like the frog who only stays in the pond and thinks the sky is round. Mobility in one's thinking and emotional landscapes is healthy.

I see the moon rising right now and it is a slight pink full moon this autumn. There is a calmness descending upon me, and I thank all the women in both direction of the past and the future, and I include the women of today....I am grateful for the mysteries of the moon!

It is apt to pay homage to the moon and the cycles of women for I have found that my womb had led me into relationships, as well as gave me the signal to leave them. Our wombs are our antennas, and when we listen, they give us messages. It is our second heart. The uterus and the heart are the only parts of the body that share a similar kind of muscle.

Here is a poem about lovers:

Portals of my heart

My lovers knocked one by one
at the portals of my heart
He was yesterday
he is today
he will be tomorrow.

There was he
Puer Aeternus
the eternal child
who hid surprises behind paintings
hidden love notes in matchboxes
that I may know the moments of delight anytime.

There was he
who was shy, so it seemed,
watched and studied me from afar
until he felt I was ready to receive him.

There was he
an older experienced man
who knew i could not see.
He planted roses by my bedroom window
that i may remember the perfume of his love.

There was he
a bricklayer who intimated to build a house together.
Only too many storms came
and I had to accept that even strong trees break.

There was he
a virgin, full of promises
with doe eyes
ideals that pittered like rain on tin roof.

There was he
I shared dreams of mother hood
utterings that punctuated years of longing.

There was he
still heartbroken from his last love
I helped him pick the pieces
watering a fresh seedling shoot in his longing.
Preparing the better version of him for the next one.

There was he
the young Krishna with his flute
who left love notes in the bag of frozen berries
reminding me of his passion in the coldest of winters.

There was he
the dancer that leapt
churning the fire within
wild in his eyes, hot in his loins
his heart so big
yet trembling in his confidence

would i meet his love?

There was he
the cowboy
in his zen sports car
wanted me with adventure
together we saw forever
is one now, one now, one now.

There was he
who mourned with me
as we lit candles at my father and brother's graves
sharing a pint of chocolate ice cream
while the sunset held silence
in the desert graveyard.

There was he
the mystic
proclaiming
he met God in me.

There was he
a loyal dog
sent carefully selected cards
with chosen funny stamps
with the same message
say YES to me!

There was he
the actor
bigger than life
for years i believed the lines.
Finally, it delivered me to courageously faced my lies.

There was he
the truthsayer
dialoged with me in areas i could bear no longer
held me courageously in his arms

leeching the rage, bitterness and sadness
showing me for that moment
there was light at the end of the tunnel.

There was he that is you
the he that is me
The me that is you
The he that is a she
The she that is a he

the lover that is the loved
there is the lover that inspires
there is the lover that expires

really
truly
there is only
there is only
one LOVE.

    My story is not different than many. In relationships with men, I have experienced magic, believing the impossible, felt the strength of togetherness, been accepted in ways I have not even accepted parts of me. There were tenderness, play, appreciation and inclusion. Relationships gave me the gift of wonder and the gift of surprise of what men are capable of. I also saw what I was capable of. I got to see myself through other's eyes, and spread my wings alongside their wings. I met men's commitment, their longing, their generosity and care, their capacity to be who they truly are. I saw my virgin and my whore, and loved both. I have held men laugh in my arms and also wept with despair, knowing that my arms were a safe place for them. I have stood in front of angry men bigger than I and fought for my right to voice my opinions. I have learnt to fight, and not just run away. Boy it took me a while, but when it happened, was it a relief!! I have lovingly surrendered my exit strategies, and come to difficult dialogs around true intimacy. I have come to know my fears and revulsions around intimacy. I have learnt in relationship how to be vulnerable and soft and true all at the same time, and invite that in the other. In relationships with men, I also have experienced death, affairs, lies, betrayals and deep disappointments. I have come to accept the imperfections of human beings, the other and myself. I have come to accept that it is not what we bring to the table, but how willing we are to truly work and make it work together. Colluding with each other's shadows and weaknesses is not the answer. It is not honest. It is not loving. Love is a choice and a gift. The continuing sharpening of capacity and ability allows one to experience the true distillation of love.

On being a woman: positive sex

When I make love, I make a prayer. A penis is not a sword that cuts. It is soft.

you begged me
giving my soul to you
is giving my soul to me

I say all of me is for me

In madness hearts racing
Racing to be one

The dawn kissing my lips
Petals blossoming
Opening her heart
To the warmth long hidden
Yearning

There were many funny stories of which I could write a book for men on how to best pick up (or not) women. Gosh, there had been so many kinds of lines, depending on the men, and of course, the culture I was in. At this age, I have come to accept that men's biological urges and predisposition resemble that of arrows going for a target. I just happened to be a woman. It wasn't personal. There were poetic men who "were carried away by my perfume" to men who propositioned in subtle or gross ways. I learnt a great deal about men's entitlement this way. There were those who just wanted sex and convinced me every which way why I should take them on this offer. "Have you dated an athlete?" to all the "positive sex" discussions. Essentially it came down to this for me: what is authentic and what is appropriate for the given moment? Sex is not about a mutual masturbation of each other alone. Sex is about truly meeting who is in front of you. It is good to check in whether you are connected or disconnected in the act of pleasure with another. Are you seeing your partner in the form that he/she comes in? Or are you looking for a form from the past whereby the present can be molded into? Surrendering somatically in a relationship requires two people to come home in themselves.

Connection and lostness are two sides of the same coin. I have repeatedly enquired into how the lostness I felt as a child in my family showed up in the lostness in my love relationships as an adult. What is the color of lostness? Its texture, sound, taste? I saw deeply that lostness for me is essentially a lost of connection. And love for me is connection. They are opposite each other.

When you drop to that place of acceptance and truly meet each other, both your hearts open and the energetic centers and pathways of your subtle body open up, and together you create a key to a higher dimensional experience of love. Relationships carry such a potential for deep healing and transformation.

We all have those moments in our lives when in a gasp we stop and simply marvel. I remember walking through the community garden in San Anselmo in the late summer. There was an old pomegranate tree and up above it a fruit had split. The plump ruby jewels caught the sunlight, and at that instant, I tasted its nectar.

POWER in relationship

The holy trinity in relationship are power, sex and money. They usually come together.

Do I choose my juiciness and be real or do I choose numbness of niceties to stay familiar? Am I seeking safety, approval or acceptance whenever I make a decision with another? Why do I bend backwards so much? Why do I want to work at it, even as friends? What's so bad about just being strangers? The tension between the spiritual superego of harmony and just moving on plays out. I keep returning to my tendency for optimism, looking at the best and expecting more. I accept that two people can love each other deeply and no longer choose each other.

Love is a garden. You both take care of the garden. You don't take a tender flower and crush it. You leave your big black boots outside. Patience and understanding need to be held in a commitment. This is the paradox of love at this time and place in our history. I've tried to own things as much as I can, and see the other person as a dynamic being with their own abilities and capacities. What is the distinction between cutting edge growth and abuse? What is my level of toleration for behavior that points to one being a jerk? I am cracking my love denial codes. Hope and fear are the same coin. I am cracking my hopes. I am cracking my false desires. I am cracking my secrets. I give up the role to save anyone.

Practical Application for you:

Questions for you in your relationship

Is this a source of joy or stress for you?
Are you happy?
Do you feel accepted as you are?
Are you accommodating? Is the other accommodating you?
Are you being rejoiced for who you are?
Are you wooed? Do you woo?
Are you welcomed for your gifts?
Are you elevating each other?
Are your requests honored? Or are they belittled and ridiculed?
Is there harmony in your life? Alone? Together?
Is she/he generous with you? In what ways? Are you generous with him/her? In what ways?
Do you feel included? Do you include others?
How does she/he make you feel loved? How do you make yourself feel loved? How do you make her/him feel loved?

Do you send her/him cards in the mail to say funny loving thoughts?

How do you surprise each other?

How do you appreciate each other? Is it coffee in the morning, water by the bedside, brushing your hair, toothpaste on the toothbrush or/and cute texts?

Does she/he adjusts things in the house/work/events to accommodate your sensitivities?

Ask yourself: is this the relationship you want? If yes, then what? If no, then what?

Do you dream together? Of the future? Of a shared future? Do you want to?

Are you spontaneous with each other?

Are you critical of yourself? Do you accept yourself?

Are you cherished?

Are you taking each other into consideration when you plan your weekends, your future, your dreams?

Is there congruency in your life?

Why do you stay when you are consistently uncomfortable?

What are your beliefs about loving, loyalty and coupleship?

What do you have to prove?

Do you allow yourself to believe? Are you angry at yourself for allowing yourself to believe?

How do you give up your sense of self? Transparency vs. engulfment?

What would you be doing with your life force if you weren't involved in this conflict?

CHAPTER 24: DANCING THE BEAST

I began dancing wildly in my room when the spiritual emergency exploded. I would play different evocative music and allow my soul to move. I placed huge swaths of butcher paper on my floor and would paint while I danced and moaned and sang. I laughed, I cried, I growled. I did it alone for many years.

Then I joined a group who loved to dance. I joined the Five Rhythms group, or better known as "Sweat your Prayers." Even though the room was full of people, I still danced alone for the first few years. I didn't want to dance with anyone. I faced the black wall and moved my grief, anger, passion. The movements did not look like a dance choreographed in a nightclub. There were the movements of life moving spontaneously. They were the embodiment of my emotions expressed dynamically. I danced alone for I didn't want anyone to interfere with this authentic movement. I didn't want someone else's agenda to guide or block what was being birthed.

This was a tough place to dance as not everyone comes here for this purpose. Some come to this dance because they want to connect with another person socially and romantically.

Then I started to dance with others, and my journey of relating, outside of just interference, opened. I accepted the invitation to bring relational passion and stillness together...not just within myself, but in relation to another person with his/her own agenda along with mine. I was relating real time, and seeing my responses in action. The dance floor became my practice ground for life in the real world. In the dance floor, I saw relationship and power dynamics even within a few minutes of dancing. There were so many negotiations around sharing/creating space, needs/ wants, following yearnings and demarcations placed arbitrarily, unconsciously. Deep questioning as to who made these rules up anyways, and now, do I really need to abide by them. The answer was no. The distinctions and nuances as to relating with another were so powerful and initiated me into further individuation. The basic foundation of how relating meant became the meta stories that were revealed. The grid that was "me" deconstructed.

I saw it as a wonderful gift to redefine myself.

I found it very useful for me to combine awareness and re-sourcing of the self together. In relationship, it is important to have a healthy sense of self.

This especially became apparent with my relationship with men. How do I go out of my center when I am in relationship? This is a common question women ask themselves being predominantly relational beings. Do I do what I truly desire versus what I think I desire? I noticed the energetic, action and speech patterns in relationships. Were there resonance, congruency and discord? How did that look like and what were the signs for me to recognize them? What do I do with vulnerability, mine and theirs? In the communication with each other, we bring our excitement and our hesitations. In the onslaught of mixed sensations, how do I tolerate this jumble? How to hold the capacity and longing to love fully like a dog leaping so excitedly without any thought, and then the other end of it of, being so scared that I would be eaten into oblivion? There was the fear that I will disappear as I merge into the other in love and when it ends, my essence disappears. What is left is a languishing in grief for I have been dismembered. Take One. That is one scenario.

Journal 11/13/09

"Moderation is a need, not a luxury for me. Too much excitement amplifies my system."

Love hits all the defended places in me, and I want to run away so fast? I haven't even been kissed and already all these abandonment issues are full blown in my face. I see myself planning, strategizing how to get out, albeit gracefully, dating others I'm not really into, not dating at all, running into a monastery, traveling, hiding away…anything but being with the pain of separation….my separation from myself. What do I do when he fails me? What do I do when I fail me?

There were times where the bottom line was that I didn't trust myself with longing. I disappeared when I longed! Where do I go? How do I find home in my longing? I am afraid to lose myself when I merge. In desiring a man passionately? Somehow, wanting becomes linked with pain and so to avoid pain, I avoid wanting. How do I stay home in the wanting? How do I stay home in the pain? How to stay home in both simultaneously? All these questions rapidly fire within all of us. Sometimes, we have enough space and nuance to hear them. Most of the time, we dismissed them or numb ourselves to them. Waking up is not done only when we are alone. We get to clearly see directly those places where we are slumbering in relationship to others. Remember, spirituality is not divorced from life. We may take time up the mountain, but we still return to the market in the valley. We chop wood, carry water, fall in love, burp and fart. How do we bring the clarity of being to the dynamic relations we have in life? I took life as an invitation to see the intersection of personality and being. Where in life is one taste not present?

I saw that it wasn't only about asking for a commitment from the man, but really asking the commitment from me. How much do I want to be available? Can I be fully me in relation? It is really about two dialoging, not one overlapping the other. Autonomy and merging need to dance together. Who stirs the ship of relating?

Within this combustion, I entered a process of emotional intelligence in relationship.

I began to observe the shifts from freeze to collapse and the anxious waiting in my being. How much distance do I need to feel safe, relaxed in my body without going to freezing? How do I cope with this sense of powerlessness and what strategies arise?

I took an honest look at how I seize my power and control. I saw how much I judged men. I have a long list to measure them by, and lots of booby traps instead of just connecting for who they are and who I am. I scared them as a purpose to test and see if they really would stick around. I had so many stories if they chased me too much or not enough. I looked at the mirror and peered at intimacy. I wanted them to be like women and was disappointed when they weren't. Then I wanted them to be like men and was disappointed when they weren't. What I saw was confusion of so many personal and cultural stories about men and women. Living in the bay area with the current questioning of gender roles added to the challenge and the gifts. I looked at the cultural assumptions of what a woman was supposed to be and how did I get rewarded for being/acting as that. Was it satisfactory? Then the lie revealed itself more. The journey underground uncovered the shadows that prevented the girl from maturing into a woman. Digital seduction was one way to flirt with feeling safe, yet it got boring very quickly. It was still playing games rather than really exploring connections. I began to find my way through this quagmire, and trust the conflicting paradoxical aliveness of the soupy mix of what is.

We live in a culture where to be a woman is really not a safe place. One only has to walk down to the coffee shop and sense how tightly the belly and pelvis are held when encountering a man bigger than us to notice this. Our pelvises are own seat of power and when we constrict them, we cut our power down. Our ovaries and wombs are our antenna, our allies, our teachers and guides. Yet, we tense this whole area and made inaccessible that which is our, by birthright, our power. How much projection do we take upon ourselves, from the media, from the strangers we meet, from the people close to us? I was once sick with a flu and had to go get something at the drug store. I hadn't washed my hair, I had a mask as to not infect other people, and I felt lousy. While waiting for my turn at the cash register, the man behind me commented, "You look good in a mask!" I almost lost it. Was he blind?

October 16, 2009 journal entry

There has been so much change these last years that I am not seeing how much stability I've actually learned and created. I've had to continuously learn a new point of stability through all these changes. Because I've had so many constraints, I've had to find freedom where I didn't have before. That is the process of discovery. I had to go from imbalance to balance to imbalance to balance and so forth.

Not only did my physical health collapsed many times in different ways, my social and relational life also thwarted. It affected the financial and the emotional well being of confidence. So many rugs underneath were being pulled away, that I had to find another center every time. Then I got it that the center is constantly moving, and that freedom is about being able to dance with and in a moving center!!

I had to apprentice myself as an adult on how to say yes, after I learnt to say no. I gave myself permission to be happy even if others were miserable. I saw that happiness is a gift to self and other.

There was also a deeper layer underneath it all. Looking at my commitment to myself, I began to see those breaks of allegiance especially when someone crossed my boundaries. Do I protect myself, tend to my comfort or do I tend to the comfort of another because I don't want to appear bitchy or shaming? I had to be willing to say anything even if I don't look spiritual, cute or nice. I looked at my allegiances. I have had a history of allegiance to the other and dismiss myself, as many women are socialized to throughout time. Giving one self up is a "value" that is expected of women. What is the baseline of your comfort and space (in relation to another)? Are you willing to listen to this boundary of comfort that comes from within you and not from someone else? So what motivates you to say something to another who's violated your sense of space? My belief at one time was: If I say something, I will shame the other and shaming was not okay, especially in public. Looking at this, I saw my unconscious commitment to protecting another, to keeping peace and harmony, to be a pleaser, and leaving myself behind. I felt sad. I declared that I am now meeting my own needs, and comfort is my guideline, and I changed it!!!

I am looking around my home and enjoying the orchids and the sage permeating the air, mixed with the sweetness of chai and fresh tomatoes. There is an Indian American story of coyote and the hummingbird. Coyote will always come with her tricks. Our power lies in drinking hummingbird nectar so the love flowers in our heart will keep growing. I pray that my love flowers will keep growing. When true love flowers, the lovers disappear, for only love remains. We are all drawn home that is why we can't stop loving. Love is home.

There was an exercise of taking a day and just saying "YES" to everything coming in. I decided that I was going to experience a "YES" week so I said yes to naps, yes to someone asking to draw my portrait, yes to a facial, yes to a conversation with a stranger, YES!

When we open our old selves into something new, it is natural that we will feel unbounded, unfamiliar, even strange and some feelings may come up of anticipation and excitement. How could you not feel these feelings? How can someone choose something new if that is not even present already? How does a child/an infant learn a new movement? We find out by accident. By trying many new ways, not by design but by multiple times of explorations. Fear of "failure" prevents one from venturing outside what one considers "successful" – identity is stuck in the idea of "safety" – but that is really just a protection of the status quo, or/and of protecting what one doesn't want or have the resource to see or feel."

Questions to play around with include:

Where do you feel your anticipation? In the pit of your stomach or the grinding of your jaws? Do you know what your tenderness feels? How do you deepen my tenderness as opposed to hiding your tenderness? These questions encourage you to know your vulnerability. How can you meet newness with curiosity? Does excitement signify pleasure or pain for you? Is your seeking of pleasure connected to frustration? Now as an adult? Then as a child?

Observe how this is true or false when you are alone or/and in relation to another. Notice whether the expansion is somehow connected to reflex and recoil in your visceral experience of yourself. Is there a little bit of fear with excitement? If this is so, notice how your sense of safety is associated with getting rid of excitement or pleasure? Tedious as it may sound, sharpening these skills will help you regulate your parasympathetic nervous system and make better choices in your life.

You will learn a lot about yourself when you can identify how you meet change and transitions in your daily life. Learn the textures of your tenderness – both in its expansive and contracted forms? You have just given yourself an opportunity to experience yourself and the world differently. This is your renovation period.

Practical Application for you:

As I explored relationships, many questions for enquiry arose. These questions helped me. Try them on for size. Let go of what you need and let go of the rest.

What is the meaning of emotional investment?
What is it and the threads of it, attachment?
How do you interpret sexual instinctual impulses?
Look at it from a cultural, religious, familial, social? Whore/saint complex?
What is the taboo around pleasure with another?
What is your sexual superego?
What is the relationship of your heart with your sexual instinct?
How do you interpret desire? Touch? Dating?
What are your guiding posts and recognition to enter relationship?
How do you block intimacy? What do you get from blocking intimacy?
What do you do when you can't tolerate an issue?
Where do you go and what do you get from that?
How can you live your life as openly, as generously, as lovingly as you can?

CHAPTER 25: CONCLUSION

Although the kundalini rising was significant in my life, I really want to emphasize that life itself, in its most ordinariness is the teacher and the path. I was forced by all my unconscious material exploding and my familiar life disappearing to look deeply at the ways I was not home to my self. I faced and accepted both my light and dark aspects. I took an honest assessment of how I kept giving myself away because I thought that was the way to be. Even when I was aware of that, I still had to unlearn that particular habit and learn better coping habits. It wasn't of course who I truly was. Essentially the take away is that it is about love: loving ourselves, loving others and loving the world. When we come from a place of love, we think, speak and act differently than when we come from a place of fear. It is simple.

It was no surprise that this shell (how many shells?) would shatter so that I can fly free, and find my place here on earth willingly and happily. In my search for the spiritual early in my life, there was such a division between good and bad. That was part of my journey. The kundalini rising invited me to see where I didn't have one taste. I am a present day 21st century yogini who lives in the modern world. As Yeshe Tsogyal beautifully sang in her retreat, "Every appearance and every event are the mind's miraculous display." To see all activity as adornment and radiance has been the invitation.

I accepted the invitation to look at my whole humanity, including shadowy personality structures. It is all light displaying itself in form. Of course, the cycles of maturing, loving and aging bring in their many challenges and gifts. I openly shared very personal material (detailed self-analysis covering decades) in order to illustrate that darkness and light are the two sides of the same coin. My hope is to illustrate that who we think we are really is only made up of patterns. On the most fundamental and absolute level, is not who we truly are. On a relativistic reality, patterns of behavior do serve or hinder us. They can be changed if they don't benefit us. Patterns of behavior are no different than patterns of piano playing or the sounds of a foreign language or learning the new apps on the cell phone. As I develop more in subtlety, I see how this identity goes so far as the familiarity of the experience of density and the space between these densities as a body. There are many different ways to look at identity and how we grab it. Do we choose suffering or ease?

My lifestyle continues to be that of a contemplative. As a result of these changes, shakti (life force) streams gentler in my system just it did in the monastery in my younger years, and the journey on a nuanced level deepens. I now help and teach people how to explore their consciousness which includes themselves as bodies. I assist individuals through private work how to use chronic pain, grief, spiritual emergence and life itself as a path to awakening. I am a healer using awareness, touch, movement, sound and energy medicine as a medium. I see people remotely as well as in person. The kundalini has taught me how to be with others in this capacity.

I have used the whole of life in its most ordinariness to constantly look at dynamic consciousness. The human journey is beset with our addictions to beliefs, labels and habits we have about ourselves, others and the world. We get a lot from our identities. There comes a time, however, when the conditions shift and what seems comfortable actually suffocates our life force. Remember that we are dynamic, not static, and the impetus to our fluid nature beckons us to discover ourselves as we play, work, love, explore and be who we truly are. As much as we crave stability and security, inherently we are dynamic, changing beings and that which wakes us up from our complacency and rigidity can come in many forms. It could be a death of someone we love, an accident, an illness, an addiction, a divorce, a job loss or any number of possibilities. For me, it was a myriad of ways. Now I can look back and am very grateful for these gifts inviting me into transformation. I am more real than I have ever been. I like myself with all my edges. I am happier as well.

In the year 2014 in San Francisco, I write this passage appropriate for all of us in the path of awakening.

Gossamer luminous stillness greeted me as I sat for an hour in front of Mark Rothko's black and gray painting. This was one to be immersed in and be taken over as a lover takes her beloved completely until only surrender remains.

We all have those moments in our lives when in a gasp we stop and simply marvel.

There are these moments when unabashed we be ourselves unapologetically. The moments we stand transparent, in integrity, in connection and one with creation.

Appendix A

Spiritual Emergence/cy: the interplay of mysticism and psychosis

"The term *spiritual emergence* refers to the normal life-enhancing aspect of human development which seeks meaning and connection beyond our personal identity. This leads to a greater capacity for wisdom, compassion, and respect for all life as well as a deeper sense of personal security and inner peace. This growth can be challenging, even tumultuous, at times turning into a crisis known as *spiritual emergency*." (as quoted from CPHS website)

There is a long standing battle between biopsychiatry and transpersonal psychology in regards to labeling mystical experiences as psychosis. This discord has a long history even before the advent of these relatively new fields. The struggle in symptomatizing signs as degenerative and a disease ("schizophreniform disorder" at best) as opposed to a "hero's journey" into greater health and wholeness has had tremendous impact on the lives of individuals. Listed below is a short history that sheds light on the existing problem. The literature review will explore what different authors have said in the field of spiritual emergence. There is ample material in the literature of individual descriptions of spiritual emergence while undergoing the process, yet a long term view of its implications has not been explored in depth. Using this history as a foundation for my study, I would like to pursue a heuristic, narrative longitudinal study of individuals (in this book, I am using myself) who had experienced spiritual emergence/cy 10-20 years ago. My aim is to explore the long-term implications of psychospiritual crisis. Let us hold the Chinese meaning of crisis being both a breakdown and a breakthrough, an opportunity to be more of who we are.

History: Split between spirit and science

The occident's views on visionaries have not always been what it is today. In the past, nature was infused with divine presence. "Angels/gods/goddesses/daemons were seen as emissaries and agents of divine spirit." The old testament as well as Iliad and Odyssey along with other books illustrated the existing beliefs of the times. There flourished a long tradition of visionaries in twelfth and thirteenth century Christian Europe. Visionary imagination flowered in the "building of great cathedrals... wide dissemination of the grail legend... black Madonna pilgrimages..." Dante wrote the Divine Comedy and mystics such as St. Francis and Hildegarde of Bingen were alive and revered. "The 14th century black death, the long terror of Inquisition (13th-19th centuries), silenced visionaries, the Dissolution of the Monasteries and the Protestant Reformation." (Barring, 2001, no pagination)

Disenchantment with the church as well as the philosophical shift of the mindset of the culture resulted more of the split between spirit and science. Science reduced the universe as mechanistic, lifeless and arising by chance. The censorship that began four hundred years ago continues today to delineate what is rational and not. With the radical philosophical shift in the scientific revolution, all of a sudden, the physical universe was not real, and therefore, the definition of a visionary also shifted to someone who sees something which is not real.

Psychological denigration of psychotic experience

Today, consciousness and visionary experiences are being relegated simply as by products of the brain. Worse still is the pathologizing of visionary experiences. The biomedical model dismisses visions in terms of chemistry and uses medication as a form of chemical lobotomy which destroys the brain's higher mental centers, and consequently, the destruction of the clarity of its etiology. (Nelson, 1990) By suppressing the visions, science today dismisses any exploration of its symbolism and metaphor, thereby losing access to its significance. As a consequence, recurrent themes of death and rebirth, "delusions of grandeur", and world destruction have been relegated to mere "hallucinations" and "delusions". Upon further deliberation, I ask: does reducing vision to chemistry deny individuals access to its deeper meaning and importance?

A visionary is often seen as "someone who suffers form delusions or hallucinations, who is at worst psychotic, at best emotionally unstable." (Barring, 2001)

A visionary, seer or shaman – the word means "one who knows" –is traditionally called to this role by a life experience which weakens his or her focus on the usual concerns of society. It could be an illness, a psychotic episode, an experience of catastrophic loss, a powerful visionary dream, and out of the body or near death experience. Whatever it is, it will shatter the pattern of so-called normal life and the structures of defense we have built against the terror and disorientation of such an experience. Our culture may see this experience as a symptom of mental illness. Other cultures may see it as a rite of initiation into a transcendent world – a break-through rather than a breakdown. There are many kinds, levels and degrees of visionary experience. Such experience is an encounter with the numinous and can be overwhelming and terrifying as well as exalting and inspiring. The line separating the visionary, the genius and the psychotic is very fine. All three have a psychic thresh hold which is permeable to deeper levels of experience, to non-ordinary states of consciousness. A culture may confirm or deny the validity of this kind of experience and it may be the fear and denial of it which may actually drive certain people into psychosis who in other cultures would be confirmed and supported in their calling as a healer and spiritual guide to the community. (Malidoma Some, 1994 as quoted in Barring, 2001)

As can be seen clearly, the radical metaphysical shifts of the scientific revolution reverberate to our current times. The clinical insensitivity to spiritual emergence is rooted in its founding father's views. Sigmund Freud in Future of Illusion referred to religion as, "A system of wishful illusions together with a disavowal of reality, such as we find nowhere else...but in a state of blissful hallucinatory confusion." (as quoted from David Lukoff's website) In Civilization and Its Discontents, Freud (1962) reduced the "oceanic experience" of mystics to "infantile helplessness" and a "regression to primary narcissism." It is no wonder that clinical psychology denigrates the psychotic experience. Another interesting point to add here is the current western pre-occupation and im-

285

portance with self control. Of course, it makes sense that "loss of ego control" will then be seen as pathological. (adapted from Natalie Tolbert in Clarke, 2001, p. 43)

According to Richard Maurice Bucke (1901) in Cosmic Consciousness, mystical experience includes:

Feelings of unity, feelings of objectivity and reality, transcendence of space and time, a sense of sacredness, deeply felt positive mood- joy, blessedness, peace and bliss,

containing paradox – mystical consciousness which is often felt to be true, despite a violation of Aristotelian logic, ineffability – language is inadequate to express the experiences, transiency, positive change in attitude or behaviour following the experience. (Clarke, 2001, p. 20)

William James (1958) defines mysticism as the height of unifying with a higher power (divine). Richard Neumann (1995) adds, "...religious mysticism is the art of union with divine reality...the mystic does not ask, what is reality. The mystic answers the question by discerning the results of contacts with that reality. The results are a wider, sharper consciousness and a more profound understanding of our own existence."

James also notes, although briefly, on "negative mysticism" which refers to frightening experiences, such as demonic possessions. There is of course what is called "The Dark Night of the Soul" in the Christian contemplative practice. (Underhill, 1969, p. 381) I will refer to these frightening altered states of consciousness as connecting with the "depth" rather than the "height" spoken of earlier. (Clarke, 2001) I propose that the depth and the height are both part of the same continuum, just as the mountain peaks belong in the same context as the valleys and canyons. In this vein, I propose further that the "negative mysticism" James points is the same as what western clinical psychology terms psychosis. Psychotics and mystics experience both the height and depth. The difference is in the integration that may lead to a freer and happier life or a rumination of narcissistic tendencies.

According to David Lukoff (Stahlman, 1992), a psychologist, "psychosis is considered a disruption to the normal functioning of consciousness." The psychotic thinks and behaves in culturally and socially unacceptable ways. Moreover, "The phenomenology (imagery, cognitions) of the psychotic condition shares many characteristics with dream experiences (Hall, 1977), hallucinogenic drug trips (Kleinman et al, 1977), spiritual awakenings (Assigioli, 1981), near death experiences (Grof & Grof, 1980) and shamanic experiences (Halifax, 1979)." (as quoted in Stahlman, 1992)

It is clear from the definitions listed above that what religious orders aspire to is pathologized by clinical psychology. Given this split in labeling and the harmful impact of its consequences, it is no surprise that this is a difficult and debated topic. It is also no wonder that even though a great many individuals have had mystical experiences, they don't tell others about it for fear of being labeled mentally ill. (c.f. Greely and McCready: Are we a nation of mystics?) As William James dramatically put it, "medical materialism finishes up St. Paul by calling his vision…a discharging lesion of the occipital cortex….It snuffs out St Theresa as a hysteric; St Francis of Assisi as a hereditary degenerate; George Fox with the sham of his age." (quoted in Clarke, 2001: 109)

Transformation in the midst of chaos: an alternative model
So here we are walking on a double edge sword. I am proposing as others have done beforehand (Jung (1964), Lukoff(1991), Laing (1965), Neumann (1973), Campbell (1969), Perry (1953), Assagioli (2000), Grof (1989)) that individuals experiencing these signs/ symptoms are not "diseased", but are actually in the throes of deep transformation that has value not only for the individuals in question, but for the society at large.

As part of this movement, Lukoff fought to have the term "spiritual problems" as a diagnosis included in the DSM IV.

Spiritual Problems:
This category can be used when the focus of clinical attention is a religious or spiritual problem. Examples include distressing experiences that involve loss or questioning of faith, problems associated with conversion to a new faith, or questioning of spiritual values that may not necessarily be related to an organized church or religious institution. (DSM IV,1994)

Before we go further, I would like to present some of the signs and symptoms/descriptions of what may be happening that the psychiatric establishments are relegating as pathological on one hand, and the religious orders are aspiring towards on another hand. Stan Grof (1989), a leading transpersonal psychiatrist, describes these experiences in a term he and his wife, Christina, had coined: spiritual emergence/emergency.

- Feelings of oneness with the entire universe. Visions and images of distant times and places. Sensations of vibrant energy coursing through the body, accompanied by spasms and violent trembling. Visions of deities, demigods, and demons. Vivid flashes of brilliant light and rainbow colors. Fears of impending insanity, even death.

- Some of them involve certain extreme emotions and physical sensation that cannot easily be understood in terms of the individual's childhood history or later events. Here belong, for example, visions and experiences of engulfment by the universe, diabolic tortures, disintegration of the personality, or even destruction of the world. Similarly, abysmal guilt feelings, a sense of eternal damnation, or uncontrollable and indiscriminate aggressive impulses in many cases cannot be traced to specific events or conditions in the patient's life (p. 5)

According to the Grofs, these individuals are undergoing a spiritual emergence – an awakening to one's spiritual nature. However, there are instances, when this awakening accelerates to a degree that the individuals experiencing them cannot handle it in a spacious way. When the experience becomes a crisis, then it is called spiritual emergency. It is important to point out here that despite the danger involve, there is also the inherent possibilities of awakening present.(Grof, 1989) Sensing the need both of individuals experiencing difficulties associated with spiritual experiences and therapists, the Grofs founded the Spiritual Emergency Network(SEN) at the Esalen Institute in 1980.

The enquiry into the transformative potentialities of a psychic breakdown began earlier with Carl Jung and his own personal exploration with the psyche. According to him, the "psyche is not of today; its ancestry goes back many millions of years. Individual consciousness is only the flower and the fruit of a season, sprung from the perennial rhizome beneath the earth." (p. xxiv 1976) In the decades he explored consciousness, Jung presented a map unlike his teacher Freud. He described the individual personality to include not only the ego, but also the personal unconscious with its complexes, and the collective unconscious with its archetypes. In the disorganization and dissolution of the ego, the collective unconscious comes to the foreground. The archetypes loaded with a large element of affect predominate the consciousness of the individual in a breakdown.(Whitmont, 1978)

In Spiritual Emergency: When Personal Transformations Becomes a Crisis, the Grofs (1989) delve into varieties of spiritual emergencies pointing out the individuality of each emergence. In so doing, the Grofs are seeing the person and not just the signs as labels. They discuss the "triggers" of transformational crisis as well as describing the different forms of breakdowns that may occur: shamanic crisis, Kundalini awakening, episodes of "unitive" consciousness, near-death experiences, possession states, experiences of close encounters with UFOs and the other major types of experiences. Because this is book is in a part a helping manual, the Grofs elucidate on, "The Stormy Search for the Self" by describing the difficulties and pitfalls that accompany spiritual emergence. This same title became a book published in 1990. Following Grofs' trail is Emma Bragdon (1988, 1993). She compiled a manual, A Sourcebook for Helping People with Spiritual Problems, to assist those undergoing spiritual emergence. Bragdon explores the interplay between spirituality and psychology. She is not shy in examining pathology and its relation to spiritual awakening. This book elucidates on supportive environments that can help one through spiritual emergence

Roberto Assagiolli (1989, 2000) first noted that disturbances on the way to spiritual awakening may arise and how inflation and grandiosity may result in said individuals. "Instances of such confusion are not uncommon among people who become dazzled by contact with truths too great or energies too powerful for their mental capacities to grasp and their personality to assimilate." (p. 36)

He added though that diagnostic labels do not shed light in understanding these complications. To Assagiolli, these physical, emotional and mental complications are part of a process of inner growth and regeneration. "Even though from the limited point of view of the personality it may seem a setback, or an undesirable phase – "as if God had set Himself against it and itself were set against God" – from the much broader perspective of the Transpersonal Self this phase, often rightly called "purgation" is in fact one of the most useful and rewarding stages of growth. The light of the Self shines on the "impurities" and brings them to the consciousness of the individual to facilitate his process of working them out." (p. 40-41)

Unfortunately, the western materialistic worldview does not allow room for material that is not measurable or tangible. As a result, many of the experiences discussed here are in question because they do not fit the cultural agreement of what is reality. As I mentioned earlier, our metaphysical assumptions of self, birth, death, health and sickness are simply that – assumptions. Our society has constructed reality based on these assumptions, and consequently, anyone who has experiences outside of these constructs must be delusional. I have illustrated this point earlier with the discussion on what constitutes an "ego". Ego is not solid, rather it is a constellation of different tendencies. Ego is a conventional construction, not an absolute structure. One only has to look at the metaphysics of different cultures such as Buddhism, Hinduism, Taoism, and so forth to understand that our beliefs are just beliefs, not reality. Transpersonal psychologists also point to this observation.

I am hammering this point because it is essential if we are to understand spiritual emergence. A person undergoing acute "psychosis" is exploding his/her beliefs and assumptions of who is the self. S/he is breaking out of paradigms and being forced to come to terms with what is not real. The conventional constructions of individual solidity and separation fall apart. This is not different when one undertakes a serious, continuous spiritual practice. The content of the experiences may be biographical (relating to the individual's personal history) or transpersonal (relating to images outside of individual's personal history). The content will vary, but the context of this is a healing beyond our cognitive dualism. It is what all religions aspire towards. What makes it a psychosis as opposed to a healthy mysticism boils down to the individual's attitude and quality of integration of these experiences.

R.D. Laing, a British psychologist commented, "Instead of the mental hospital, a sort of reservicing factory for human breakdowns, we need a place where people who have traveled further ... can find their way further into inner space and time, and back again. Instead of the degradation ceremonial of psychiatric examination, diagnosis and prognostication, we need...an initiation ceremonial, through which the person will be guided with full social encouragement and sanction into inner space and time." (as quoted in Fadiman and Kewman, 1973, p. 69) Moreover, Joseph Campbell's (1982) research into mythology illustrates these breakdowns/throughs as the "Hero's Journey" –an "inward and backward journey to recover something missed or lost, and to restore, thereby, a vital balance." (p. 209)

I echo Laing and Campbell's concerns and hopes. Afterall, what would have happened if sages/mystics such as Ramakrishna, Muktananda, Moses, Yogi Ram Surat Kumar, St. Teresa of Avila (just to name a few) would have been institutionalized. I shiver at the thought of the loss to humanity of the gifts these individuals have offered. I, myself, have benefited so much from their teachings. There is an intelligence that takes over the individual and re-organizes who s/he is in order that s/he may be more of who s/he really is. This time is critical and not easy.

Another visionary psychiatrist, John Perry (1953), named this process of disintegration the "renewal process." According to Perry (1999),

> In acute psychosis individuals undergo a profound reorganization of the self, effected by a thorough going reintegration through utter disintegration. The concept of the acute "psychosis" is that, when we speak of a self-healing process, we do not mean that the faults to be healed are these unusual expressions of the devices the psyche uses to

attain its goals. Instead, the problems needing solution are in the limitations of the personality prevailing before the episode; the psyche is trying to break free from constrictions, from a markedly negative self-image, a rather impoverished world outlook, and an unsuitable cultural set. The upheaval takes place in those persons whose nature cannot tolerate such limitations. The visionary devices set in motion by the psyche therefore do not constitute the disorder or pathology. In the turmoil the psyche's process is not what needs healing, but rather, the healing is accomplished by the "psychotic" process itself.(p. 26-27)

Perry had opened two alternative psychiatric institutions in the bay area in the 1970s, Diabasis and Soteria (1999, p. 12). In his experience and research, first time acute psychotics can be contained that helps them integrate their experiences in a transformative way. He noticed that given the natural course of unfolding, the individuals went through their process in the space of 7 weeks (40 days). Perry did not give medication nor did he pathologize the individuals. When individuals enter Diabasis, this statement is read to them. "This is not a disease, illness, or psychopathology. It is a rich inner experience in a visionary state that may be turbulent and scary at times, sometimes nightmarish and sometimes sublime, yet that's all tending to move toward a goal that is favorable for a better life. We're here to help you with it." (p. 39)

What Perry noted was that pathologizing these experiences is what actually causes the madness, not the initial experiences itself. "...A central source of people's distress is their (culturally sanctioned) assumptions, attitudes and beliefs about what is '(ab)normal'- which they apply like a template to themselves, discover a mismatch between their belief(s) about 'normality' and their own self experience, and then distress themselves about the mismatch. On this view, such 'secondary' distress is, then, at the very least an active contributor towards their experienced 'symptoms' of distress-and, at least sometimes, even the central factor." (Perry, 1999, p. 121)

It is the crazy making that makes a person crazy. The western worldview of denying reality to dimensions not consensually sensed by the majority does not mean that these dimensions do not exist. Peter Magaro (1976) explores "the construction of madness" in his book of the same title and questions whether the "help" the establishment is giving the "patient" is really help. Richard House, in his article , *"Psychopathology, psychosis and the kundalini: postmodern perspectives on unusual subjective experience"* added that, "if personal identity 'amounts to the assimilation of socially available theories and templates' and if 'How we reflect upon and define ourselves is determined and constrained by the structures of knowing available to us', then 'psychiatric patients, through the course of repeated assessments, come increasingly to define their experiences in accordance with a professional definition of 'psychiatric illness'. In short, 'clinical' discourses impact upon individual autobiography, thereby influencing both the types of subjectivity and identity that are brought into being'. Professional elites and their 'regimes of (professional) truth' are seen as constructing people's realities through language, and 'the ubiquity of particular types of discourse makes it impossible for their subjects to 'think'or even imagine an 'elsewhere'. " (Clarke, 2001, p. 110)

James Fadiman and Donald Kewman (1973, 1979) also had compiled an anthology Exploring Madness: Experience, Theory, and Research. More recently, Isabel Clarke (2001) has done a beautiful job of exploring Psychosis and Spirituality. This book with 14 different contributions challenges conventional frameworks that box a set of experiences either on one extreme or the other. Clarke elucidates on the neuropsychological perspectives as well as the mystical side of psychosis. British psychology acknowledges in the "schizotypy" model that certain individuals are born with tendencies towards transliminal experiences and that this is not pathology.(Clarke, 2001)

As noted earlier, there are also mystics that are revered with these experiences. Traditions such as shamanism not only encourage, but honor and privilege these healers in their societies. "Spirit release" and "retrieving the soul" are commonplace in shamanic culture. This brings an important point to this topic. The western metaphysical belief of birth and death does not allow room for the spirit. Natalie Tobert (Clarke, 2001), an anthropologist, questioned the current psychiatric establisment's assumptions. "What happens if we start to believe in reincarnation and the pre-existence of souls? If there is reincarnation, could there be spirits of the dead? Could there be discarnate beings? Can spirits manifest in the slipping into a non-physical dimension and picking up material and confusing it with common consensus reality? It may be easier for both sufferers and therapists to believe in the reality of the sickness called psychosis, since the other possibilities are so challenging to our belief systems about the nature of existence." (p. 39) I agree with Tolbert in her questioning of the western perception of the "porousness" and "boundedness" of the human body? I do not believe the skin is the boundary between the individual inside and the world outside." (p. 39)

Lee Sanella's (1978) classic book, Kundalini: Trascendence or Psychosis, was one of the first books written by a psychiatrist upholding the integrity of spiritual experiences against the onslaught of the medical model. John Nelson (1994), Healing the Split Madness or Transcendence?: A New Understanding of the Crisis and Treatment of the Mentally Ill, is another book on spiritual psychiatry. Nelson, a psychiatrist, elucidates on the distinction between regressive illness and progressive transformation. Using his understanding of both Eastern philosophy (Tantric chakras) and Western neuroscience, Nelson integrates his knowledge in his psychotherapeutic applications. With his experience and understanding, Nelson does not turn away from the medical model of prescribing medication, yet adds to it spiritual practices. It is important to note that the example he gave does not include a first time acute psychotic break that Grof and Perry had alluded to in their research. An example is prescribing both lithium and a spiritual practice to a manic patient. He believes that simply prescribing medication that deletes the magical wonder associated with mania defeats the purpose. By prescribing a spiritual practice, the patient still has a way to connect with the infinite. Like Michael Washburn (1988), he believes that individuals may undergo 'regression in the service of transcendence'. Nelson accedes that spiritual growth may be mistaken for mental illness. On the same note, not all disorganization and disillusion are mystical and healthy. He is also careful to not fall into the pre/trans fallacy Ken Wilber (1998) had

294

elucidated. Nelson believes that "modern psychiatry is more ready to integrate spiritual concepts that non-psychiatrists generally acknowledge" (p. 415).

Following on the footsteps of Nelson and Sanella, Russell Shorto, Saints and Madmen, another psychiatrist presents a well researched narrative about the interplay of mysticism and psychosis. Using "science of the soul", he delves into the shifting meanings of "self," "soul," "mind," and "brain". He embarks the spiritual dimension of psychotropic drugs as well as the spiritual longings inherent in addictions and depression. The case studies he used point to the complexity of mind.

It is interesting to note that it is not only contemporary men of science that have deliberating this split. Emmanuel Swedenborg (1758, 1971) challenged many of the western notions of non-physical entity. In the 18th century, Swedenborg, a famous Renaissance scholar of all fields, spent the last 27 years of his life, speaking with spirits on a daily basis. His findings, since then validated through a psychological qualitative research of William Van Dusen (1974), reflect an acknowledgment of the existence of spirits. According to Swedenborg, there are two orders of spirits: the lower order and the higher order. The lower order spirits possess "limited vocabulary and range of ideas" and are "incapable of sequential reasoning. They seem imprisoned in the lowest level of the patient's mind," (Fadiman & Kewman, 1973, p. 139) exploring madness and tend to hark on the individual's weaknesses.

> The speech of an angel or spirit with man is heard as sonorously as the speech of man with man, yet not by other who stand near, but by himself alone. The reasons that the speech of an angel or spirit flows first into man's thought and by an internal way into his organ of hearing thus affecting it form within....
> To speak with spirits at this day is rarely granted, because it is dangerous; for then the spirits know that they are with man, otherwise they do not know it, and evil spirits are such, that they regard man with deadly hatred, and desire nothing more than to destroy him, both soul and body. This in fact is done with those who have indulged much in phantasies, so as to remove themselves from the delights

proper to the natural man. Some also who lead a solitary life occasionally hear spirits speaking with them. (Swedenborg, 1971, P. 248-49)

The higher order spirits, on the other hand, are "more likely to be symbolic, religious, supportive, genuinely instructive, and communicate directly with the inner feelings of the patient". (p. 140) According to Swedenborg, "The speech of the angels is also full of wisdom, because it proceeds from their interior thought; and their interior thought is wisdom, as their interior affection is love, their love and wisdom uniting in speech. Consequently it is so full of wisdom that they can express by one word what man cannot express by a thousand words." (1971, p. 239)

Further Thoughts

Given the contributions of different thinkers in the field, I find this area of enquiry very rich and pregnant with enormous possibilities. I also see the dangers of the limitations of our own metaphysical beliefs illustrated in our fears as well as our hopes and dreams. After all, are not these constructions the very anchors that keep our ego intact and allow us full functioning in this very world we have created. There is a tendency to take one camp over the other, spiritualizing pathology or pathologizing spirituality. It is my hope that my own psycho-history does not delineate and limit my presentation to one side over the other. Rather, it is my aspiration that I keep an open mind and make connections where similarities may occur under the guises of differing, if not opposing language.

In lieu of what Swedenborg's 27 year findings, I consider it very interesting that he points that lower order spirits hammer on the individual's weaknesses. Clinical psychology also indicates the role of early abuse and its effects of poor self esteem in psychotic patients. What strikes me is the similarity as well as the potential to use resources to illuminate this weakness in the break of the self. It is important that the findings of clinical psychology not be dismissed fully for I do acknowledge its importance and function in certain circumstances. I do not believe that all individuals who undergo psychosis are mystics nor vice versa. On the same token, I am aware of the limited understanding clinical psychology displays in the regard to the full psychic spectrum. I suggest that some situations actually include both and need spiritual and psychological guidance and resources to help the individuals involved. Nobody will disclaim that dis-ease is present in the breakdown of the self. The question is: how do we hold it that self is birthed more into ease.

Even within shamanism, there is a distinction between an individual who is going through "a healer's illness" and a psychotic. Moreover, contemplative traditions from both east and west do not stop with visions and powerful manifestations called siddhis. In fact, there are warnings regarding these states and one's tendency to attach to them. To the spiritual aspirant, the goal is not these states, but rather to perceive the true nature of self and other. As Ram Dass aptly points out, "The journey of consciousness is to go to the place where you see that all of them are really relative realities and these are merely perceptual vantage points for looking at it all...you have to be able to go in and out of all of them, that any one you get stuck in is the wrong one." (Fadiman & Kewman, 1973, p. 129)

What is essential here is to recognize that a psychotic process is no different than Campbell's "Hero's Journey". A death-rebirth is reenacted. I agree with Perry(1973) in his analysis.

> It is an appalling experience to undergo when it actually is a "death trip". The expression is no mere simile or figure of speech; it is an actual coming to the end of something and not knowing at all what is ahead. One only knows that one simply losing many familiar ways to which one has become accustomed, having no idea what is going to appear to replace them. Hence the experience really is like death, but it concerns the self-image, and hand in hand with that it becomes also the death of the world-image. (p. 46-47)

It is my sincere hope that by doing the longitudinal study of the long term psycho-spiritual effects of spiritual emergence that I may contribute to a part of this dialectic. More importantly is my wish that this study may be one of the guides that contain and help those undergoing psycho-spiritual crises. May my story, decades after the initial waking, serve as a rail to stairs unknown and its readers come to a deeper acceptance and understanding that this psychic chaos actually has an order. I share with you a description of Gopi Krishna's attitude of his own psycho-spiritual crisis, "He let the ego sleep in its world of dreams; he observed merely what was going on, trusting...and letting the process transform him. Rather than let his ego integrate the luminous other world, he let the luminous other world integrate him. His approach...was just the reverse of what we assume in the west." (Clarke, p. 118-119)

Bibliography

Aurobindo, Sri, *Integral Yoga: Sri Aurobindo's Teaching & Method of Practice*, 1993.

Assagioli, Roberto. (1986). Self-realization and psychological dis turbances. *ReVision*, 8(2), 21-31.

Becker, M.D., Robert, and Selden, Gary, *The Body Electric, Electromagnetism and the Foundation of Life,* Quill, 1985.

Bragdon, E. *The Call of Spiritual Emergency*. 2nd ed. USA, ebookIt.com, 2012. (#2).

Campbell, J. *The Hero with a Thousand Faces*. 3rd. ed. 1973.

Clarke, I. (Editor) *Psychosis and Spirituality: Consolidating the New Paradigm,* 2010.

Corthright, Brant. *Integral Psychology: Yoga, Growth, and Opening the Heart* (Suny Series in Transpersonal and Humanistic Psychology), 2007.

Frankel, Viktor. *Man's Search for Meaning,* New York: Washington Square Press/Simon and Schuster, 1963.

Fromm, Erich. *Escape from Freedom.* New York: Avon, 1965.

Gopi, Krishna, *Kundalini: The Evolutionary Energy in Man*, 1997.

Greenwell, Bonnie, *Energies of Transformation,* Shakti River Press, 1990.

Grof, Christina, & Grof, Stanislav. *Spiritual emergency: The un derstanding and treatment of transpersonal crises. 1986.*

Grof, Christina & Grof, Stanislav, S*piritual Emergency: When Personal Transformation Becomes a Crisis,* 1989.

Hafiz and Ladinsky, Daniel, *The Subject Tonight is Love,* Penguin Contrast, 1999.

Harrigan, Joan Shivarpita, *Kundalini Vidya,* Patanjali Yoga Care, 1996.

Hixon, Lex, *Coming Home, The Experience of Enlightenment in Sacred Traditions,* Larson Publications 1995.

Jung, C.G., *Mysterium Coniunctionis,* Bollingen Series/Princeton, 1989.

Jung, C.G. *Memories, Dreams, Reflections.*1989.

Laing, R.D., *The Divided Self: An Existential Study in Sanity and Madness,* Penguin Psychology.

Ledi Sayadaw, *Manual of Insight,* The Wheel Publication, 1961.

Lukoff, David, The diagnosis of mystical experiences with psy chotic features. *Journal of Transpersonal Psychology,* 17(2), 155-181, 1985a.

Maharishi, Ramana, *Be as You Are: The Teachings of Sri Ramana Maharshi (Compass), 1989.*

Metzner, Ralph. *The Unfolding Self. Varieties of Transformative Experience,* Novato, CA: Origin Press, 1998.

Mookerjee, Ajit, *Kundalini, The Arousal of the Inner Energy,* Destiny Books, 1986.

Muktananda, S. *Kundalini: The Secret of Life (erd ed.).* U B S Publishers' Distributors Ltd., 1995.

Nelson, John E. (1994). Madness or transcendence? Looking to the ancient East for a modern transpersonal diagnostic sys tem. *ReVision,* 17(1), 14-23.

Nisargadatta, Maharaj. *I Am That.* 1999.

Perry, John Weir. (1986). Spiritual emergence and renewal. *ReVi sion,* 8(2), 33-38.

Radhakrishna, S, *Dhammapada: With Introductory Essays, Pali Text,* English Translation and Notes (Oxford India Paperbacks), 1996.

Rinpoche, S. *The Tibetan Book of Living and Dying, 1994.* (#1, 5).

Sannella, Lee, *Kundalini-Psychosis or Transcendence.* San Fran cisco, CA: H.S. Dakin, 1977.

Satprem, *The Mind of the Cells, or Willed Mutation of Our Species,* IER, 1982.

Satprem, *Sri Aurobindo or the Adventure of Consciousness,* 2008.

Tagore, Rabindranath, *Collected Poems and Plays of Ra bindranath Tagore,* Macmillan Publishing, 1952.

Weir, John, *The Far Side of Madness,* Prentice-Hall, 1974.

Yogananda, Paramahansa, *The Autobiography of a Yogi.* Self-Realization Fellowship, 1995.

About the author

Kathrina Peterson was trained in Buddhist monasteries in Thailand, Burma, Sri Lanka and Nepal. In her search for wholeness, she continued her training in psychology, energy medicine, movement education and how they relate to make effective change in the plastic malleable behavior of the brain. She is a holistic healer and teacher helping others realize their authentic selves. She teaches meditation groups and workshops dedicated to empowering people to awaken. Kathrina offers integral body-mind approaches based on the integration of western psychology, eastern philosophy, somatic and energy medicine to assist transformation. She facilitates others to integrate being with personality through the body. She works individually in person as well as long distance by skype.

She lives in the San Francisco Bay area in California. She loves gardening, traveling around the world, walking in nature and baking.

To contact her, please visit:

Marin Mindful Body
205 Camino Alto Suite 250
Mill Valley, CA 94942

email: kathrinapeterson@yahoo.com
web: www.marinmindfulbody.com

Made in the USA
San Bernardino, CA
17 March 2015